ADVICE AND DISSENT

THE CONTROVERSY: ABORTION ON REQUEST

"The objective for American society should be to make the child-bearing decision as free as possible of unintended societal pressures."

The Majority Recommends—

ABORTION: Women should be free to control their own fertility. State laws prohibiting abortion should be liberalized; federal, state, and local funds be made available to support abortion services; and abortion costs be covered by health insurance.

CONTRACEPTION: States should actively encourage teen-agers to receive contraceptive services. Responsible sex education should be widely available to all.

VOLUNTARY STERILIZATION: Hospitals should relax their policies concerning voluntary sterilization and make it easier to obtain.

The Minority Dissents—

ABORTION ON REQUEST will encourage irresponsible sexual activity. It does not account for the legal or moral right of the unborn child to live.

POPULATION AND THE AMERICAN FUTURE— THE GREAT DEBATE CONTINUES

More MENTOR and SIGNET Titles On Ecology

POPULATION AND THE AMERICAN FUTURE

The Report of

The Commission on Population Growth
and the American Future

A SIGNET SPECIAL from

NEW AMERICAN LIBRARY

TIMES MIRROR

This is an advance copy of the Commission's Report and is subject to revisions and corrections in the official version to be published by the Government Printing Office.

Library of Congress Catalog Card Number: 72-77389

One of the most serious challenges to human destiny in the last third of this century will be the growth of the population. Whether man's response to that challenge will be a cause for pride or for despair in the year 2000 will depend very much on what we do today. If we now begin our work in an appropriate manner, and if we continue to devote a considerable amount of attention and energy to this problem, then mankind will be able to surmount this challenge as it has surmounted so many during the long march of civilization.

Richard Nixon
July 18, 1969

Commission on Population Growth and the American Future

726 Jackson Place, N. W.
Washington, D. C. 20506

March 27, 1972

To the President and Congress of the United States:

I have the honor to transmit for your consideration the Final Report, containing the findings and recommendations, of the Commission on Population Growth and the American Future, pursuant to Sec. 8, PL 91-213.

After two years of concentrated effort, we have concluded that, in the long run, no substantial benefits will result from further growth of the Nation's population, rather that the gradual stabilization of our population would contribute significantly to the Nation's ability to solve its problems. We have looked for, and have not found, any convincing economic argument for continued population growth. The health of our country does not depend on it, nor does the vitality of business nor the welfare of the average person.

The recommendations offered by this Commission are directed towards increasing public knowledge of the causes and consequences of population change, facilitating and guiding the processes of population movement, maximizing information about human reproduction and its consequences for the family, and enabling individuals to avoid unwanted fertility.

To these ends we offer this report in the hope that our findings and recommendations will stimulate serious consideration of an issue that is of great consequence to present and future generations.

Respectfully submitted for the Commission

John D. Rockefeller 3rd
Chairman

The President
The President of the Senate
The Speaker of the House of Representatives

THE COMMISSION ON POPULATION GROWTH AND THE AMERICAN FUTURE

CHAIRMAN
John D. Rockefeller 3rd

VICE CHAIRMAN
Grace Olivarez
Executive Director, Food for All, Inc.

VICE CHAIRMAN
Christian N. Ramsey, Jr., M.D.
President, The Institute for the Study of Health and Society

Joseph D. Beasley, M.D.
The Edward Wisner Professor of Public Health
Tulane University Medical Center

David E. Bell
Executive Vice President, The Ford Foundation

Bernard Berelson
President, The Population Council

Arnita Young Boswell
Associate Field Work Professor
School of Social Service Administration
University of Chicago

Margaret Bright
Professor, Dept. of Behavioral Sciences, and
Professor, Dept. of Epidemiology
School of Hygiene and Public Health
The Johns Hopkins University

Marilyn Brant Chandler
Housewife, Volunteer, Student

Paul B. Cornely, M.D.
Professor, Dept. of Community Health Practice
College of Medicine Howard University, and
Assistant to the Executive Medical Officer
Welfare and Retirement Fund,
United Mine Workers of America

This report represents the official views of the Commission, particularly as to the listed recommendations. Clearly, in the case of a Commission with such diverse membership, not every Commissioner subscribes in detail to every suggestion or statement of policy.

COMMISSION STAFF

Executive Director
Charles F. Westoff

Deputy Director
Robert Parke, Jr.

Directors of Research
Sara Mills Mazie
Elliott R. Morss
A. E. Keir Nash
Ritchie H. Reed*
Dianne Miller Wolman

Director of Policy Coordination
Carol Tucker Foreman

Assistant to the Chairman
David K. Lelewer

Director of Public Information
Gerald Lipson

General Counsel
Ben C. Fisher

Administrative Officer
Lois A. Brooks

Editorial Coordinator
Carol F. Donnelly

Press Officer
Rochelle Kutcher Green

Professional Staff
Gail E. Auslander
Phyllis Coghlan
Florence F. Einhorn
Duane S. Elgin
Dorothy Mann
Susan McIntosh
Steve W. Rawlings

Special Consultants
Daniel Callahan
Lenora T. Cartright
Robert F. Drury
Edgar M. Hoover
Frederick S. Jaffe
Peter A. Morrison
Ronald G. Ridker
Norman B. Ryder
Irene B. Taeuber

Support Staff
Mary Ann Ferguson
Mildred G. Herald
Kathryn E. Herron
Mac Arthur C. Jones
Kituria D. Littlejohn
Betty Marshall
Pearl R. Phillips
Diane O. Sergeant
Judith M. Stock
Mary C. Wilcher

* Deceased

Because he deepened our conviction that each individual has a unique contribution to make to the dignity and worth of all mankind, the Commission and staff dedicate this report to the memory of our colleague, staff member, and friend.

Ritchie H. Reed
1941-1971

PREFACE

For the first time in the history of our country, the President and the Congress have established a Commission to examine the growth of our population and the impact it will have upon the American future. In proposing this Commission in July 1969, President Nixon said: "One of the most serious challenges to human destiny in the last third of this century will be the growth of the population. Whether man's response to that challenge will be a cause for pride or for despair in the year 2000 will depend very much on what we do today." The Commission was asked to examine the probable extent of population growth and internal migration in the United States between now and the end of this century, to assess the impact that population change will have upon government services, our economy, and our resources and environment, and to make recommendations on how the nation can best cope with that impact.

In our Interim Report a year ago, the Commission defined the scope of our mandate: ". . . to formulate policy for the future"—policy designed to deal with "the pervasive impact of population growth on every facet of American life." We said that population growth of the magnitude we have experienced since World War II has multiplied and intensified many of our domestic problems and made their solution more difficult. We called upon the American people to begin considering the meaning and consequences of population growth and internal migration and the desirability of formulating a national policy on the question.

Since then, the Commission and staff have conducted an extensive inquiry. We have enlisted many of the nation's leading scientists in more than 100 research projects. We have heard from more than 100 witnesses in public hearings across the country and have met with experts in many days of executive meetings. And we are aware that population has become an active subject of consideration in a number of states in our country concerned about their future. We have come to recognize that the racial and ethnic diversity of this Commission gives us confidence that our recommendations—the consensus of our members—do indeed point the way in which this nation should move in solving its problems. Because of the importance of this matter, the Commission recommends that future federal commissions include a substantial representation of minorities, youth, poor citizens, and women among their members, including congressional representatives, and that commission staffs and consultants include significant numbers of minorities, youth, and women.

We offer this report in the hope that our viewpoints and recommendations will stimulate serious consideration and response by the citizens of this nation and of nations throughout the world to an issue of great consequence to present and future generations.

CONTENTS

Separate Statements 259

CHAPTER 1. PERSPECTIVE ON POPULATION

In the brief history of this nation, we have always assumed that progress and "the good life" are connected with population growth. In fact, population growth has frequently been regarded as a measure of our progress. If that were ever the case, it is not now. There is hardly any social problem confronting this nation whose solution would be easier if our population were larger. Even now, the dreams of too many Americans are not being realized; others are being fulfilled at too high a cost. Accordingly, this Commission has concluded that our country can no longer afford the uncritical acceptance of the population growth ethic that "more is better." And beyond that, after two years of concentrated effort, we have concluded that no substantial benefits would result from continued growth of the nation's population.

The "population problem" is long run and requires long-run responses. It is not a simple problem. It cannot be encompassed by the slogans of either of the prevalent extremes: the "more" or the "bigger the better" attitude on the one hand, or the emergency-crisis response on the other. Neither extreme is accurate nor even helpful.

It is a problem which can be interpreted in many ways. It is the pressure of population reaching out to occupy open spaces and bringing with it a deterioration of the environment. It can be viewed as the effect on natural resources of increased numbers of people in search of a higher standard of living. It is the impact of population fluctuations in both growth and

1

distribution upon the orderly provision of public services. It can be seen as the concentration of people in metropolitan areas and depopulation elsewhere, with all that implies for the quality of life in both places. It is the instability over time of proportions of the young, the elderly, and the productive. For the family and the individual, it is the control over one's life with respect to the reproduction of new life— the formal and informal pronatalist pressures of an outmoded tradition, and the disadvantages of and to the children involved.

Unlike other great public issues in the United States, population lacks the dramatic event—the war, the riot, the calamity —that galvanizes attention and action. It is easily overlooked and neglected. Yet the number of children born now will seriously affect our lives in future decades. This produces a powerful effect in a double sense: Its fluctuations can be strong and not easily changed; and its consequences are important for the welfare of future generations.

There is scarcely a facet of American life that is not involved with the rise and fall of our birth and death rates: the economy, environment, education, health, family life and sexual practices, urban and rural life, governmental effectiveness and political freedoms, religious norms, and secular life styles. If this country is in a crisis of spirit—environmental deterioration, racial antagonisms, the plight of the cities, the international situation—then population is part of that crisis.

Although population change touches all of these areas of our national life and intensifies our problems, such problems will not be solved by demographic means alone. Population policy is no substitute for social, economic, and environmental policy. Successfully addressing population requires that we also address our problems of poverty, of minority and sex discrimination, of careless exploitation of resources, of environmental deterioration, and of spreading suburbs, decaying cities, and wasted countrysides. By the same token, because population is so tightly interwoven with all of these concerns, whatever success we have in resolving these problems will contribute to easing the complex system of pressures that impel population growth.

Consideration of the population issue raises profound questions of what people want, what they need—indeed, what they are for. What does this nation stand for and where is it going? At some point in the future, the finite earth will not satisfactorily accommodate more human beings—nor will the United States. How is a judgment to be made about when that point will be reached? Our answer is that now is the time to

2

confront the question: "Why more people?" The answer must be given, we believe, in qualitative not quantitative terms.

The United States today is characterized by low population density, considerable open space, a declining birthrate, movement out of the central cities—but that does not eliminate the concern about population. This country, or any country, always has a "population problem," in the sense of achieving a proper balance between size, growth, and distribution on the one hand, and, on the other, the quality of life to which every person in this country aspires.

Nor is this country alone in the world, demographically or in any other way. Many other nations are beginning to recognize the importance of population questions. We need to act prudently, understanding that today's decisions on population have effects for generations ahead. Similarly, we need to act responsibly toward other people in the world: This country's needs and wants, given its wealth, may impinge upon the patrimony of other, less fortunate peoples in the decades ahead. The "population problem" of the developing countries may be more pressing at this time, but in the longer perspective, it is both proper and in our best interest to participate fully in the worldwide search for the good life, which must include the eventual stabilization of our numbers.

A DIVERSITY OF VIEWS

Ultimately, then, we are concerned not with demographic trends alone, but with the effect of these trends on the realization of the values and goals cherished as part of the American tradition and sought after by minorities who also "want in."

One of the basic themes underlying our analysis and policy recommendations is the substitution of quality for quantity; that is, we should concern ourselves with improving the quality of life for all Americans rather than merely adding more Americans. And unfortunately, for many of our citizens that quality of life is still defined only as enough food, clothing, and shelter. All human beings need a sense of their own dignity and worth, a sense of belonging and sharing, and the opportunity to develop their individual potentialities.

But it is far easier to achieve agreement on abstract values than on their meaning or on the strategy to achieve them. Like the American people generally, this Commission has not been able to reach full agreement on the relative importance

3

of different values or on the analysis of how the "population problem" reflects other conditions and directions of American society.

Three distinct though overlapping approaches have been distinguished. These views differ in their analysis of the nature of the problem and the general priorities of tasks to be accomplished. But, despite the different perspectives from which population is viewed, all of the population policies we shall recommend are consistent with all three positions.

The first perspective acknowledges the benefits to be gained by slowing growth, but regards our population problem today primarily as a result of large numbers of people being unable to control an important part of their lives—the number of children they have. The persistence of this problem reflects an effective denial of freedom of choice and equality of access to the means of fertility control. In this view, the population problem is regarded more as the sum of such individual problems than as a societal problem transcending the interests of individuals; the welfare of individuals and that of the general society are seen as congruent, at least at this point in history. The potential conflict between these two levels is mitigated by the knowledge that freedom from unwanted childbearing would contribute significantly to the stabilization of population.

Reproductive decisions should be freely made in a social context without pronatalist pressures—the heritage of a past when the survival of societies with high mortality required high fertility. The proper mission for government in this matter is to ensure the fullest opportunity for people to decide their own future in this regard, based on the best available knowledge; then the demographic outcome becomes the democratic solution.

Beyond these goals, this approach depends on the processes of education, research, and national debate to illuminate the existence of any serious population "problem" that transcends individual welfare. The aim would be to achieve the best collective decision about population issues based on knowledge of the tradeoffs between demographic choices and the "quality of life," however defined. This position ultimately seeks to optimize the individual and the collective decisions and then accepts the aggregate outcome—with the understanding that the situation will be reconsidered from time to time.

The second view does not deny the need for education and knowledge, but stresses the crucial gaps between what we claim as national values and the reality experienced by certain

4

groups in our society. Many of the traditional American values, such as freedom and justice, are not yet experienced by some minorities. Racial discrimination continues to mean that equal access to opportunities afforded those in the mainstream of American society is denied to millions of people. Overt and subtle discrimination against women has meant undue pressure toward childbearing and child-rearing. Equality is denied when inadequate income, education, or racial and sexual stereotypes persist, and shape available options. Freedom is denied when governmental steps are not taken to assure the fullest possible access to methods of controlling reproduction or to educational, job, and residential opportunities. In addition, the freedom of future generations may be compromised by a denial of freedom to the present generation. Finally, extending freedom and equality—which is nothing more than making the American system live up to its stated values—would go far beyond affecting the growth rate. Full equality both for women and for racial minorities is a value in its own right. In this view, the "population problem" is seen as only one facet, and not even a major one, of the restriction of full opportunity in American life.

The third position deals with the population problem in an ecological framework, one whose primary axiom asserts the functional interdependence of man and his environment. It calls for a far more fundamental shift in the operative values of modern society. The need for more education and knowledge and the need to eliminate poverty and racism are important, but not enough. For the population problem, and the growth ethic with which it is intimately connected, reflect deeper external conditions and more fundamental political, economic, and philosophical values. Consequently, to improve the quality of our existence while slowing growth, will require nothing less than a basic recasting of American values.

The numbers of people and the material conditions of human existence are limited by the external environment. Human life, like all forms of life on earth, is supported by intricate ecological systems that are limited in their ability to adapt to and tolerate changing conditions. Human culture, particularly science and technology, has given man an extraordinary power to alter and manipulate his environment. At the same time, he has also achieved the capacity virtually to destroy life on earth. Sadly, in the rush to produce, consume, and discard, he has too often chosen to plunder and destroy rather than to conserve and create. Not only have the land, air, and water, the flora and fauna suffered, but also the individual, the family, and the human community.

This position holds that the present pattern of urban industrial organization, far from promoting the realization of the individual as a uniquely valuable experience, serves primarily to perpetuate its own values. Mass urban industrialism is based on science and technology, efficiency, acquisition, and domination through rationality. The exercise of these same values now contain the potential for the destruction of our humanity. Man is losing that balance with nature which is an essential condition of human existence. With that loss has come a loss of harmony with other human beings. The population problem is a concrete symptom of this change, and a fundamental cause of present human conditions.

It is comfortable to believe that changes in values or in the political system are unnecessary, and that measures such as population education and better fertility control information and services will solve our population problem. They will not, however, for such solutions do not go to the heart of man's relationship with nature, himself, and society. According to this view, nothing less than a different set of values toward nature, the transcendence of a laissez-faire market system, a redefinition of human identity in terms other than consumerism, and a radical change if not abandonment of the growth ethic, will suffice. A new vision is needed—a vision that recognizes man's unity with nature, that transcends a simple economic definition of man's identity, and that seeks to promote the realization of the highest potential of our individual humanity.

THE IMMEDIATE GOAL

These three views reflect different evaluations of the nature of the population problem, different assessments of the viability of the American political process, and different perceptions of the critical values at stake.

Given the diversity of goals to be addressed and the manifold ramifications of population change throughout society, how are specific population policies to be selected?

As a Commission and as a people, we need not agree on all the priorities if we can identify acceptable policies that speak in greater or lesser degree to all of them. By and large, in our judgment, the policy findings and recommendations of this

6

Report meet that requirement. Whatever the primary needs of our society, the policies recommended here all lead in right directions for this nation, and generally at low costs.*

Our immediate goal is to modernize demographic behavior in this country: to encourage the American people to make population choices, both in the individual family and society at large, on the basis of greater rationality rather than tradition or custom, ignorance or chance. This country has already moved some distance down this road; it should now complete the journey. The time has come to challenge the tradition that population growth is desirable: What was unintended may turn out to be unwanted, in the society as in the family.

In any case, more rational attitudes are now forced upon us by the revolutionary increase in average length of life within the past century, which has placed modern man in a completely different, historically unique, demographic situation. The social institutions and customs that have shaped reproductive behavior in the past are no longer appropriate in the modern world, and need reshaping to suit the new situation. Moreover, the instruments of population policy are now more readily available—fuller knowledge of demographic impacts, better information on demographic trends, improved means by which individuals may control their own fertility.

As a Commission, we have come to appreciate the delicate complexities of the subject and the difficulty, even the impossibility, of solving the problem, however defined, in its entirety and all at once. But this is certainly the time to begin: The 1970's may not be simply another decade in the demographic transition but a critical one, involving changes in family life and the role of women, dynamics of the metropolitan process, the depopulation of rural areas, the movement and the needs of disadvantaged minorities, the era of the young adults produced by the baby boom, and the attendant question of what their own fertility will be—baby boom or baby bust.

Finally, we agree that population policy goals must be sought in full consonance with the fundamental values of American life: respect for human freedom, human dignity, and individual fulfillment; and concern for social justice and social welfare. To "solve" population problems at the cost of such values would be a Pyrrhic victory indeed. The issues are ethical in character, and their proper solution requires a deep sense of moral responsibility on the part of both the individual family and the national community: the former in

*A separate statement by Commissioner James S. Rummonds appears on pages 299-305.

7

considering another birth, the latter in considering appropriate policies to guide population growth into the American future.

For our part, it is enough to make population, and all that it means, explicit on the national agenda, to signal its impact on our national life, to sort out the issues, and to propose how to start toward a better state of affairs. By its very nature, population is a continuing concern and should receive continuing attention. Later generations, and later commissions, will be able to see the right path further into the future. In any case, no generation needs to know the ultimate goal or the final means, only the direction in which they will be found.

CHAPTER 2. POPULATION GROWTH

The tremendous growth in the world's population is a recent development in the history of mankind. In pre-industrial times, birthrates were high; but hunger, ignorance, and disease combined to stack the odds against an infant surviving to the age of parenthood. Societies required high birthrates simply to keep themselves going.

In modern times, the reductions in mortality have given the average person a longer, healthier life and have inaugurated a phase of rapid population growth. The world's population grew from one-half billion around 1650, to about 1½ billion by 1900, to 2½ billion in 1950, and had already surpassed 3½ billion by 1970. The world's total has doubled during the last 50 years.

From the beginning of the Christian era to 1650, mankind increased by an average of 150,000 persons a year. Today, the world total is increasing by about 78 million persons annually. If current rates of growth continue for another 50 years, the world's population will number some 10 billion.

The same civilization that achieved a lengthening of life in Europe and America also evolved an urban way of life in which the institutional supports to high fertility were gradually eroded, and developed a technology that reduced the role of ignorance and error in reproduction. The technology of mortality control was exported to the rest of the world. There was far less exporting of the underlying social and economic changes which gave rise to this technology, and only recently have efforts been made to export reproduction control.

Because of declining birthrates, the advanced nations have been narrowing the gap between birthrates and death rates in the 20th century. These nations have been approaching a stabilized population—one in which births and deaths have come into balance. The historical transition has been from a stabilized population maintained by high birthrates, high and erratic death rates, and short lifetimes, toward a stabilized population characterized by low birthrates, low death rates, and long lifetimes. When birthrates once again equal death rates, these nations will have completed the demographic transition.

Ultimately, this transition must be completed. Population growth at our current rate of about one percent per year would double the population every 70 years. Such growth leads to "standing room only" if continued indefinitely. By one means or another, such an impossible result will be avoided. An average of zero growth over the long term—a stabilized population —must and inevitably will be reestablished.[1] The question is when it will happen, and how. In this, we in the United States may exercise choice.

THE UNITED STATES

No country has completed the demographic transition, and the United States will probably not be the first to do so. A discussion of our prospects for completing it requires some appreciation of the dynamics of our population during the first 70 years of the 20th century.

Even a cursory examination of the data reveals that, since 1900, the United States has undergone something of a demographic revolution. (See table on page 11.) In terms of total numbers, our population has increased from about 76 million in 1900 to almost 205 million in 1970. This represents an additional 129 million people that our society has been called upon to accommodate over the past 70 years. By mid-1972, our country will have about 209 million people.

The growth of population is sustained only as long as the yearly number of new entrants (births and immigrants) exceeds the number required to replace those who die or emigrate. Although the United States has always been a growing population, the rapid growth rates characterizing our early years began to taper off in the 19th century.

In the 20th century, we have seen substantial changes in all three components of population growth—fertility, mortality,

10

Demographic Perspective of 20th Century United States

	Around 1900	Around 1970
Population	76 million	205 million
Life expectancy	47 years	70 years
Median age	23 years	28 years
Births per 1000 population	32	18
Deaths per 1000 population	17	9
Immigrants per 1000 population	8	2
Annual growth	1¾ million	2¼ million
Growth rate	2.3 percent	1.1 percent

SOURCES: U. S. Bureau of the Census, *Historical Statistics of the United States, Colonial Times to 1957*, 1961. U. S. National Center for Health Statistics, *Vital Statistics of the United States*, Volume II Section 5, *Life Tables*, 1968. Irene B. Taeuber, "Growth of the Population of the United States in the Twentieth Century" (prepared for the Commission, 1972).

and migration. First, consider the birthrate. It is important to understand that this measure simply indicates the average level of yearly births in the population. Although it obscures a considerable amount of variation associated with such factors as age and socioeconomic status, it is nevertheless a useful measure of the contribution of births to population growth. The birthrate was about 32 births per 1,000 population in 1900, and declined fairly steadily to about 18 per 1,000 in the depths of the Depression. Just when the experts had become convinced—some even concerned—that our level of fertility would soon dip below the level required for replacement of the population, couples began increasing their rates of childbearing. This aberration in the history of American fertility, of which we will have more to say shortly, came to be called the "baby boom." By 1947, the birthrate stood at 27 per 1,000, and it remained at around 25 per 1,000 for a decade before resuming its long-term decline. By the early 1960's, the boom had run its course, and our birthrate today is below pre-World War II levels.[2] (See chart on page 13.)

A second basic determinant of how fast a nation grows is the degree to which it succeeds in preserving and extending the lives of its people. We have seen dramatic progress toward reducing the threat of early death. The death rate has fallen from about 17 per 1,000 population at the turn of the century, to its present level of about nine per 1,000. The average life expectancy today is about 70 years,[3] or 23 years longer than in 1900. Most of these declines in mortality were achieved prior to 1960, and all segments of our population have gained some, though not equal, benefits in terms of increased longevity.

In the United States, mortality during the early years of life is already so low that any substantial further improvements in life expectancy will have to come primarily among persons over the age of 50. Since this segment of the population is generally beyond childbearing, the extension of their life span would not result in any significant increase in births. Consequently, further additions to the duration of life in this country would simply result in somewhat larger numbers of people at the older ages, where they still can be quite productive members of society.

The third factor associated with growth is, of course, immigration. Only the Indians, who numbered less than one million[4] when the first English colonists settled in Massachusetts and Virginia, can rightfully claim original status. Our population is comprised primarily of immigrants and their descendants. Since 1900 alone, 20 million more people have moved into this country than out of it. Approximately 40 percent of the population growth in the first decade of this century was attributable to immigration. During the 1930's, the number of immigrants was slightly lower than the number of people leaving the country. Immigration once again increased following World War II, and during the 1960's, it accounted for about 16 percent of our national growth.[5]

When all of these demographic credits and debits are tallied, we are left with either net population growth or net decline. The United States has had a long history of diminishing growth rates. Our annual rate of growth dropped from about 3.3 percent in the second decade of the 19th century to 2.1 percent by the first decade of this century, to an average of around 0.7 percent during the 1930's. It then rose to about 1.9 percent during the fifties, before falling to its present level

12

TOTAL FERTILITY RATE
CHILDREN PER WOMAN

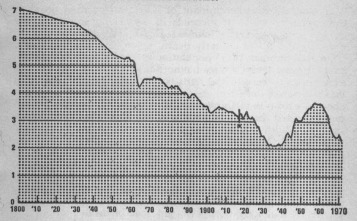

*Prior to 1917 data available only for white population; after 1917, for total population.

Annual births expressed in terms of implied completed family size, declined until the 1930's, rose, and fell again.

SOURCES: Prior to 1917—Ansley J. Coale and Melvin Zelnik, *New Estimates of Fertility and Population in the United States,* (Princeton: Princeton University Press) 1963. 1917 to 1968—U. S. National Center for Health Statistics, *Natality Statistics Analysis,* Series 21, Number 19, 1970. 1969 to 1971—U. S. Bureau of the Census, *Current Population Reports,* Series P-23, No. 36, "Fertility Indicators: 1970," 1971. The figure for 1971 is based on an unpublished Census staff estimate.

of 1.1 percent. However, the size of our population is now so large that even our low current rate of growth translates into about 2¼ million people added to our society each year— more than enough to fill a city the size of Philadelphia.

We cannot predict how fast our population will grow in the years ahead, but we can be sure that, barring some unforeseen catastrophe, substantial additions to our numbers lie ahead. Our population has a potential for further growth greater than that of almost any other advanced country. The reasons for this are a pattern of early and nearly universal marriage and childbearing, fertility levels above those required to replace the parental generation, and a preponderance of youth in the population. The youngsters born during the baby boom are reaching adulthood today and beginning to do many of the things their parents and grandparents did before them

13

—finishing school, seeking jobs, developing careers, getting married, and having children of their own.

THE "BIRTH DEARTH"

In the summer of 1971, the news media spread a report that, because women were having fewer babies than had been expected, we were in the midst of a "baby bust." That story was based on data for the first six months of 1971, which showed a drop in birthrates at a time when most of the experts had expected them to rise again as the baby-boom generation reached adulthood. These expectations seemed to be realized when the birthrate, after reaching a new low of 17.5 in 1968, moved up to about 18.2 in 1970.[6] But, instead of continuing upward in 1971, the rate dropped back to about 17.3, and so was born the idea of the "birth dearth."

This phenomenon is notable because birthrates are showing declines at a time when everyone was expecting them to increase. It had long been assumed that birthrates would rise during the 1970's as potential parents who were born during the baby-boom years came of age. If general fertility (the rate of childbearing among women aged 15 to 44) remained constant, there would be an unavoidable "echo boom" in the birthrate of the total population, as larger and larger numbers of potential parents reached childbearing age. The increase in the number of people entering the childbearing ages is, however, presently being offset by a decline in the level of general fertility.

Two factors seem to account for this recent decline. One is temporary; the other may or may not be permanent. The first element arises from the fact that we are now in a period of gradually rising age at childbearing. This means that, in any given year, some fraction of the births is, in effect, postponed to a later year. The effect is temporary because the age at childbearing will not rise indefinitely; when it stabilizes, the postponement will stop and the birthrate will rise again.

The other and more important element is that today's young people expect to have far fewer children than people a few years their senior. On the average, women now in their late thirties already have more than three children. According to a 1971 Census Bureau survey, married women 18 to 24 say that they expect to have an average of 2.4 children before they complete their families.[7] Not everyone will marry, so the total for this generation could ultimately be lower. On the

14

other hand, experience with similar surveys in the past indicates that women usually end up having more children than they estimated when they were young. The baby-bust phenomenon is significant and somewhat surprising, but it would be premature to say that we are on the verge of a fertility level that would ultimately stabilize the population.

The baby-bust psychology may give rise to unwarranted complacency born of the notion that all of the problems associated with population growth are somehow behind us. Our population growth has developed its own momentum which makes it very difficult to stop, no matter how hard the brakes are applied. Even if immigration from abroad ceased and couples had only two children on the average—just enough to replace themselves—our population would continue to grow for about 70 years. (See charts on pages 15-16.) Our past rapid growth has given us so many young couples that, to bring population growth to an immediate halt, the birthrate would have to drop by almost 50 percent, and today's young generation of parents would have to limit themselves to an average of about one child.[8] That is just not going to happen.

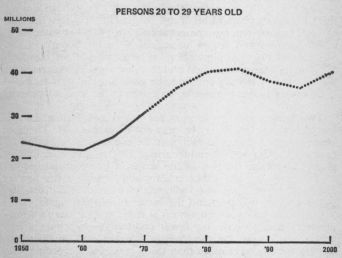

PERSONS 20 TO 29 YEARS OLD

AN AVERAGE OF 2 CHILDREN PER FAMILY WOULD SLOW POPULATION GROWTH, BUT WOULD NOT STOP IT SOON BECAUSE THE NUMBER OF PEOPLE OF CHILDBEARING AGE IS INCREASING.

SOURCE: U. S. Bureau of the Census, *Current Population Reports*, Series P-25.

15

SO, EVEN IF FAMILY SIZE DROPS TO A 2-CHILD AVERAGE, THE RESULTING BIRTHS WILL CONTINUE TO EXCEED DEATHS FOR THE REST OF THIS CENTURY

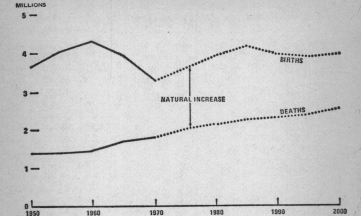

SOURCE: U. S. Bureau of the Census, *Current Population Reports*, Series P-25.

SO THE POPULATION WILL STILL BE GROWING IN THE YEAR 2000, BUT AT A DECREASING RATE.

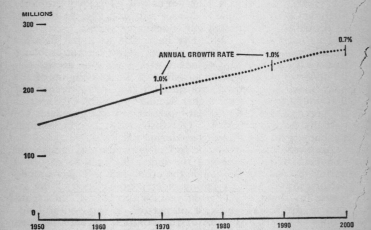

SOURCE: U. S. Bureau of the Census, *Current Population Reports*, Series P-25.

THE BOOM GENERATION

The postwar baby boom is over, but those born during the boom period are still very much with us. Our society has not had an easy time thus far in its attempts to accommodate the baby-boom generation, and their impact is not likely to diminish in the near future. Over the past couple of decades, most of the problems have been associated with providing for their schooling. Shortages of classrooms and teachers began to plague our elementary schools in the mid-1950's.

Similar difficulties have become commonplace in our secondary schools and colleges as the bulk of the boom generation advances to higher levels of education. At the same time, primary schools are now having to cope with smaller enrollments. The number of children entering first grade has stopped escalating, and is now declining. Furthermore, in contrast to the serious teacher shortage of the 1950's, we are now faced with more teachers than the system can readily absorb. The National Education Association recently observed that, during the remainder of this decade, there will be at least two qualified graduates seeking a teaching position for every available job.[9] Thus, the baby boom has left us with a legacy of problems attendant on both rapid increases and decreases in the flow of people passing through our educational system.

This new wave of humanity has made itself felt in areas outside the educational arena as well. Many current problems that we do not normally associate with population growth can be understood, in part, as an effect of the growing-up of the baby-boom generation. For instance, it is generally recognized that young drivers have higher accident rates than the rest of the population. Hence, recent increases in traffic accidents are partially attributable to the fact that many of those born in the baby boom became drivers during the 1960's.

An awareness of the same sort of population dynamics can also help us to understand the increasing volume of crime during the past decade. Since the crime rate is higher among persons under 25 than among older people, much of the increase in crime during recent years is traceable to an expansion in the relative number of persons in the youthful age groups. About 28 percent of the reported increase between 1960 and 1970 in the number of arrests for serious crimes can be attributed to an increase in the percentage of the population under 25. Another 22 percent of the increase can be

17

explained by the growing size of the population and other demographic factors. Thus, population change alone accounted for about half of the reported increase in the number of arrests for serious crimes over the past decade.[10]

Now, as the youth culture of the sixties evolves into the young adult society of the seventies, the impact is being felt in the housing and job markets. In the two decades before 1965, about 48 million Americans reached the age of 20. Between 1965 and 1985, over 78 million will cross this important threshold.

As those born during the baby boom move off the campus or leave their parents' homes, we can expect a 33-percent jump in annual household formation by the end of this decade. Between 1950 and 1966, the number of households grew at a relatively steady rate of around 900,000 per year. After that, the rate began to climb, and last year we added well over the million households. Our research shows that the rate will increase to almost 1.5 million households added each year by the end of the seventies, and will remain at that level until about 1985. These figures understate future demand for the construction of new housing, since additional new housing units will be required to replace part of the older housing stock.

Along with increased housing demands will come greater demand for employment opportunities. The highest rates of joblessness are found among the young. Consequently, one factor to be considered, irrespective of the state of the economy itself, is the sheer increase in the numbers of young people seeking work. The Bureau of Labor Statistics tells us that we can expect about 3½ million persons to make their initial entry into the labor force each year during the 1970's. This level of prospective job seekers exceeds the annual average for the 1960's by about 700,000 persons a year. Here again, we can attribute the large numbers to a heavy influx of new jobseekers who were born during the baby boom.[11]

The boom generation will continue to exert a heavy impact on our society as they move up the age ladder. Eventually, they will reach retirement age; at that point, we can expect added pressure on retirement systems as the proportion of beneficiaries in the population increases. Today, we have an estimated 20 million senior citizens. About 50 years from now we will have an estimated 40 million, twice the present number.

In sum, it should be evident that, even if the recent unexpected drop in the birthrate should develop into a sustained trend, there is little cause for complacency. Whether we see

18

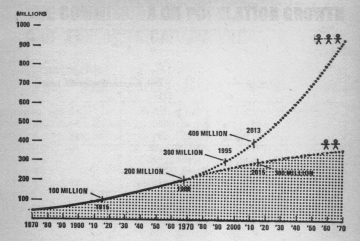

The population of the United States passed the 100-million mark in 1915 and reached 200 million in 1968. If families average two children in the future, growth rates will slow, and the population will reach 300 million in the year 2015. At the 3-child rate, the population would reach 300 million in this century and 400 million in the year 2013. (Projections assume small future reductions in mortality, and assume future immigration at present levels.)

SOURCES: Prior to 1900—U. S. Bureau of the Census, *Historical Statistics of the United States, Colonial Times to 1957,* 1961. 1900 to 2020—U. S. Bureau of the Census, *Current Population Reports,* Series P-25. 2021 to 2050—unpublished Census Bureau projections. Beyond 2050—extrapolation.

it or not—whether we like it or not—we are in for a long period of growth, and we had best prepare for it.

IMPLICATIONS OF GROWTH

It is clear that we are confronted with a continuing legacy of population growth in this country. Much of it is unavoidable, but its full extent will depend upon choices made by American couples in the years immediately ahead.

If families in the United States have only two children on the average and immigration continues at current levels, our population would grow to 271 million by the end of the century. If, however, families should have an average of three children, the population would reach 322 million by the year

UNITED STATES POPULATION, 1970 AND 2000

(Numbers in Millions)

	1970	2000	
		2-child average	3-child average
All Ages	205	271	322
Under 5	17	20	34
5 to 17	53	55	80
18 to 21	15	17	24
under 18	70	75	114
18 to 64	115	167	179
65 and over	20	29	29
Dependency Ratio[a]	78	62	80

[a]Number of persons 65 and over plus persons under 18 per 100 persons aged 18 to 64.

These data are based on the Census Bureau's *Current Population Reports*, Series P-25, No. 470, "Projections of the Population of the United States by Age and Sex: 1970 to 2000." These projections served as the basis for much of the research reported in this volume. We examined how the population would grow between now and the year 2000 under the 2-child family projection (Census Series E) and under the 3-child projection (Census Series B).

Series B assumes that in the future, women will be giving birth at an "ultimate" rate averaging out to 3.1 children per woman over her lifetime. The transition from the 1969 rate of 2.4 to the "ultimate" future rate is not instantaneous in the projections, but most of the change is assumed to occur by 1980. The 3.1 figure is an average for all women, regardless of marital status. In the United States today, almost all women (95 percent) marry at some time in their lives, so the Series B rate of childbearing represents a reasonable approximation to an average family of 3 children.

Series E assumes an ultimate rate of childbearing that works out to an average of 2.1 children per woman over a lifetime. This is the rate at which the parental generation would exactly replace itself. The extra 0.1 allows for mortality between birth and the average age of mothers at childbearing, and for the fact that boy babies slightly outnumber girl babies.

Different generations born in the 20th century have reproduced at widely varying average levels, some exceeding three children (as did the women born from 1930 to 1935) and some approaching two (as did women who were born from 1905 to 1910). The fact that major groups in our modern history have reproduced at each of these levels lends credibility to projections based on either of these averages.

It is assumed in both projections that future reductions in mortality will be slight. The net flow of immigrants into the United States is assumed, in the projections, to continue at the present level of about 400,000 persons annually.

2000. One hundred years from now, the 2-child family would result in a population of about 350 million persons, whereas, the 3-child family would produce a total of nearly a billion. (See chart on page 19.) Thus, a difference of only one extra child per family would result in an additional 51 million people over the next three decades, and if extended over a century, an additional two-thirds of a billion people.

When we speak of 2- or 3-child families, we are talking about averages which can be made up by many possible combinations of family sizes, ranging from childless couples to those with many children.

The total size of our future population is not our sole concern. Perhaps just as important are the changes which lie ahead in the size of various age categories that play an important role in the demands placed on our society.

If families average three children, we can expect to find about 46 percent more young people of elementary and secondary school age (5 to 17 years), and 36 percent more persons of college age (18 to 21 years) in the year 2000, than would be the case if families average only two children. (See table on page 20.) Thus, a difference of only one child per family will have important consequences for the magnitude of the load on our educational system.

The burden placed on those in the economically active segment of the population, traditionally considered to be those aged 18 to 64, will also be influenced by future family size. The dependency burden is determined chiefly by the proportion of the population in the childhood and adolescent years. Projections indicate that the number of persons in the dependent ages under 18 in the year 2000 would be 52 percent greater if families average three children than if the 2-child average prevails. The size of the population 65 and over in the year 2000 would be unaffected by changes in the average number of children, since everyone who will be over the age of 30 at the end of this century is already born. Consequently, the numbers in the dependent ages, relative to persons of working age, would be about one-third larger under the 3-child than under the 2-child projection.

To understand the importance of these prospects, we need first to see how the social and economic transformation of the United States has altered the geographic distribution of population and to assess the likely effect of alternative population futures on our economy, resources, environment, government, and social conditions. We turn to these in the following chapters.

21

CHAPTER 3. POPULATION DISTRIBUTON

Americans are a metropolitan people. Most families live in metropolitan areas; most births, deaths, and migration take place in them. But the traditions and nostalgia are farm and small town.

Our transition from rural to metropolitan has been rapid. At the beginning of this century, 60 percent of the people lived on farms or in villages. When people now 50 years old were born, half the population was rural. In fact, it is only those below age 25 whose life experience is more attuned to a society that is two-thirds metropolitan and becoming more so. Perhaps we have been slow to cope with life in the metropolis because it is so new on the American scene. We struggle to solve the new problems of a metropolitan nation using old institutions suited to a simpler past. As one expert said to the Commission: "Small wonder we have an urban crisis; we are still trying to learn to live in this new demographic and technological world."[1]

This country has experienced a demographic revolution in population distribution as well as in national population growth. Today, 69 percent of the American people live in metropolitan areas—cities of 50,000 or more, and the surrounding county or counties that are economically integrated with the city. Between 1960 and 1970, the population of the United States grew 13 percent, while the metropolitan population grew 23 percent.[2] Nearly all metropolitan growth took place through the growth of suburbs and territorial expansion into previously rural areas. The United States has become mainly a nation of cities and their environs.

The surroundings in which metropolitan people live vary considerably, ranging from inner city to open country. And the metropolitan influence, through the highway and communications systems, affects people far beyond the central cities and adjacent counties. Distinctions between rural and urban people are diminishing. Some "urban" people reside in the countryside, and "rural" people can be found in the poverty areas of our cities.

Metropolitan population growth is a basic feature of the social and economic transformation of the United States—the transition from an agrarian, to an industrial, and now to a service-oriented economy. Metropolitan growth is the geographical dimension of these changes. Reflected in this process are increases in the productivity of agriculture, and the new dominance of commercial, professional, and industrial activities that thrive where people, equipment, money, and know-how are concentrated in space. It is a universal experience. As one of our consultants observed:

> The concentration of national population within limited areas of national territory appears to be characteristic of practically all developed countries. It has little to do with overall population size or density . . . but rather is a reflection of the massive reorientation of population growth and life styles associated with the industrial and technological revolutions of the last two centuries. Enormous changes in modes of population settlement, land use, and resource exploitation accompany these revolutions.[3]

Metropolitan growth is the form that national and regional population growth have taken. The national population grew by 24 million in the 1960's. The metropolitan population grew by more than 26 million, while the nonmetropolitan population declined as migration continued, rural areas became suburban, and many smaller cities grew to metropolitan size. The states with rapid population growth—for example, California, Florida, and Arizona—have been states with rapid growth of metropolitan population. The regional shifts in population, from north to west and south, from the midcontinent to the coasts, have been focused in rapidly growing metropolitan areas.

The process has brought efficiency and confusion, affluence and degradation, individual advancement and alienation. The buildup of transport and communications has made possible increased contact and exchange, increased concentration and dispersal, and increased segregation of activities and people.

24

While the metropolitan economy has reached new heights of productivity, the people who staff it, their families, and the businesses and roads that serve them, have settled miles and miles of formerly rural territory, creating a new enlarged community—a real city with common problems but no common government to manage it. Minority migrants have found better jobs and education, but in so doing have traded the isolation imposed by rural racism for the isolation of the inner city and the institutional racism of metropolitan America. And, the growth and dispersion of the metropolitan population has brought wholly new problems of environmental management as well as social organization.

Population growth *is* metropolitan growth in the contemporary United States, and it means different things to different people.

To the man in Los Angeles, it means rapid growth throughout Southern California. The outcome is often unplanned and haphazard development that falls far short of realizing the full aesthetic potential of the climate and natural surroundings. Tract housing developments are marked off by smoggy and noisy expressways. It is the "good life" colliding with a fragile environment under palm trees.

To a housewife in Nebraska, it means the loss of population in her small farming town—it reached its peak population in 1920. Family, friends, and neighbors, particularly the young and better trained, have moved away. Tax revenues are shrinking and essential public services are becoming more limited. She and her husband can remain where they are, but only at the cost of a difficult and uncertain livelihood.

To a black person in Harlem, the process of metropolitan growth means discrimination that keeps him in a ghetto area with crumbling old apartments and abandoned houses. And, it means that it is harder than ever to reach the jobs opening up in the suburbs as companies shift their operations outward.

Each of these problems relates to a different part of the country and a different set of circumstancces. All are related to the evolution of a metropolitan America.

METROPOLITAN GROWTH[4]

In its geographical dimension, population growth has been a dual process of concentration on a national scale and dispersion and expansion at the local level. More and more of our people live in metropolitan areas. At the same time, the greatest central cities have been losing population, and the territory of metropolitan settlement has expanded even faster than population. Consequently, average metropolitan densities have declined somewhat.

The older industrial areas of the north were the first to develop a high degree of metropolitan concentration. Two-thirds of the northeast was urban in 1900; by 1970, this proportion was four-fifths, and more than one of every two Americans residing in a metropolitan area lived in the north. Recently, however, the north has lost much of its magnetism. Instead, the most rapid growth has been in the south and west where migration, supplementing growth from natural increase, has produced high metropolitan and regional growth rates.

In 1900, more than four-fifths of the south was rural. By 1970, over half was metropolitan. The Atlanta area grew 37 percent during the 1960's. In Texas, the metropolitan population grew 24 percent from 1960 to 1970 and accounted for virtually all of the state's growth. At the end of the decade, three-fourths of the state population was metropolitan. In the west, the Arizona metropolitan population grew 42 percent from 1960 to 1970. Migration contributed as much to Arizona's growth as did natural increases—the balance of births over deaths. Over 80 percent of the growth was concentrated in the state's two metropolitan areas—Phoenix and Tucson—so that in 1970 three-fourths of the population was metropolitan. Migration accounted for half of California's growth in the 1960's; but, by the end of the decade, there were signs that the annual net migration from other states was very low if not zero. Still, because past migrants included so many young adults at the beginning of their childbearing years, state growth remained high. The degree of metropolitan concentration in California was also high. In 1970, it was the highest in the nation at 93 percent.

The most rapid growth in the past decade occurred in metropolitan areas with populations of one to two million. As a class, these areas grew an average of 27 percent, twice the rate for the total population of the United States. Thirteen of the 21 areas in this size class are in the south and west, and all areas of this size that grew *more* than 27 percent are in the south and west. (See table on page 27.)

The 12 areas having more than two million people grew at an average rate of 12 percent, slightly under the rate for the total population of the United States. As a class, they grew just enough to retain their natural increase. Because they are so large, their slow growth rate nonetheless resulted in the addition of six million people. These large areas are mainly the old urban centers of the north. Of the 12 areas in this class, only Los Angeles and San Francisco are in the west, and only Baltimore and Washington are in the south.

Metropolitan Area Population, 1970	Number of Areas, 1970	Population in 1970 Boundaries (millions)	Population Increase, 1960 to 1970 (in 1970 boundaries)	
			Number (Millions)	Percent (Increase)
All Areas	243	139	20	14
2,000,000 or more	12	52	6	12
1,000,000 to 2,000,000	21	28	6	27
500,000 to 1,000,000	32	22	3	18
250,000 to 500,000	60	20	3	16
Under 250,000	118	17	2	14

SOURCE: U. S. Bureau of the Census, *Census of Population and Housing: 1970, General Demographic Trends for Metropolitan Areas, 1960 to 1970,* Final Report PHC(2), 1971. The figures shown in this table differ somewhat from those cited elsewhere in the text due to differences in areal definitions. If one compares the population of metropolitan areas as defined in 1960 to the corresponding population within areas as defined in 1970, there is an increase of 26 million people. But, if we look at growth occurring within fixed metropolitan boundaries as defined in 1970, as in this table, there is an increase of 20 million. The latter figure does not allow for territorial extension of existing areas or the growth of additional areas to metropolitan status between 1960 and 1970.

SOURCES OF METROPOLITAN GROWTH[5]

The total metropolitan population grew by 26 million in the 1960's. About one-third of this growth was from territorial expansion of existing centers and the emergence of other communities into metropolitan status; two-thirds was the result of population growth within constant boundaries.

Within metropolitan boundaries as defined in 1960, 74 percent of growth was natural increase—the excess of births over deaths—and 26 percent was net migration, consisting of immigrants as well as migrants from nonmetropolitan areas of the United States. As the nonmetropolitan population becomes a smaller fraction of the nation's total, its relative importance as a source of migration declines. If current trends continue, other parts of the United States will contribute four million migrants to the metropolitan population between now and the year 2000, while immigrants will add about 10 million.[6]

The dominance of natural increase and the smaller role of

27

migration show how far metropolitan growth has advanced. When two-thirds of the people are metropolitan, their fertility has a greater effect on the growth of metropolitan population than does migration from nonmetropolitan areas. Natural increase is the dominant source of metropolitan growth because we have had so much migration to metropolitan areas in the past.

MIGRATION

We are a geographically mobile society. Expansion and movement have been central themes in a history in which metropolitan growth is but a recent chapter.

Migration is basically a process of adjustment. For the individual, it represents a personal adjustment to changing life circumstances and opportunities. For most of us, moving has led to better things. Whether across town or across the country, movement provides access to areas of greater opportunity. Immobility of people often reflects their isolation from opportunities available in the mainstream of society—social, economic, and political.

For the nation as a whole, migration helps achieve a balance between social and economic activities on the one hand and population numbers on the other. As we move about the country, our actions create broad social, economic, and political realignments, as well as adjustments in our personal lives. Balance is achieved through three broad types of movement: (1) the shift from economically depressed regions, often rural, to areas of expanding employment and higher wages, usually metropolitan; (2) the movement of the population within metropolitan areas—the flight from the central city to the suburbs—historically an adjustment to changing housing needs and a desire for more space; and (3) the system of migration flows among metropolitan areas by which migrants participate in a nationwide job market, moving to areas offering economic advancement and often personal environmental preferences.

Nearly 40 million Americans, or one in five, change homes each year. Roughly one in 15—a total of 13 million people—migrates across a county line.[7] These rates have remained virtually unchanged over the quarter century for which data are available. In part because of the relative decline in rural population, the majority of people moving to metropolitan

28

areas, especially those moving long distances, are now coming from other urban areas.

Whether it is a short or a long haul, those who move are typically the better educated, more skilled young adults, seeking a better life. Nearly a third of all migrants are in their twenties, and they bring with them young children: A tenth of all migrants are between the ages of one and four.

Migration, then, represents more than the numbers suggest. Where five million young adults take their young children and reproductive potential each year affects where future population growth will take place, and where heavy demands for housing and health and educational services will be felt. It also determines where some of our most capable young people, with most of their productive lives ahead, will contribute to the nation's future.

Especially since World War II, metropolitan migrations have included large numbers of blacks. Their transition from rural to metropolitan life has been faster, more recent, and more extensive than that of whites; 74 percent of the black population of the United States is now metropolitan, compared with 68 percent of whites. Blacks, more than whites, tend to live in the larger metropolitan areas, and four-fifths of them live in the central cities.[8]

Recent streams of migration among regions also have varied substantially by race. In the 1960's, there was a net movement of whites out of the north, to the west and south. Blacks moved from the south to the north and west. The net effect was an exchange of population between the north and south, with the west experiencing net in-migration of both whites and blacks. In the south, it was the nonmetropolitan areas that experienced the heaviest outmigration of blacks. The main areas receiving white in-migrants were Florida, the Washington-Baltimore area, and large metropolitan areas in Texas.[9]

LOCAL VARIATIONS

Differences in migration produce large differences in the rates at which individual metropolitan areas grow. The Washington, D.C. area, for example, grew 39 percent in the 1960's, but Pittsburgh's population declined. Although the total metropolitan population of Texas grew 24 percent, three-fifths of its metropolitan areas grew slowly or not at all.[10]

Most migrants to an individual area come from other metropolitan areas. What is happening is that a small number of areas are attracting a disproportionate number of people moving from one metropolitan area to another. Between 1960 and 1965, some 60 metropolitan areas, accounting for 25 percent of all the metropolitan population, drew migrants at a rate at least twice that for the total system of metropolitan centers, and absorbed nearly half of all metropolitan growth. In this same period, 82 other metropolitan areas had more people leaving than arriving. The population size of the fastest growing areas ranged from small to very large, but the lion's share of metropolitan growth was taken by the larger of these fast-growing areas.[11]

With the drying up of nonmetropolitan sources of migration and a general decline in the rate of natural increase, migration among metropolitan centers might result in some 60 to 80 metropolitan areas actually losing population by 1980. Many others would simply not grow. We indicate later in this report why we believe that the usual apprehensions over this prospect are ill-founded. But we also believe that far more research is needed to understand the potential consequences of such trends.

RURAL AREAS AND SMALL TOWNS

Over the decades, there has been an immense transfer of population and reproductive potential through migration from town and countryside to urban areas. The total rural population in 1900 was 46 million, or 60 percent of the population of the United States. Seventy years later, rural population had risen by only eight million to a total of 54 million, while the total national population had nearly tripled. By 1970, the rural population was only 26 percent of the total.[12]

High fertility rates in rural areas would have produced pressures for outmigration in any event. But the mechanization of agriculture made a small number of workers very productive, reduced the job market, and added to migration pressures. Since 1940, the farm population has dropped from 32 million to less than 10 million. Today, farmers, farm workers, and their families are only five percent of the nation's population.[13]

Early in the century, those who moved were mainly white—the children of rural immigrants of the late 19th century, and people from Appalachia, the Ozarks, and other depressed rural areas. More recently, there was the great movement of rural blacks from the south to the largest cities of the north and west.

Most migrants, regardless of race, bettered themselves economically, and in terms of their standard of living. In a recent government survey, most said their move was a success: They were better off financially, and were happier as a result of the move.

Here is Mrs. Mariah Gilmore, aged 60, who lived in the tiny hamlet of DeValls Bluff, 30 miles from Little Rock until her husband died in 1967:

> I was without an income. After his death, I looked for work, but was unable to find anything other than ironing, which didn't pay enough money to maintain a house and buy groceries, too.
> There were months that I might pick or chop cotton, but due to this being seasonal work, I couldn't make a living . . . I had to come to Little Rock to see about finding a job because I didn't have nothing to live on.[14]

Mrs. Gilmore found a job as a maid in a hotel for $35 a week. She also found her way into a federally funded work-training program operated by Pulaski County. She was eventually able to take a better position at the University of Arkansas Medical Center in Little Rock. Although she improved her economic status, Mrs. Gilmore confesses she would really prefer to live in DeValls Bluff, if she could have the same job. DeValls Bluff is still home to her.

The migration from rural areas has been such that in the past decade nearly half of all counties lost population. These losses occurred in a belt from Canada to the Rio Grande between the Mississippi River and the Rockies, in the deep south, and in the Appalachian Mountains. For example, four-fifths of the counties in West Virginia declined in population in the 1960's, with virtually all counties losing population through net outmigration. West Virginia lost one-third of its people in their twenties by migration during the decade.

The territory involved in this rural exodus is immense; but, relative to the national population, the number of people leaving is small. The growth of the nation has been so great that even if all rural counties were repopulated to their historical maximum, they would absorb a population equivalent to no more than five years of national growth.[15]

Nationally, decline in the farm population has been offset

by growth in the nonfarm rural population, made possible by growth in nonfarm employment. These people now outnumber the farm population by five to one. If this employment trend should spread, rural population may begin to stabilize in some areas where depopulation has been the rule. Such signs are already apparent, as in the recent reversal of the trend in Arkansas.

Paralleling the decline in the rural percentage of population has been a decline in the proportion of the population located in towns and cities of less than 50,000. Population growth has pushed many of these places into the metropolitan category, but others have lost population. Such is the history of many small towns in Iowa and the Dakotas. In such towns, population decline reflects a national system that increasingly requires critical minimum concentrations of economic activities in one location. Lacking adequate roads, power lines, sewers, proximity to large urban centers, and other advantages that would attract new kinds of economic activity and revive growth, they suffer from chronic high-level unemployment and a shrinking economic base. This triggers outmigration, mainly of the young and better educated, and leaves behind an older population that is disadvantaged in terms of education and training and less likely to depart, even in the face of economic hardship. In this case, migration removes surplus population, but it also tends to weaken further the town's competitive position. The future of these places and, more important, the future of the people who live in them, present problems that need continued government attention.

Yet this decline is far from universal. More than half of all nonmetropolitan municipalities grew during each of the last three decades. Between 1940 and 1970, the number of nonmetropolitan places increased from 12,800 to 13,800 and their total population grew from 23 to 33 million. An increasing percentage of this population is in places over 10,000. The places closest to metropolitan areas were more likely to grow than those situated in remote locations.[16]

Nor is it clear that population growth is good for all small towns or cities any more than for all metropolitan areas. For some types of activities, recreation for example, many rural areas may already have more people than desirable, even though density and population size are well below urban levels. The typical small college town, which has experienced rapid growth in the last decade, might well benefit from stabilization of its population as college enrollment levels off.

The continued growth of some small towns and cities, and the vitality of others whose populations are not growing, challenge the popular notion that small town life is disappearing. On the other hand, the association between growth and proximity to a metropolitan center indicates that many of the small towns are growing because they are part of an extensive metropolitan area whose influence goes beyond the census-defined boundaries. Although rural in physical setting, the life style is urban. Many of these areas have become part of the process of metropolitan growth and dispersal.

METROPOLITAN DISPERSAL

The territory of metropolitan America has expanded even faster than its population. Roads and communications extend the reach of today's metropolitan areas deep into their hinterland. Villages and towns become part of the city-system, grow, and the metropolis expands. At the same time, internal changes sharpen differences within areas. Major variations in ethnic diversity, environmental hazard, socioeconomic status, and income, as well as in fertility and mortality exist within rather than between metropolitan areas. Moreover, the most extensive depopulation in the contemporary United States is occurring in central cities of metropolitan areas.

Fifteen of the 21 central cities with a 1960 population of one-half million or more had lost population by 1970.[17] In fact, declining central cities lost more people in the 1960's than were lost by declining rural counties. Over half the 1970 metropolitan population lived outside the central city, and suburban areas captured almost all the metropolitan growth during the decade. Continuing dispersal and expansion means that the density of the central cities and of the great metropolitan areas as a whole is falling slightly as the border gets pushed further and further outward.

The territorial expansion of metropolitan areas has resulted from the movement of business and the more affluent and white population out of the central city, and from a shift in the locus of new growth—residential, industrial, commercial —to the expanding periphery. These changes have been so pervasive that many suburban areas now provide all the basic services and facilities generally found in the city—shopping, jobs, and entertainment, as well as residences. The suburban resident has a decreasing need to come into the city. Many work at industries along the beltways circling many cities.

33

Others, particularly white-collar workers, commute daily to the city, but otherwise live essentially a suburban life.

Simultaneous with this dispersal has been the concentration of the black population in the central city, entrenching the already established pattern of racial separation. Even among relatively affluent blacks, the proportion living in the suburbs is low compared to their white counterparts. In the 1960's, the black population increased by a third. By 1970, 41 percent of metropolitan whites and 78 percent of metropolitan blacks lived in central cities. Suburbs continued to be almost totally white. Six central cities were over 50 percent black, and this number is expected to increase over the next decade.[18]

Outside the central city there is an extensive sorting-out process. Suburban communities typically are internally homogeneous, but differ from one another along social and economic lines, with the rich in some, the less affluent in others. Variations among suburbs are becoming as important as those between the central city and suburbs as a whole.

These processes—expansion and differentiation—pose critical problems for the contemporary United States. They do so in part because of the multiplicity of governmental jurisdictions encompassed and created by the expanding metropolis, and because of the ease with which the city line becomes the border between "them" and "us."

The first problem is racial and economic separation—blacks and the poor in the inner city, whites and the better off in the suburbs. While job opportunities have been moving to suburban areas, the disadvantaged remain locked in declining areas of the central city. These areas have many of the same characteristics as the depopulating rural areas: a population with low skills and inadequate education, deteriorating and abandoned housing, poor public facilities. Conditions are aggravated by selective outmigration. Those who can, leave. Those unable to cope with the problems of social and economic isolation remain.

The demography of racial separation is grim. Blacks and other nonwhites, now 22 percent of central-city populations, are projected to comprise about 40 percent by the year 2000.[19] Long before this average is reached by all cities, it will have been surpassed by many. At least in a geographical sense, the "two societies" envisioned by the Kerner Commission are emerging.

A second problem is the relationship of the "real city"—the functionally integrated metropolitan area—to the legal entities that are supposed to govern it. Since the turn of the century,

34

the legal boundaries of the central city have remained relatively fixed, while the functional city has expanded to include many suburban jurisdictions as well. The Secretary of the Department of Housing and Urban Development recently referred to this problem, pointing to the need to deal with problems of transportation, housing, and location of jobs in relation to other daily activities at the metropolitan level.[20] Instead, we are trying to cope with the problems arising from a new form of collective living—metropolitan—with a fragmented political structure suited to the needs of an earlier era. Disparities exist between the resources and responsibilities of different units of local government. Core cities with limited and sometimes shrinking tax bases are still responsible for needy elements of the population—the elderly, poor, unemployed, and nonwhite —left behind by the suburban exodus.

A third problem lies in the expanding periphery of metropolitan areas. During the rapid expansion of suburban areas since World War II, we failed to plan for anticipated growth; instead, we allowed it to spread at will. Whether or not we are past a population explosion, it is clear that the land-use explosion of "spread city" is currently in full bloom. In the 1970's and 1980's, the baby-boom generation will marry, have children, and set up house in the suburbs, creating a tremendous demand for the conversion of rural land to urban use. Without proper efforts to plan where and how future urban growth should occur, and without strong governmental leadership to implement the plans, the problems of sprawl, congestion, inadequate open space, and environmental deterioration will grow on an ever-increasing scale.

PUBLIC ATTITUDES

Partly because of the problems of urban living, partly as an expression of nostalgia for what is perceived as the "good old days," and perhaps partly in anguish over the condition of modern life—for whatever reasons—Americans express dissatisfaction with the city and think something should be done. When asked where they would prefer to live, they show pronounced preferences for small towns and rural areas. Following are some of the results from our survey of public information and attitudes:

	Where do you live now? (Percent)	Where would you prefer to live? (Percent)
Open Country	12	34
Small Town or City	33	30
Medium-Sized City or Suburb	28	22
Larger City or Suburb	27	14
Total	100	100

SOURCE: National Public Opinion Survey conducted for the Commission by the Opinion Research Corporation, 1971.

Thus, 34 percent of people surveyed said they would prefer to live in open country, but only 12 percent of them were classified as actually living there now.[21] These results correspond to the results of many similar national surveys. What do they mean?

A recent survey of Wisconsin residents asked the same questions, but added a question on preferred proximity to a large city. The results show a preference to live in smaller places *within commuting distance of a metropolitan central city*. In fact, if we take them at their word, 70 percent of the Wisconsin survey respondents would prefer to live near a metropolitan area, whereas only 54 percent now do.[22]

We do not know if the results of the Wisconsin survey reflect national attitudes. If they do, it means people want the best of both worlds—the serene and clean environment of rural areas and the opportunity and excitement of the metropolis. Perhaps it is not accidental that much metropolitan growth in fact occurs in peripheral areas with a semi-rural environment. Ironically, people moving to such areas typically find that they soon lose their more desirable aspects—semi-rural areas rapidly become suburban.

Even if current trends should prove to reflect majority preferences, about one-fourth of the population in medium- and large-sized metropolitan areas think that the place where they live is too big. Over half of the population feel that the federal government should "discourage further growth of large metropolitan areas" or should "try to encourage people and industry to move to smaller cities and towns." One-third disagree, and the rest express no opinion. Americans are urban and becoming more so, but many people evidently dislike the trend.[23]

36

WHERE DO THE TRENDS LEAD US?[24]

In 1970, about 71 percent of our population was metropolitan; it is expected to be 85 percent by the year 2000. (The census figure for 1970 was 69 percent. Our projections were based on a modified definition of metropolitan areas; hence the difference.)

Natural increase is the primary factor affecting the growth of metropolitan population as a whole. To measure its effect, we asked the Census Bureau to project growth within fixed (1960) metropolitan boundaries, supposing there were no additions to metropolitan population through territorial additions or migration from within the United States or from abroad. Even assuming growth at the 2-child rate, we found that the metropolitan population would grow by nearly 40 million people between 1970 and the year 2000, through natural increase alone.[25] If to this we add migration, territorial expansion of existing areas, and the growth of other centers to metropolitan size, it is clear that a metropolitan future is assured.

If the national population should grow at the 2-child rate, projections based on recent trends indicate that there will be 225 million people living in metropolitan areas by the end of the century. This would represent the addition of 81 million people to the 144 million persons who comprised our metropolitan population in 1970. An average of three children per family would cause our metropolitan population to swell to a total of 273 million by the year 2000, an increase of 129 million over the 1970 figure. Thus, our metropolitan population at the end of the century will be nearly 50 million greater if American families average three rather than two children.

Where will these people live? In 1970, more than four out of every 10 Americans were living in a metropolitan area comprised of one million or more people. By the year 2000, the projections indicate that more than six of every 10 persons are likely to be living in these large areas. Not all of the additional people will be added to the 29 metropolitan areas of one million or more that existed in 1970. In the year 2000, there will be a total of 44 to 50 such places, depending on how fast the total population grows. If present trends continue, the locus of continued increases in our total population will be large metropolitan areas. This is to be expected so long

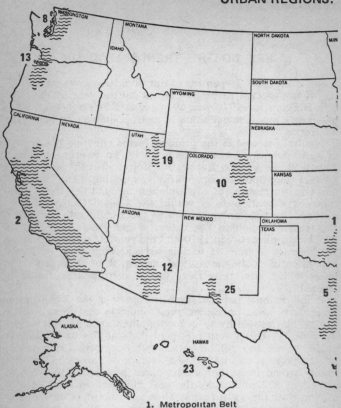

URBAN REGIONS:

1. Metropolitan Belt
   1.a. Atlantic Seabord
   1.b. Lower Great Lakes
2. California Region
3. Florida Peninsula
4. Gulf Coast
5. East Central Texas—Red River
6. Southern Piedmont
7. North Georgia—South East Tennessee
8. Puget Sound
9. Twin Cities Region
10. Colorado Piedmont
11.. Saint Louis
12. Metropolitan Arizona
13. Willamette Valley

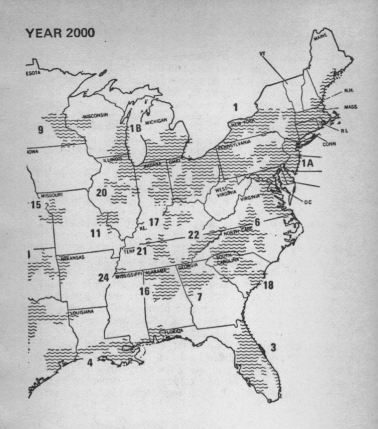

YEAR 2000

14. Central Oklahoma—Arkansas Valley
15. Missouri—Kau Valley
16. North Alabama
17. Blue Grass
18. Southern Coastal Plain
19. Salt Lake Valley
20. Central Illinois
21. Nashville Region
22. East Tennessee
23. Oahu Island
24. Memphis
25. El Paso—Ciudad Juarez

Based on 2-child family projection

SOURCE: Jerome P. Pickard, "U. S. Metropolitan Growth and Expansion, 1970-2000, With Population Projections" (prepared for the Commission, 1972).

as the total number of people in metropolitan areas keeps on growing.

We tried to learn how much the growth of the large metropolitan areas might be reduced if the growth of smaller, less congested places were stimulated. Commission researchers picked 121 places ranging in size from 10,000 to 350,000 whose growth in the past decade indicated that they might be induced to grow more rapidly in the future. They listed all places of this size that had grown faster than the national average during the 1960's and were located more than 75 miles from any existing or projected metropolitan area of two million people or more.

Such places had a total population of 14 million in 1970. If they were to grow by 30 percent each decade, their population in the year 2000 would be about 31 million. If this were to happen, our calculations suggest that these places might absorb about 10 million of the growth which is otherwise expected to occur in areas of one million or more, assuming the 2-child national projection. However, these large areas would still increase by 70 million under the 2-child projection, and by 115 million under the 3-child projection. If the smaller areas were to grow faster than 30 percent, they would, of course, divert more growth from the large areas. But to obtain substantial effects, these smaller places would have to grow 50 percent per decade.[26] At that point, one must ask if the cure is any better than the disease.

Moreover, most of the smaller areas which are capable of attracting many people are in urban regions, or would be by the year 2000. Thus, stimulating their growth would have the useful effect of decongesting settlement in urban regions, but would do little to retard urban region growth.

URBAN REGIONS[27]

The evolution of urban communities has proceeded from farm, to small town, to city, to large metropolitan area. It is now proceeding to the urban region—areas of one million people or more comprised of a continuous zone of metropolitan areas and intervening counties within which one is never far from a city. The reach of the urban economy has so increased that the most logical scale at which to grasp the trend is at the urban region level.

There have been tremendous changes in the geographic

scale at which we live. Transportation technology, particularly our extensive highway system, permits us to move great distances within a short period. Some people commute daily between New York and Boston or Washington. Urban people in search of open space and recreation travel considerable distances to enjoy a weekend camping trip. A century ago, Central Park was the city park for New York. Now the "city" is the urban region along the Atlantic seaboard and its park is the Shenandoah National Park on Skyline Drive. It is perhaps a weekend park, not one visited daily; but, on a three-day weekend, the license plates on visiting cars will be from Pennsylvania, New York, D.C., and Virginia. The scale at which we live is expanding well beyond formal metropolitan boundaries. In the future, our daily experience may well reach out into the far corners of urban regions and beyond.

An urban region is not a single "supercity"; it is a regional constellation of urban centers and their hinterland. Although substantial portions are comprised of more or less continuous geographic settlement, the urban region offers—and continues to provide—a variety of residential settings within the functional sphere of a metropolitan economy. This mosaic of environments ranges from rural (southern New Hampshire or Indio, California) to cosmopolitan (Chicago or Los Angeles). Such environments coexist within a common functional framework without intruding spatially on each other. Even in the largest urban region, running along the Atlantic coast from Maine to Virginia, and westward past Chicago, it is estimated that only one-fifth of the area is currently in urban use.

These regions grow not only through the increase of population but by geographic expansion. In effect, they are a product of the automobile era and new communication technology which encouraged the outward movement of industries and residences from the city proper. Density within these regions has remained relatively constant and low, even though population size has increased.

Urban regions appear to be a prominent feature of the demographic future of this country. In 1920, there were 10 urban regions with over one-third of the total population. By 1970, about three-fourths of the population of the United States lived in the urban regions which already exist or are expected to develop by 2000.

The total land area encompassed by urban regions is estimated to double in the period 1960 to 1980, while the number of such areas is expected to increase from 16 to at least 23. By 2000, urban regions will occupy one-sixth of the conti-

EXPANSION OF URBAN REGIONS

SQUARE MILES

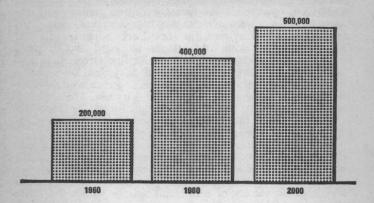

The territory of urban regions is doubling in the period 1960 to 1980. By the year 2000, urban regions will encompass one-sixth of the United States land area (excl. Alaska and Hawaii).

SOURCE: Jerome P. Pickard, "U. S. Metropolitan Growth and Expansion, 1970-2000, With Population Projections" (prepared for the Commission, 1972).

nental United States land area, and contain five-sixths of our nation's people. (See bar graph above.)

If our national population distributes itself according to these projections, 54 percent of all Americans will be living in the two largest urban regions. The metropolitan belt stretching along the Atlantic seaboard and westward past Chicago would contain 41 percent of our total population. Another 13 percent would be in the California region lying between San Francisco and San Diego. (See map on pages 38-39.)

Even if the broad trends have been projected accurately, the experiences of individual metropolitan areas may differ considerably from the estimates prepared for us. Within the general system of metropolitan centers, some will probably stabilize or decline; others, having a disproportionate number of young people, or attracting much migration, will continue to grow rapidly, even if national population stabilizes. Finally, there may well be new frontiers of growth that have not yet been established or discovered by social scientists. Our projections, then, should be taken as a description of a possible future—one that is essentially the outcome of trends now observable—but not as a prediction of what will happen or a prescription of what is desirable.

POPULATION STABILIZATION, MIGRATION, AND DISTRIBUTION

How would stabilization of the national population affect migration and local growth? First, shifts in population composition—chiefly age and family structure—would alter the tempo of migration. Second, changes in the balance between natural increase and migration would influence local growth. Because of the momentum of past growth and the time it will take to achieve a stabilized population in the United States, the full effects will be long range.

An older population with smaller families would be slightly less mobile. Long-distance moves would be relatively less numerous because of the decline in the proportion of the population aged 20 to 24, which is most apt to move. Smaller families would reduce the need of repeated residential moves, since such moves are often an adjustment to changing housing needs.

Perhaps the most significant effect of population stabilization on the distribution of population is the most obvious: Zero growth for the nation will mean an average of zero growth for local areas. It may be that the most effective long-term strategy for stabilizing local growth is through national stabilization, not redistribution.

Stabilization would slow the growth of the largest metropolitan centers, which are already growing only at the same rate as the nation, and it would shift somewhat more of the available growth to small- and intermediate-size centers. Replacement-level fertility would mean that migration in and out of a metropolitan area would be an extremely important component of local growth; and continued selective growth through migration would tend to accentuate uneven growth among different metropolitan areas. Natural increase would no longer balance out net outmigration, so a significant number of metropolitan areas could be expected to lose population.

However, even if the population of our country were to stop growing today, we would still have problems associated with rural depopulation and metropolitan growth. Our large metro-

43

politan areas would still have problems of congestion, pollution, and severe racial separation.

According to the Commission's survey, 54 percent of Americans think that the distribution of population is a "serious problem"; half believe that, over the next 30 years, it will be at least as great a problem as population growth.[28] This is in accordance with our belief that to reduce problems of population growth in no way absolves us of the responsibility to address the problems posed by the distribution of population.

CHAPTER 4. THE ECONOMY

Does a healthy economy require a growing population? Would slower population growth hurt business or threaten workers' jobs? Would it help? How would the average person fare in economic terms if the rate of population growth approached zero?*

We have conducted research to determine what effects different rates of population growth are likely to have on the economic well-being of the nation. We compared the effects of the 2-child population projection with the effects of the 3-child projection. Our overall conclusions from this research are:

1. Major economic changes are on the horizon regardless of future changes in population growth rates.

2. The nation has nothing to fear from a gradual approach to population stabilization.

3. From an economic point of view, a reduction in the rate of population growth would bring important benefits, especially if the United States develops policies to take advantage of the opportunities for social and economic improvement that slower population growth would provide.

*Separate statements by Commissioners Otis Dudley Duncan, with Paul B. Cornely, M.D., concurring (pp. 274-275), John R. Meyer (p. 288), and James S. Rummonds (pp. 305-307), appear on the indicated pages.

INCOME

Between now and the year 2000, increases in the productivity of workers are likely to result in such a large rise in average income that styles of life in the year 2000 will be qualitatively different from what they are today. It is expected that by the year 2000 average family income, now about $12,000, will exceed $21,000, in terms of today's dollars.[1] This is the projection, even if the work week were reduced to 30 hours, and even if the population grew at the 3-child rate.

The average individual's consumption is expected to be more than twice what it is today, whether the population grows at the 2-child or the 3-child rate. As income increases, people show an increased preference for services, such as education and health services, as compared with manufactured goods. So, the population of the year 2000 will boost its consumption of services faster than its consumption of manufactured goods.

The rate of population growth will have a significant effect on per capita income. Our research indicates that in the year 2000, per capita income may be as much as 15 percent higher under the 2-child than under the 3-child population growth rate. The main reason for the higher per capita income under the 2-child projection is the shift in the age composition resulting from slower population growth; as we saw earlier, people of working age will constitute a larger fraction of the total population under conditions of slower population growth. A secondary reason is that with lower birthrates the percentage of women in the labor force is expected to rise somewhat faster than it would otherwise. Taken together, these trends mean relatively more workers and earners, and relatively fewer mouths to feed.

The age effect arises from the fact that population replaces itself from the bottom up; and, if it is growing, it is adding more and more at the base of the age pyramid. However, growth in the population of working age is drawn from the smaller numbers of births that occurred 15 to 20 years earlier. When growth slows, it slows first at the base, and before long we see a narrowing of the difference between the number of births and the numbers annually entering the working ages. The ratio of workers to youthful dependents rises, the income they produce is spread among fewer people, and the average income available per person in the population consequently increases.

Of course, the same process eventually causes a rise in the percentage of old people in the population—those who have passed working age. But because of higher death rates at these ages, the increase in aged dependency offsets only part of the decline in youth dependency, and the overall result is still a major drop in total dependency and an increase in income available per person in the population.

ECONOMIC GROWTH
AND THE QUALITY OF LIFE

The use of income or output per capita as an indicator of the quality of life has been criticized on a number of grounds. One such criticism is made by people who are concerned about environmental deterioration. They maintain that higher output levels for the economy *as a whole* will cause a greater drain on natural resources and more pollution.

Accordingly, we examined the effects that the 2- and 3-child growth rates would have on GNP—the gross national product—which measures the total volume of goods and services produced. GNP is expected to more than double by the year 2000, whether the population grows rapidly or slowly.[2] This is the prospect implied by the projected increases in per capita income and the further growth of population resulting from the baby boom.

However, if families average three children in the future, GNP will grow far more than if they average two children. In the year 2000, the difference in GNP resulting from different population assumptions amounts to as much as one-fourth of the total GNP today. Rapid population growth will cause more rapid growth in the size of the economy, and correspondingly greater demands on resources and the environment. People will not be better off economically with more rapid population growth—we have already seen that income per person is higher under the slower population growth assumption. Rather, increases in the number of people simply multiply the volume of goods and services produced and consumed. In the next chapter, we examine the meaning of these trends for resource consumption and deterioration of the environment.

POVERTY

Income or output per capita is an average, and it conceals some gross disparities. We need to be concerned with these, especially at the lower end of the income scale—the people in poverty.

We have estimated the effects that slower population growth would have on poverty in the United States in the year 2000. We have found that the general improvement in average income associated with slower population growth would assist in reducing poverty, but would not eliminate it. This is not good enough.

There are today, by official estimate, 26 million Americans living in poverty conditions.[3] This is 13 percent of our population. Improvements in the average income of the population do something for these groups, but not enough. Their problem is that too many of them are not part of the system that generates and distributes income.

Over six million poor people are working adults who simply do not make enough money to meet even the minimal official income standard. Over three million of the poor are persons aged 14 to 64 who are sick or disabled, in school, or unable to find work. Nearly five million are over age 65, and over eight million are children. Finally, more than two million are female heads of family whose responsibilities at home keep them from taking jobs.

What this adds up to is that more than nine out of 10 poor people are excluded—because of age, incapacity, poor training, family responsibilities, fiscal disincentives, or discrimination in the labor market—from the system that produces and distributes income and the things income buys. Real improvements in their lot will be reflected in a changing distribution of income. But, while average income has risen dramatically and the number of poor has declined as a result, the relative distribution of income has changed little in the 25 years the Census Bureau has been measuring it.

In a country as wealthy and resourceful as ours, there is no excuse for permitting deprivation. For the working poor and those who cannot find work, the solution is to eliminate racial and sex discrimination in employment, and to improve education and training. Beyond this, we need a serious reexamination of the status of the aged. Old people are healthier and

48

better educated than ever before. They are often forced to stop working far before the end of their productive lives, because of outright discrimination and outdated restrictions against older workers, and because of fiscal disincentives against work built into our social security laws and other pension arrangements.

Nevertheless, the country still has a number of people who cannot be helped by better access to the labor market. For these, the answer should be an increased public responsibility for maintaining a decent standard of living.

Measures to achieve an improved distribution of income should be beneficial demographically as well as socially. Evidence indicates that levels of childbearing—both wanted and unwanted—decline as income rises.

LABOR FORCE GROWTH

Thirty-five million new workers will be seeking their first job in the decade of the 1970's.[4] That is seven million more than in the 1960's. This is one of the legacies of the baby boom. As that generation comes of age, swelling numbers of job applicants put an extra burden on full employment policy.

The pressure should be off in the 1980's. The number of new entrants to the labor force will probably be close to the figure for the 1970's, due to declining birthrates in the past decade. Once all the new entrants and women resuming work after their children are grown are balanced out against withdrawals through retirement and death, the labor force in 1990 should number some 114 million, or 28 million more than the 1970 figure.

What happens thereafter depends mainly on the number of births in the 1970's. If fertility should follow the 2-child projection, the number of people looking for their first job in the 1990's should be about the same as in the 1980's. However, if fertility follows the 3-child projection, the number of job seekers in the 1990's will jump 10 million, to a total of around 44 million; and by the year 2000, the total labor force will number some 136 million. Beyond 2000, the difference in labor force growth between the two projections becomes immense.

It seems clear that labor-force trends under the 3-child projection can be expected to generate greater pressure for increased production, employment, and consumption, and correspondingly greater problems associated with the social and environmental consequences of such increases. The 2-child projection does not imply that these problems can be avoided, only that they will be less pressing. It implies not only smaller numbers to be accommodated, but also a context in which the urgency of competing priorities will be muted.

We have seen that slower population growth causes a gradual increase in the percentage of old people and a decline in the percentage of youth—hence, a rising average age of the population. The same process also causes the labor force to age.

Concerns have been expressed that an older labor force will lack the energy, flexibility, and imagination of a younger one. Despite the absence of evidence for these concerns, their existence is further reason to support programs desirable on other grounds, such as the provision of continuing education of our labor force. Indeed, in light of the rapid changes occurring in all aspects of life, the idea that education should be completed by the age of 18, 22, or even 30, is clearly out of date.

BUSINESS

Will a slower rate of population growth hurt specific industries, particularly those which cater to young people? Does it threaten jobs?

While it is certainly true that there would be a faster increase in the sales of certain products, for example baby foods and milk, under conditions of higher population growth, it is also true that other products and services, for example convenience foods and airline travel, would be relatively favored by the faster rise in per capita income associated with slower population growth rates. More important, it does not appear, for several reasons, that a lower population growth rate will cause serious problems for any industry or its employees.[5]

First, regardless of the rate of population growth, total income, and hence demand, will rise.

Second, slower population growth will actually cause total as well as per capita income to be higher over the next 10 to 15 years than would a more rapid population growth rate. In other words, during the next 10 to 15 years total GNP in the 2-child projection would probably be slightly larger than in the 3-child case.

Third, it is important to note that under the 2-child family projection, there is no year in which there would be fewer births than there were in 1971. In other words, a gradual approach to population stabilization would not reduce demand from current levels for any industry we studied. (We studied the effect of the 2-child and 3-child population projections on demand for housing starts, mobile homes, domestic cars, imported cars, men's suits, frozen foods, power boats, credit, furniture and household equipment, food and beverages, beer, clothing and shoes, steel, dishwashers, railroad travel, and airline travel.)

Beyond the next 10 to 15 years, the adjustments businesses must make to changes in consumer tastes and technological developments should far exceed the problems of adjusting to a lower population growth rate. The loom tender in the diaper factory is hurt more by the competition from synthetic disposables than by the recent decline in births. Large fluctuations in birthrates will require larger adjustments by business than will small ones; still, we can have fluctuations around a 3-child as well as a 2-child growth rate. In declining communities, small businesses will not do as well economically as they would if there were more people around—some adjustments will be required. But other changes that are unpredictable today will require far more important adjustments by individuals, as well as by entire industries.

Past experience should lead to confidence that such adjustments can be made. Here is the Board Chairman of Atlantic-Richfield, testifying at our public hearing in New York:

> There is a habit of thinking in some segments of the business community, of course, that population increase is somehow essential to the maintenance of vigorous demand and economic growth, just as there is an instinctive reaction against any important new cost factors being added to the processes of production and distribution. But our economy has already, and in many ways, shown its tremendous adaptability to new social demands and necessities. I have not the slightest doubt that it can meet this new challenge.[6]

THE GROWTH MYSTIQUE

In short, we find no convincing economic argument for continued national population growth. On the contrary, most of the plusses are on the side of slower growth. This finding is at variance with much opinion, especially in the business com-

51

munity and among many civic leaders. We have sought to find the reason for this seeming contradiction.

Periods of rapid population growth in this country have generally been periods of rapid economic expansion as well. It is not surprising, therefore, that we associate population growth with economic progress. However, the historical association of population growth with economic expansion would be an erroneous guide to the formulation of population policy for the future.

This connection reflects in large part the fact that periods of rapid economic expansion attracted immigrants to our shores and thus quickened population growth as a result. Additions to population through immigration are far more stimulating to economic growth than are additions by natural increase. This is because, while babies remain dependent for many years before beginning to contribute to output, many immigrants are of working age and thus become immediately productive. Immigration made a major contribution to rapid population growth up to World War I, but its effect since then has been much diminished. In the years 1861 to 1910, the average annual immigration rate per 1000 Americans was 7.5; the rate for the period 1911 to 1970 dropped to 1.8. The rate for the recent period reflects a rise from the 1930's, when there was a net outflow of migrants, to the 1960's when the rate was 2.2.[7]

This answer may not satisfy the gas station owner, local food retailer, or banker, to whom it seems obvious that "more people" means more customers or more savings accounts. Once again, however, we need to examine the *kind* of growth that means more business, and its relationship to local economic expansion. The rapid local population growth that means more business results chiefly from other people moving in, not more people being born and raised. Adults moving in make ready customers and ready employees. They have grown up elsewhere, their education has been paid for elsewhere, and being young, they impose few of the demands of the dependent aged. Since mobile people are, on the average, better qualified than those who do not move, it is no surprise that they provide an extra boost to local establishments.

We have studied the effects of lower national population growth rates on the economic well-being of urban and rural areas within the nation. Is there reason to fear that the ills typical of areas of population decline today would become more serious or widespread if national population growth rates declined? We conclude that there is not; such fears are based on a mistaken belief that population decline causes economic decline. In reality, the chain of causation in distressed areas

52

runs from (1) the decline of regional competitive capability to (2) unemployment to (3) net outmigration to (4) population loss.[8] Accordingly, there is little reason to suppose that local problems of unemployment or obsolescence of physical facilities would be more serious in a situation of zero or negative national population growth than they would be at any positive level of national population growth. In the future, as in the past, areas of relatively high unemployment will tend to be areas of relative population loss; but the relative population loss will be the consequence and not the cause of local unemployment.

The diminished burden of providing for dependents, and for the multiplication of facilities to keep up with expanding population, should make more of our national output available for many desirable purposes: new kinds of capital formation, including human resources investment; public expenditure involving qualitative improvement and modernization; and greater attention to environmental and amenity objectives. Thus, whatever the future problems of urban areas and regions may be, we should have more ample per capita resources to attack them in a situation with a lower rate of population growth than we would have with a higher rate.

SUMMARY

We have looked for, and have not found, any convincing economic argument for continued national population growth. The health of our economy does not depend on it. The vitality of business does not depend on it. The welfare of the average person certainly does not depend on it.

In fact, the average person will be markedly better off in terms of traditional economic values if population growth follows the 2-child projection rather than the 3-child one. Slower growth will give us an older population, and this trend will require adjustments well within the ability of the nation to provide. Beyond this, however, we point out that the fruits of slower population growth will be denied to those most in need of them unless deliberate changes are made in distribution of income to those who lack it by reason of discrimination, incapacity, or age.

CHAPTER 5. RESOURCES AND THE ENVIRONMENT

What are the likely future impacts of population growth on the demand for resources and on the environment in the United States? Here again, we have examined the consequences of the population growing according to the 2-child projection and the 3-child projection, and compared the results. For problems such as air pollution, where local concentrations are important, we have examined the implications of population growth in local areas as well as in the nation as a whole.

For several resource and environmental topics, we have extended the analysis beyond the year 2000 to the year 2020; in so doing, we have identified some important effects that do not become particularly noticeable in the shorter period. Beyond the next 50 years, we do not know enough to make quantitative projections. Nonetheless, it is obvious that there are ultimate limits to growth. We live in a finite world. While its limits are unknown because technology keeps changing them, it is clear that the growth of population and the escalation of consumption must ultimately stop. The only questions are when, how, and at what level. The answers to these questions will largely be determined by the course of world population growth, including that of the United States.

Several general conclusions* emerge from our research:

*A separate statement by Commissioner Alan Cranston appears on pages 267-268.)

1. Population growth is one of the major factors affecting the demand for resources and the deterioration of the environment in the United States. The further we look into the future, the more important population becomes.

2. From an environmental and resource point of view, there are no advantages from further growth of population beyond the level to which our past rapid growth has already committed us. Indeed, we would be considerably better off over the next 30 to 50 years if there were a prompt reduction in our population growth rate. This is especially true with regard to problems of water, agricultural land, and outdoor recreation.

3. While the nation can, if it has to, find ways to solve the problems growth creates, we will not like some of the solutions we will have to adopt. With continued growth, we commit ourselves to a particular set of problems: more rapid depletion of domestic and international resources, greater pressures on the environment, greater dependence on continued rapid technological development to solve these problems, and a more contrived and regulated society. So long as population growth continues, these problems will grow and will slowly, but irreversibly, force changes in our way of life. And there are further risks: Increasing numbers press us to adopt new technologies before we know what we are doing. The more of us there are, the greater is the temptation to introduce solutions before their side effects are known. With slower population growth leading to a stabilized population, we gain time to devise solutions, resources to implement them, and greater freedom of choice in deciding how we want to live in the future.

4. The American future cannot be isolated from what is happening in the rest of the world. There are serious problems right now in the distribution of resources, income, and wealth, among countries. World population growth is going to make these problems worse before they get better. The United States needs to undertake much greater efforts to understand these problems and develop international policies to deal with them.

HOW POPULATION AFFECTS RESOURCES AND THE ENVIRONMENT

The pressure that this nation puts on resources and the environment during the next 30 to 50 years will depend on the size of the national population, the size of population in local areas, the amounts and types of goods and services the population consumes, and the ways in which these goods and services are produced, used, and disposed of. All these factors are important. Right now, because of our large population size and high economic productivity, the United States puts more pressure on resources and the environment than any other nation in the world.

We have attempted to separate these factors and estimate the impact of population on resources and the environment using a quantitative model which shows the demand for resources and the pollution levels associated with different rates of economic and population growth. The seriousness of the population-induced effects has then been assessed by evaluating the adequacy of resources to meet these requirements and the environmental impacts of pollution.

In discussing the economy, we indicated that under any set of economic projections, the total volume of goods and services produced in the United States—the gross national product—will be far larger than it is today. It is expected to be at least twice its present size by the year 2000, and in 50 years, with rapid population and economic growth, it could be seven times as large as it is now. Regardless of future population growth, the prospect is that increases in output will cause tremendous increases in demand for resources and impact on the environment.

What happens to population growth will nevertheless make a big difference in the future size of the economy. In the year 2000, the difference in GNP resulting from the different population assumptions could amount to one-fourth of today's GNP. By the year 2020, this difference amounts to more than the total size of today's GNP.

In short, total GNP, which is the principal source of the demand for resources and the production of pollutants, will become much larger than it is now. But if population should grow at the 3-child rate, GNP will grow far more than it will at the 2-child rate.

MINERALS

In our research, we examined the demand for 19 major nonfuel minerals: chromium, iron, nickel, potassium, cobalt, vanadium, magnesium, phosphorous, nitrogen, manganese,

57

molybdenum, tungsten, aluminum, copper, lead, zinc, tin, titanium, and sulfur.

Resource consumption will rise more slowly if population grows more slowly. Our estimates indicate that the amount of minerals consumed in the year 2000 would average nine percent lower under the 2-child than under the 3-child population projection. The difference in annual consumption would be 17 percent in the year 2020, and would grow rapidly thereafter.

Population growth exerts an important effect on resource consumption compared with the effect of economic growth. Our research shows that in the year 2000, if GNP per capita were one percent less than projected, the consumption of most minerals would be 0.7 to 1.0 percent less; the consumption of four minerals—cobalt, magnesium, titanium, and sulfur—would be reduced relatively more. In the year 2000, if population were one percent less than projected, minerals consumption would be 0.5 to 0.7 percent less. The population effect, while substantial, is smaller because of an important offsetting effect. As we saw earlier, slower population growth induces higher output per person because of the favorable ratio of labor force to total population. This offsets somewhat the effect that smaller numbers have on the conservation of resources.

While there are clear resource savings from slower population growth, our research supports, with certain qualifications, the view that the United States would have no serious difficulty acquiring the supplies it needs for the next 50 years, even if the population were to grow at the 3-child rate. This is the prospect, even assuming, as we have done, that the resource demands of the rest of the world grow more rapidly than those of the United States, as has been the case in recent years. Although growing demand may pose some problems of adjustment, adequate supplies of all the minerals we studied can be achieved through tolerable price increases. Price increases will equalize supply and demand by stimulating exploration or imports (increased supply) and by stimulating recycling and the use of more plentiful substitutes (reduced demand). The earth's crust still contains immense quantities of lower grade minerals which can be called into production at levels of costs which we could afford to pay, even if the demands of the rest of the world should rise as projected and our population were to grow at the 3-child rate.

This expectation could be altered by several developments. First, prices could fail to anticipate impending shortages; that is, they might not rise long enough in advance to stimulate the changes necessary to avert shortages. Second, mining operations are heavy polluters, and mineral needs could conflict with environmental policy. Finally, and most serious, there are worldwide imbalances in access to resources. While the United States will remain among the "haves," relatively speaking, disparities between world regions may affect international power balances in ways that would involve us.

ENERGY

Energy makes the difference between poverty and affluence. The reason per capita income in the United States is so high is that the average American worker has at his command more energy, chiefly in the form of electricity, than any other worker in the world. With energy we refine aluminum, make rubber, shape steel, form new synthetic chemical compounds, propel automobiles, and heat our homes.

How much energy we have available depends on the availability of the necessary fuels and on our ability to convert the fuels to energy—the greatest advance in this regard was the development of inexpensive methods of electricity production. The technology of fuels acquisition and the technology of energy conversion are both critical. So is purchasing power —the ability to pay for domestic development of fuels or to import them. The original inhabitants of North America occupied a continent rich in energy fuels. But they neither knew how to get the fuels out of the ground nor how to convert them to energy. Some modern countries with advanced means of energy conversion lack their own fuel supplies; they buy them from other countries.

The ability of the United States to meet its future energy needs will be determined chiefly by developments in technology—the technology of conversion and the technology of fuels acquisition. A major question will be whether we can find methods that are environmentally safe. Virtually every stage of energy use—fuel production, delivery, conversion, and consumption—has a significant environmental impact. For example, one-third of all coal is produced by strip mining, and the consequence is a scarred landscape and severe runoff into streams and rivers. Oil spills which contaminate the oceans and beaches may result from offshore drilling. Much airborne pollution comes from the use of such relatively dirty fuels as coal and oil. Some scientists are beginning

59

to raise the possibility of thermal pollution resulting from concentrated use of energy in local areas. Nuclear power generation requires the disposal of radioactive atomic wastes. Because of these problems, the development of energy-production capacity could be impaired.

The increase in our energy needs will be immense under any projection, although not as large under the 2-child population projection as under the 3-child projection. The relative difference in energy demands under the different population projections is about the same as for minerals, and it becomes very large after the population with the lower rate of growth stabilizes. Whether population growth will strain fuel supplies, or cause serious environmental damage in the process of acquiring and using the necessary fuels, depends on future developments in technology.

With no major changes in technology, oil and gas supplies could become a problem for the United States by the year 2000—we would be importing more and paying higher prices; and supplies would certainly be a problem for some world regions. These problems could be averted if we found inexpensive means of using such potential sources as oil shale and tar sands, but using these sources is likely to have environmental consequences as serious as those from the strip-mining of coal. If we unlock the secrets of atomic fusion, we could have an environmentally clean way of generating electricity, with no fuel supply problem. The energy from converting the deuterium contained in 30 cubic kilometers of seawater would equal that of the earth's original supply of coal and petroleum.

Our review of the energy situation indicates that high priority ought to be given to research and development in clean sources of energy production. The faster population grows, the more urgent such breakthroughs become. We turn now to several areas where population growth dominates other considerations—where we cannot be hopeful about the ability of purchasing power and technical development to avert population problems.

WATER

Water requirements already exceed available flow in the southwestern United States. Our research shows that growing population and economic activity will cause the area of water shortage to spread eastward and northward across the country in the decades ahead. Such deficits will spread faster if population growth follows the 3-child projection than if it follows the 2-child projection. (See bar graph below and map on pages 62-63.) This will occur despite large expenditures on water treatment, dams, and reservoirs during the next 50 years. Population growth will be more important than economic growth in causing these growing problems.

Our national abundance of water does not change this picture significantly. If water could be shipped across the country like oil, coal, or manufactured goods, there would be no problems of water shortage. But distances are so long and the amounts of water used so huge, that it would be prohibitively expensive to solve these regional problems by transfers of water from surplus to deficit areas. Nor is there scope for sufficiently large relocation of water users—people and industries—to regions where water is plentiful. An inexpensive method of taking the salt out of seawater could solve the problem, but such technology is not now available. Similarly, artificial control of rain is not advanced enough to be used to any significant extent. While little is known about the extent of groundwater reserves, most experts do not consider the mining of such reserves an adequate alternative.

On the other hand, there is wide scope for reducing use through rationing and the adoption of water-conserving tech-

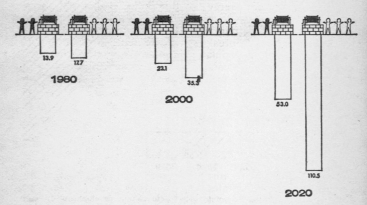

REGIONAL WATER SHORTAGES

BILLIONS OF GALLONS / DAY

13.9   12.7

1980

23.1

35.3

2000

53.0

110.5

2020

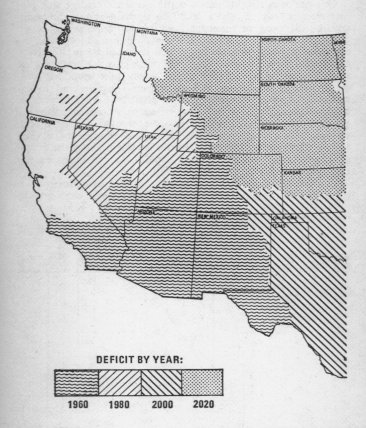

WATER DEFICIT REGIONS:

DEFICIT BY YEAR:

1960   1980   2000   2020

Estimates assume rapid economic growth, maximum development of water storage facilities, and tertiary treatment. Alaska and Hawaii not shown: Commission's data did not include these states.

3-CHILD FAMILY

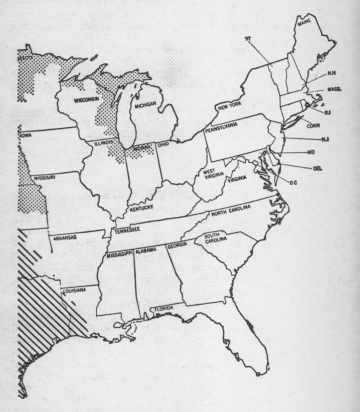

SOURCE: Ronald G. Ridker, "Future Water Needs and Supplies, With a Note on Land Use" (prepared for the Commission, 1972).

nology. Even today, most water is used virtually free of cost or is distributed on a fee basis that provides no incentives for conservation; and free use of water bodies as waste dumping grounds is more the rule than the exception. If the cost of utilizing water for these purposes were raised to more appropriate levels, factories and power plants would install techniques of production that save water instead of wasting it; farmers would modify their irrigation practices or otherwise adjust by changing location or shifting to crops using less water; and households would eventually adjust by reducing lawns and shrubbery.

Sooner or later we will have to deal with water as a scarce resource. The sooner this is done, the fewer water crises will emerge in the years ahead. However, doing this will not be easy technically or politically—most water supplies are run by local governments. And few will like the austerity created by the need to conserve on something as fundamental as water. The rate of national population growth will largely determine how rapidly we must accomplish these changes.

OUTDOOR RECREATION

On a recent holiday weekend, Yosemite National Park had a population of 50,000 people, according to a Park source. Since then, the number of campsites has been reduced and traffic has been restricted in order to reduce noise and pollution. Still, visitors are put on notice that the water in the river is undrinkable. Yellowstone, too, has far more applications than can be accommodated in the available campsites. Even so, population densities in the non-wilderness areas of the Park sometimes exceed densities in the suburbs of Dallas.

More and more Americans have the time, the money, and the inclination to enjoy the outdoors. Production of truck campers and camping trailers shot up from 62 thousand in 1961 to over one-half million in 1971. With better roads and easier travel, national parks have in effect become city parks for the residents of nearby metropolitan areas. In the past 10 years, visitors to all national park facilities more than doubled, while the area of the parks increased by only one-fifth. There are many areas to enjoy and more to be developed, but the enjoyment will depend largely on how fast the population grows.

By the year 2000, incomes will nearly double and hours of

leisure will rise. More and more people will be inclined to get away and will be able to do so. However, our research on some 24 outdoor recreation activities and the facilities for these activities indicates that population growing at the 3-child rate will exert great pressure on outdoor recreation resources —so great that, rather than "getting away" to the outdoors, people will be applying for admission to it.

In the face of rising congestion, many people will substitute organized sports, sightseeing, foreign travel, and artistic and cultural activities, if they so desire. Rising incomes and the increase in man-made facilities will make these alternatives possible. For many, these will be adequate alternatives, but for others they will not.

The prospects for recreation with the 2-child projection are much different for two reasons. First, the population will not be as large as that resulting from the 3-child rate. More important, the percentage of people in the young ages that make especially heavy use of outdoor recreation facilities will be smaller. As a consequence, we estimate that, in the year 2000, the demand for recreational facilities could be as much as 30 percent less under the 2-child than under the 3-child rate of growth.

Either way, recreation will differ from what it is now. The style of life may change with the lower rate of growth as well, shifting from more active to more sedentary pursuits. But in this case it would be voluntary, determined by the individual needs and preferences of an older population, not imposed by the desire to avoid overcrowding.

AGRICULTURAL LAND AND FOOD PRICES

At a time when the federal government pays farmers to hold land out of production, it seems absurd to be looking forward to a scarcity of good agricultural land and rising food prices. Yet these are the prospects indicated by our analysis of what rapid United States population growth implies.

This picture emerges when we combine the requirements for feeding a rapidly growing population with a sound environmental policy which restricts the use of pesticides and chemical fertilizers. There are a number of reasons for believing that the nation will wish to limit application of these chemicals. But to do so will retard improvements in per acre productivity. This means that, to produce a given quantity of food, more acres

65

must be brought into production. It is likely that, with such restrictions, all the high quality land will have been returned to production by the year 2000. Consequently, the task of feeding the more rapidly growing population would force us to bring an additional 50 million acres of relatively low-quality land into production.

This is an expensive undertaking requiring heavy investment in equipment, fertilizer, and manpower, for which farmers must be compensated. The result is that 50 years from now the population resulting from the 3-child average could find itself having to pay farm food prices some 40 to 50 percent higher than they would be otherwise. The needs of the population at the lower growth rate could be met with practically no price increase.

The larger population could avoid the price rise by shifting away from consumption of animal livestock towards vegetables and synthetic meats. Perhaps it would shift to a closed system of agriculture—food from factories. One way or another, a solution can be found. The problem for a growing population is to survey the possible solutions and select the ones it dislikes least.

POLLUTION

As the gross national product goes up, so does the production of pollutants. An irony of economic measurement is that the value of goods and services represented by GNP includes the cost of producing the pollutants as well as expenditures for cleaning up afterward. We may fill our tank with gasoline, but due to engine inefficiency, some portion of that ends up in the atmosphere as air pollution. Such pollutants are not free—we had to pay good money to put them in the air. Yet the cost of putting them there is included in our principal measure of national economic well-being.

If we clean up the pollutants, the cost of the cleanup effort is also added to GNP. But many of the costs, such as poorer health and deteriorated surroundings, are never counted at all. It is an indictment of our ignorance and indifference toward what we do to the environment, that in our national economic accounts we count so few of the "bads," and that even when we do count them, we count them as "goods."

To understand the contribution of population to pollution, we have to distinguish two broad classes of pollutants. The first class includes the major products of combustion—carbon monoxide, carbon dioxide, oxides of nitrogen, oxides of sulfur, hydrocarbons, and particulates—and several measures of water pollution, including biochemical demand for oxygen and suspended and dissolved solids. The pollutants in this group, once produced, endure in the environment for a relatively short time —short enough so that long-term accumulations are not a problem. This group contains the more massive and commonly discussed pollutants, and enough information exists about them so that we can link them to economic activity and population.

The second class of pollutants includes those which endure longer—radiation and pesticides, plus a wide variety of ever-changing chemicals emitted by our high technology industries. Most such chemicals are emitted in small, often highly poisonous amounts. For many of these pollutants, future developments depend more heavily on changes in technology than on changes in population and economic growth. In any case, they are very difficult to link to population and economic growth in a simple and quantitative fashion. For this reason, the results we present here are for the first class of pollutants, although this does not minimize the environmental damage done by the others.

In the next 30 years, most of these pollutants can be eliminated by enforcing treatment standards for pollution emissions. Slower population and economic growth would help; but over this period, by far the biggest reduction in pollution can be achieved by a head-on attack. This is illustrated in the figure showing hydrocarbons (p. 68)—a major component of auto exhaust and other combustion. In this example, the treatment standard is the Environmental Protection Agency's 1975 standard for emissions into the air. Even if this standard were not met on schedule, it certainly will be met by the year 2000; indeed, by that time, we are likely to have much tighter standards.

The relationships shown in the figure hold generally for the other pollutants we examined. The reason for the spectacular results from enforcing standards is that we have imposed so little control in the past. The results do not assume any big new technological breakthroughs. It is just that we have only now begun to fight. Many of the required changes could be implemented today. Soap could be used instead of detergent; natural-colored paper could replace heavily bleached paper in many uses; returnable bottles could be used; the horsepower of auto engines could be reduced. It is not difficult to find answers when one begins to look.

Whatever we assume about future treatment policy, pollu-

HYDROCARBON EMISSIONS
MILLIONS OF POUNDS PER YEAR

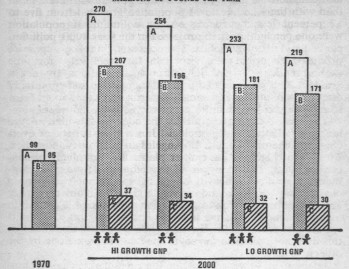

| | PRESENT TECHNOLOGY | | ACTIVE ABATEMENT POLICY |
| A | | | |

| | IMPROVED TECHNOLOGY |
| B | |

The generation and emission of hydrocarbon pollutants is shown under different assumptions about future population growth, economic growth, changes in technology, and pollution abatement policy.

The bars labeled A, shown for background purposes only, indicate the levels of hydrocarbon wastes that would be generated under present technology: These waste levels would be generated if there were no changes in technology between the 1967-1970 base period and the year 2000.

The bars labeled B show actual emissions of hydrocarbon pollutants in 1970 and expected emissions in the year 2000, assuming no change in pollution abatement policy. The difference between A and B shows the extent to which the introduction of more efficient, less wasteful technology between now and the year 2000 is expected to reduce the generation and emission of pollutants below the levels generated if technology remained unchanged. Such changes in technology are likely to come anyway; they do not depend on public pressure to reduce harmful residuals.

The B bars show that, even with improved technology, pollution levels would be much higher in the year 2000 than they are now. These levels would, however, be somewhat lower if population grew at the 2-child rate rather than the 3-child rate, and if the economy grew at a slower rate rather than a more rapid rate (lo-growth GNP vs. hi-growth GNP).

The bars labeled C show hydrocarbon emissions in the year 2000 assuming an active pollution-abatement policy. The assumed policy is the Environmental Protection Agency's 1975 standard for emissions into the air. The changes in production and waste treatment processes induced by this policy would have a greater effect than would any of the other changes shown—in technology, population growth, or economic growth.

SOURCE: Ronald G. Ridker, "The Economy, Resource Requirements, and Pollution Levels" (prepared for the Commission, 1972).

tion emissions in the year 2000 would be less with the 2-child than with the 3-child rate of population growth—from five to 12 percent less, depending on the pollutant. If population were one percent less than projected in the year 2000, pollution emissions would be 0.3 to 0.6 percent less. If GNP per capita were one percent less than projected, emissions would be 0.2 to 0.9 percent less.

Once we achieve control over the emissions from each source, pollution will once again rise in response to economic and population growth. We can already see this process at work in rapidly growing parts of the country. At our Los Angeles public hearing, meteorologist James D. Edinger described the successful efforts in Los Angeles to control air pollution from stationary sources—power plants, heavy industry, home heating—and the beginnings of the program to control pollution from motor vehicles. But, he said, in recent years:

> . . . a close race has been run between increasing numbers of sources and decreasing emissions per source. But as emission levels per source are trimmed lower and lower the effort required to achieve each new increment of improvement gets more and more difficult. The increase in the number of sources, on the other hand, is projected to rise steadily. If the race for acceptable air quality is to be won, the heroic emission control programs, present and anticipated in Los Angeles, must soon be joined by a leveling off, if not a reduction, in the number of sources.[1]

Our own research on air pollution indicates that such worries are well founded. The standard for concentrations of nitrogen oxides used by the Environmental Protection Agency is 100 micrograms per cubic meter. In 1970, the air in 36 urban areas had concentrations above this level. An active abatement policy would eliminate the problem in most areas. But if our projections of economic and population growth come anywhere close to the truth, Los Angeles and San Diego in the year 2000 will still have a problem. In Los Angeles, we estimate that even with an active abatement policy, concentrations of nitrogen oxides will still be at least 50 percent above standard, and probably well above that. In this region of the country, clearly something must give: the rate of population growth, the use of the internal combustion engine—especially for personal transport—or the standard itself.

As the case of air quality in Los Angeles illustrates, problems of environmental quality are often worse in metropolitan areas that are larger and in regions that are more densely populated.

69

This is clearly true for air pollution (and associated respiratory disease), noise, traffic congestion, and time spent getting to work. Other factors are less clear. Our research shows that sewage and water treatment costs per person decline as city size increases to about 100,000; above that, engineering data suggest that costs should be the same for conventional facilities, but the actual observed costs appear to rise. If large cities have to change their sewage facilities, costs per person will be much higher. Similarly, solid waste disposal costs either follow a U-shaped curve or increase with city size and density. There is also evidence that large cities change local climate—wind, cloudiness, temperature, and precipitation; we really do not know whether or not such changes are bad. The inner city has all these environmental problems but to a heightened degree.

Yet the underlying cause of poor environmental quality in the larger urban centers may often not be size. Most of our largest centers are the old cities of the north; their problems may arise more from urban forms and transportation systems appropriate to an earlier era, old and uncoordinated facilities, multiple governmental jurisdictions, and the injustices that lead to inadequate financing and high proportions of minority groups and poor in central cities. In new cities as well as old, environmental quality suffers from inadequate pricing of public facilities and common property resources like space and waste disposal media, such as rivers and air. The historical evidence relating environmental quality to metropolitan size may not be applicable to the building of new cities and the refitting of older cities; indeed, many such problems would remain wherever people live.

The total volume of pollutants in the United States reponds, as we have seen, to the size of the national economy, which in turn depends heavily on the size of the national population. People consume resources wherever they live. Whether in New York City or a small town in the midwest, people still drive an automobile made of steel using coal mined in West Virginia. In the process, the air in cities is fouled by smoke and the scenery and the streams of West Virginia are spoiled by strip mining. Wherever Americans live, they make huge demands on the nation's and the world's resources and environment.

RISKS AND CHOICES

As a nation, we have always faced choices and always will. What matters is the range of choice we have and the urgency with which the need to choose is thrust upon us The evidence indicates that continued population growth narrows our choices and forces us to choose in haste.

From the standpoint of resources and the environment, the United States can cope with rapid population growth for the next 30 to 50 years. But doing so will become an increasingly unpleasant and risky business—unpleasant because "coping" with growth means adopting solutions we don't like; risky because it means adopting solutions before we understand them. Within the United States, the risks are ecological and social. And, there are risks which involve our relationship with the rest of the world.

We in this country are tampering with the ecosystem in many ways, the consequences of which we do not begin to understand. The crude methods used to estimate the effect of emissions on air quality and the damages and costs of urban pollution illustrate our ignorance all too well. Worse yet is our understanding of the second class of pollutants, bypassed in our analysis precisely because we know so little about them. Because such pollutants endure longer, because they are highly poisonous in small doses, because new pollutants are continually being introduced, and because there are long time lags between emissions and the appearance of damages, we shall not quickly improve our knowledge in this area.

Radioactive wastes are an example. There will be more nuclear power plants if rapid population and economic growth occurs, but nuclear management and technology are changing so fast that there is no stable benchmark from which to estimate the amount of radioactive wastes likely to escape into the environment. We know that, once in the environment, such wastes can travel long distances through space and food chains, and we know the kinds of damage they can cause. But we do not know where they will come to rest, the extent of the damage, or when it will occur. Clearly, we need to know far more about how natural systems function when forced to absorb greater quantities of pollutants.

Beyond pollution, there are profound ecological impacts.[2] the simplification and destabilization of ecosystems associated with modern one-crop agriculture; the reduction in the variety of gene pools in our most important plants; the threat to the productivity of the sea through the filling-in of salt marshes; the unknown consequences of climate changes caused by man's activities; and many more.

Population growth is clearly not the sole culprit in ecological damage. To believe that it is, is to confuse how things are done with how many people are doing them Much of the damage

71

we do results from efforts to satisfy fairly trivial preferences—for unblemished fruit, detergents, rapidly accelerating cars, and bright colored paper products. We can and should cut back on frivolous and extravagant consumption that pollutes. The way things are done can, to a significant degree, be changed regardless of how many people are doing them. But the overall effect is a product of numbers times styles of life taken together. One multiplies the other to produce the total impact.

The real risk lies in the fact that increasing numbers press us to adopt new technologies before we know what we are doing. The more of us there are the greater is the temptation to introduce solutions before their side effects are known. It might be far better environmentally to postpone the introduction of nuclear power plants until the inherently cleaner fusion reactors are developed. When one pesticide or food additive is found to be dangerous to man, it is replaced with another about which we know less. We undertake the expenditure of billions on water treatment, without knowing whether the benefits outweigh the costs of other opportunities foregone. Slower population growth will not eliminate this situation, but it will reduce the urgency, the "crash program" character of much that we do. It will buy time for the development of sensible solutions.

We can cope with population growth for another half century if we have to; the question is whether we want to. We can cope with resource shortages—if we cannot mine a resource, we can import, design around it, find a substitute, or reduce consumption. Where water deficits threaten, we can choose between charging more for its use, transferring people and industry to other parts of the country, and constructing longer and larger canals. If pollution emissions cannot be tolerated, we can change production processes, improve treatment, separate polluters from their victims, treat the symptoms, or simply produce less of the commodity causing the pollution. Congestion during commuter hours can be handled by restricting the use of private cars, developing mass transit, and staggering work hours. Congestion at recreation sites can be handled by building additional facilities, improving management, encouraging substitutes such as foreign travel, and if necessary, by staggering vacations. Even land shortages for agriculture can be handled, given sufficient lead time, through farming the sea, changing our diet, developing synthetic foods, and so forth.

Such changes pose physical, technical, and managerial challenges that we can probably meet if we must. But in so doing we shall pay a cost reckoned not in dollars but in our way of life

Population growth forces upon us slow but irreversible

changes in life style. Imbedded in our traditions as to what constitutes the American way of life is freedom from public regulation—virtually free use of water; access to uncongested unregulated roadways; freedom to do as we please with what we own; freedom from permits, licenses, fees, red tape. and bureaucrats; and freedom to fish, swim, and camp where and when we will. Clearly, we do not live this way now. Maybe we never did. But everything is relative. The population of 2020 may look back with envy on what, from their vantage point, appears to be our relatively unfettered way of life.

Conservation of water resources, restrictions on pollution emissions, limitations on fertilizer and pesticides, preservation of wilderness areas, and protection of animal life threatened by man—all require public regulation. Rules must be set and enforced, complaints heard and adjudicated. Granted, the more we can find means of relying on the price system, the easier will be the bureaucratic task. Indeed, we ought to be experimenting right now with ways of making price incentives induce appropriate use of the environment and resources. At present, most monetary incentives work the wrong way, inducing waste and pollution rather than the opposite.

But even if effluent charges and user fees became universal, they will have to be set administratively; emissions and use will have to be metered, and fees collected. It appears inevitable that a larger portion of our lives will be devoted to filling out forms, arguing with the computer or its representatives, appealing decisions, waiting for our case to be handled, finding ways to evade or to move ahead in line. In many small ways, everyday life will become more contrived.

Many such changes will have to occur no matter which population projection occurs. But the difference, small at first, would grow with time until, a half century from now, the two societies may appear qualitatively different.

Another price we pay for having to cope with continued population growth is the pressure to keep on postponing the solution of social problems. While growth continues, top priority will be given to finding the necessary resources, controlling pollutants, correcting the damages they have done, and building ever larger water canals, highways, and mass transit systems. A large and perhaps growing fraction of our physical and intellectual capital is directly or indirectly devoted to these tasks—to finding ways to cope with the problems that continued growth generates. From past experience, we can predict with a fair degree of confidence that such priorities will continue to subordinate efforts devoted to resolving fundamental social problems When something must give because the system is becoming overloaded, it is unlikely to be the building of another dam.

The point is that continued population growth limits our options. In the case of the larger population, with less land per person and more people to accommodate, there are fewer alternatives, less room for diversity, less room for error. To cope with continued growth, technology *must* advance, lifestyles *must* change. Slower population growth offers us the difference between choice and necessity, between prudence and living dangerously.

THE UNITED STATES AND THE WORLD

The research done for the Commission showed that the United States will greatly enlarge its demands on world resources, especially minerals and petroleum, over the decades ahead. We will be requiring substantially larger imports of many minerals, such as chromium, vanadium, cobalt, and nickel, for which domestic supplies are not available or are available only at substantially higher costs.

The demand of other countries for minerals, petroleum, and other resources will certainly also rise sharply over the coming decades. This will result from rapid increases in output per person in other industrialized countries and from the rapid modernization of agriculture and industry in developing countries. The rates of increase in production in other parts of the world are likely to be higher than those of the United States. Their rates of increase in demand for mineral supplies are likely to rise even more sharply, because they are at an earlier stage of the industrialization process and because the composition of their GNP includes proportionately more goods and fewer services than does that of the United States.

Taking into account the huge increases in population which are in prospect, it seems clear that demands for natural resources in other parts of the world will rise more rapidly than demands in the United States; thus, the share of the United States in the use of world resources will steadily decline. For example, projections made for the Commission indicate that over the next 50 years the share of the United States in the world's use of aluminum may decline from 37 percent in 1968 to as low as nine percent by the year 2020. In the same time period, the share of the United States of total world copper requirements may drop from 22 percent to five percent.

While all such figures necessarily reflect uncertain assumptions about production, income, and technology, nevertheless they indicate the extremely important extent to which the United States is inextricably involved in the development and use of resources on a worldwide scale.

Our research also demonstrates that environmental issues will have to be faced increasingly on an international basis over the years ahead. There are already conspicuous cases of environmental damage and risk which cannot be solved on a national basis. The continuing problem of petroleum pollution in the oceans is such a case. Neither the oceans nor the atmosphere can be successfully dealt with if one looks only at the territory within a nation's boundary. And many additional issues of international ecological significance will be increasingly important—such as the effects of enormous increases in world use of pesticides and chemical fertilizers, the environmental impact of multi-national corporations, and many more.

The Commission has been deeply impressed by the unprecedented size and significance of the looming problems of resources and environment on a world scale. We see the need for much greater efforts than are underway now to analyze and understand these problems, and to develop international policies and programs to deal with them. We foresee potentially grave issues of clashing interests among nations and world regions, which could have very serious effects on the United States.

Therefore, we believe strongly that, in its own interest, the United States should work positively and constructively with other countries and international organizations in analyzing and solving problems related to natural resources and the environment in the world. We have made no special study of the detailed policies and programs which the United States should pursue for these purposes. We do now emphatically urge, however, that the nation join vigorously and cooperatively in solving problems of international trade, assistance to less-developed countries, and other pressing issues which will affect so sharply not only the future well-being of others in the world but the direct prospects for a sensible and respectable future for ourselves. We should not approach such problems in a spirit of charity or largesse. Our own future depends heavily on the evolution of a sensible international economic order, capable of dealing with natural resources and environmental conditions on a world scale.

LONG-TERM STRATEGIC PLANNING

Our consideration of the problems and prospects involved in this country's long-term future convinces us that an important dimension of policy formation is being overlooked. This dimension involves the identification, study, and initiation of actions with respect to future problems that may require lead times of decades rather than years to resolve. There is a need for continuous monitoring and evaluation of the long-term implications of demographic changes, of future resource demands and supplies, of possible pollution overload situations, and of the underlying trends in technology and patterns of social behavior that influence these factors.

Once future problems are identified, there is a need to undertake the necessary research and development and to formulate the policies to resolve them. We need to study our social, political, and economic institutions with a view towards recommending modifications that will reduce the discrepancy between the private and the public interest. Practical procedures for utilizing the effluent charge approach to environmental quality management and for initiating a rational system of land-use planning are important cases in point. We need to develop technologies that conserve particularly scarce physical and environmental resources. While appropriate effluent charges will encourage private business to move in this direction, government sponsorship of "yardstick" research on industrial technologies is necessary, particularly when our concern is with the problems farther in the future than private business can afford to look.

While parts of these tasks are being performed by isolated agencies, coordination and analytical assessment on a broad level are lacking. Private business firms and most government agencies are of necessity too present-oriented or mission-oriented to serve these functions adequately; nor can they be left to *ad hoc* commissions such as this one. On the other hand, we do feel that some group should be assigned central responsibility for such functions. Such a body would serve as a "lobby for the future" to identify potential population, resource, and environmental problems well in advance of their occurrence; to establish priorities and sponsor technical and social research directed towards their resolution; and where necessary to formulate and recommend policies to that end.

CHAPTER 6. GOVERNMENT

Can government adapt to the new realities and fragility of our existence as the pace of our lives accelerates, the world grows more crowded, technology multiplies life's complexities, and the environment is increasingly threatened?* Whether the economy thrives and environmental crises are avoided depend very much on government playing an active role—preparing for population change in advance of crises, and establishing and implementing appropriate policies. In fact, most of the recommendations we shall present imply government action.

We have examined the effect of different rates of population growth on the demand for key governmental services in the years ahead. The results of this research are presented below.

Beyond the question of costs, any concern with the effects of population on government requires us to raise broad questions of the relations between government and the size, characteristics, and distribution of the population it serves. These questions range from the essential characteristics of democratic government—citizen participation and representation, justice, and national security—to the adequacy and efficiency of ordinary, taken-for-granted service functions of government at all levels.

Government represents not only a universally and vitally important segment of our national life that is affected by population change; it also constitutes the channel through

*A separate statement by Commissioner James S. Rummonds appears on pages 308-310.

which a national concern with population must act to affect the causes and cope with the consequences of population growth and change. Can local, state, and federal governments cope adequately with the problems associated with population change through their traditional structure, means of financing, and allocation of responsibilities and jurisdictions? The fundamental questions we have raised transcend political party distinctions; they are concerned directly with people, how they live, and how they are governed.

Our examination of these questions gives us no cause for complacency or satisfaction. We are troubled by our assessment of the readiness and capability of government to deal with problems associated with population growth and change, as well as by the impacts of growth and change on our basic governmental institutions. The choices that face us are not easy ones, nor do we view population stabilization as any final solution to the problems raised.

PUBLIC SERVICE COSTS[1]

Regardless of how our population grows in the coming decades, we are going to spend more on public services, simply because of rising demands for new types of services and improved quality of existing services. Even if population were to remain at its current level, we would have to spend more just to satisfy present demands for better housing, education, transportation, health services, environmental improvements, and the elimination of hunger and poverty. Conversely, even if no new services or improvements in quality were demanded, costs would rise because, even at the slow growth rate, we will have a larger population requiring public services.

Different population growth rates will lead to different levels of demand for government services. The Commission has examined in detail three sectors in which government activities play a significant role—education, health, and welfare. Our studies were based on a comparison of the differences in expenditures required by different levels of demand resulting from population growth under the 2- and 3-child averages between now and the year 2000.

Our projections of government expenditures for education in the year 2000 assume that a larger percentage of people will be enrolled, and allow for improvements in the quality of education. These quality improvements include more variety in teaching methods and greater use of paraprofessionals, technical equipment, and materials. In 1970, about 7.5 percent of GNP—some $74 billion—was spent on education. Our projections suggest that, in the year 2000, the faster-growing population would spend 13 percent of its GNP, or $400 billion, on education, compared to an expenditure level of 9.7 percent of GNP, or $276 billion, with slower population growth.

Another way of expressing the impact of the 2- versus the 3-child projections is in terms of the tradeoffs between the quality of education and the number of people to be educated. Assume that we will spend 10 percent of our GNP on education in the year 2000. What type of education would this buy under the two population projections? With the larger population, this expenditure would provide seven percent of the students with our assumed higher quality education, and 93 percent would receive education comparable to quality today. With the same proportion of the GNP spent on education under the 2-child projection, all students could receive a higher quality education.

While the effect of population on educational services is large, this is not the case for expenditures in the health and welfare fields. In the health field, we looked at the demand for physician visits, dental visits, and hospital beds. We found that, for a given quality of health care, the more rapidly growing population would spend $20 billion more over the next three decades than would the slower growing population. This averages out to a difference in annual expenditure of less than $1 billion.

We examined the demand for welfare services using both today's definition of poverty and a definition that would increase at the same rate as per capital income. The evidence suggests that annual welfare expenditures, using either definition of poverty, would probably be slightly smaller under the 2-child population projection than under the 3-child projection; the difference would be no more than $2 billion and probably less. Relative to GNP in the year 2000, this amount would be insignificant.

Despite higher average incomes, a slower rate of population growth will not eliminate poverty. As we have pointed out, if poverty is to be eliminated by the year 2000, economic growth must be accompanied by policies that redistribute income.

There are additional sectors of the economy, such as housing, transportation, and energy production, in which government is involved heavily. While the Commission studied in detail only the government involvement in education, health, and welfare, a general conclusion that can be drawn is that the country will have to spend more in absolute terms to provide public services for a population growing at the 3-child rate than at the 2-child rate. Also, slower growth would produce a higher income per capita. Under our present tax systems, this would mean that per capita government revenues would be greater.

However, these benefits of slower growth will not automatically guarantee a higher quality of life. This will be achieved only if we deliberately choose to take advantage of the opportunities that slower growth presents. The wise use of these opportunities depends on public and private decisions yet to be made.

STATE AND LOCAL RESOURCES AND REQUIREMENTS

As we have seen, with slower national population growth, the provision of public services would be less of a burden on the nation. What would that mean for the state and local levels of government? The day-to-day services of state and local governments—in such fields as education, welfare, health services, police and fire protection, highways, transportation facilities, sanitation, and waste disposal—are intimately tied to the number of persons they serve and to the demographic characteristics of that population. Changes in population can have a substantial impact on requirements for public services as well as on the availability of resources to meet them.

Even if national population stabilized, there would still be changes in population size and composition in states and localities as a result of variations in natural increase and migration within the United States and from abroad.

Because the more affluent states attract migrants, characteristically in the economically productive age groups, the strains on state government from growth through migration can be accommodated relatively easily. Natural increase, however, creates demands for services without providing the necessary economic resources for meeting them. In addition, some of the highest rates of natural increase are found in the poorest states. Thus, differences in the *way* in which state populations grow—whether primarily by migration or primarily by natural increase—may be as important as growth itself in affecting a state's ability to meet increased demands for public services. Federal policies which would have the effect of lowering the birthrate and national programs which would assume a larger share of financial support for public welfare, education, and health could help reduce some of the inequities among states.[2]

Among local jurisdictions, population change shows even wider variety than among states. Some rural communities, exhibiting a high rate of natural increase and a net population loss because of high outmigration, have heavy public burdens due to relatively large numbers of children and the elderly to serve. While metropolitan suburbs draw generally more affluent residents, the central cities attract poor rural migrants and recent foreign arrivals.[3] The unequal effect on demand for local government services is illustrated in Louisville, Kentucky, where the central city encompasses less than half the population of the metropolitan area, but has more than 90 percent of the area's public assistance recipients.

While local governments adjust their expenditure and employment levels to population changes, it is not easy. They struggle to eliminate the time lags between population change and the recognition of that change by appropriate agencies, the perception of its meaning for service demands, and the provision of services. We have also found that public demand for improvement in the scope, intensity, and quality of government services has caused sharp nation-wide expansions in the level of activity of local government, at a rate far exceeding the growth in national population.[4]

These matters are cause for concern, and we are by no means satisfied that the attempts of local government to adjust service levels to population changes and respond to public demand are adequate to meet the needs of the future. The findings of the Commission's national public opinion survey add to this concern. Only 10 percent of the general public rated the performance of local government "excellent," 43 percent thought its performance "good," 31 percent "fair," and 12 percent "poor." Nor are we satisfied that present services and the taxes supporting them are sufficient and equitably distributed.[5]

There are sharp disparities among communities' resources and revenue-raising efforts. These stem largely from the combination of an excessive reliance on the property tax and a fragmented structure of governments in metropolitan areas. The restriction of local government jurisdictions to political boundaries that cut across settlement patterns leaves many local units with more than their fair share of service demands and others with a free ticket to avoid some of local governments' most difficult tasks.[6]

The imbalance between resources and demands for services is especially acute in the contrast between suburban communities and the central cities of our large metropolitan areas. Because of the lower incomes of central city residents, their lower tax capacity, and greater demand for higher cost services, a greater tax effort is required of central city residents who, at the same time, often receive a poorer quality of service than their more affluent suburban neighbors. Older, built-up suburbs close to the central city and receiving its overflow of high cost residents are also at a disadvantage with a very limited tax capacity.

We are not satisfied that levels of basic public services should be dependent on the resources yielded by the local property tax—high in rich communities, low in needy communities—and feel that greater flexibility and imagination are needed to find other revenue sources.

In addition to the mismatch between resources and need, the ability of local governments to continue to cope is clearly threatened. Taxpayer revolts, the drive for federal revenue sharing, the fiscal anguish of cities—all testify to the precariousness of the process of providing public services at a satisfactory level of quantity and quality.

It is not enough to consider only whether local governments can adjust service levels to future population changes. Ways must be found for local governments to narrow the gap between their needs and their resources and for the tax burden to rest more heavily on those best able to pay. A geographical broadening of the local tax base, at least within metropolitan areas, could both encompass the effects of population change and help narrow the fiscal disparities, if revenues were raised on the basis of fiscal capacity and distributed on the basis of expenditure needs. The responsibility of state and federal governments to help bear part of the burden needs to be expanded.

DEMOCRATIC REPRESENTATION AND PARTICIPATION[7]

Our political institutions were designed originally to govern a much smaller society, organized and oriented differently from what we have today. These institutions have changed as the society has changed. They have demonstrated remarkable flexibility and adaptability, but they also have shown some serious inadequacies. Are they capable of accommodating still more population growth in the future?

The answer to this question depends in part on maintaining and improving citizen participation and representation. Political activity and interest among urban people is as high as, if not higher than, that of rural people, according to the Commission's public opinion survey and other evidence. Still, the development of metropolitan political forms to deal with population change must include efforts to increase citizen representation and participation and the responsiveness of a larger bureaucracy.

Representation at the national level is diluted by population growth. The constituency of an individual congressman has grown enormously since the size of the House of Representatives was fixed at 435 members in 1910. Then, each congressman represented 211,000 citizens, on the average. In 1970, a congressional constituency averaged 470,000 citizens. By the year 2000, each congressman in a 435-seat House will represent 623,000 persons under the 2-child growth rate, or 741,000 persons in the 3-child case.

The size of the constituency is clearly not the sole factor in determining excellence in government. Perhaps it may not even be very important, compared with the quality of the representatives, the size and professionalism of their staffs, the size of the governing body itself, and other factors. But, it cannot be denied that the individual constituent's voice will be diminished under such circumstances. And, no increase of Congress's ability to communicate with constituents by mass media can disguise or make up for that diminution.

Population growth at the national level is just one demographic element to be considered in the adaptation of our political system to the needs of the 21st century. Population redistribution, as well as population growth, will affect the congressional profile. Representation will follow the people to metropolitan areas, away from the rural areas—to growing states like California and other coastal regions, away from the midcontinent. For example, if California continues to grow as it has in the past, its share of the seats in the House of Representatives would increase from 10 percent of the total to 14 percent by the year 2000. Thus, California would have over one-fifth of the 270 electoral votes required to elect the President.

While the strains on the political system related to large

constituencies may be alleviated somewhat by population stabilization, increased metropolitan concentration and interregional migration will continue to alter the makeup of the Congress and shift its orientation. The Commission is concerned about the uncertainties implied by these findings and believes they deserve further attention.

ADMINISTRATION OF JUSTICE[8]

The administration of justice stands as a fundamental role of government in our society. The fact that this system today is under pressure is too obvious to require demonstration. Congested court dockets, long waiting periods before trial in criminal and civil cases, the torment of the correctional system—all bear evidence to the troubles. No matter what the circumstances may be in the year 2000, the gravity of the current situation requires an immediate and aggressive effort to improve the present system of justice.

The Supreme Court of the United States is the final arbiter at the apex of the judicial system. In the nature of things, we can have only one of these. In 1824, when our population was 11 million, Daniel Webster could argue an important case before the Supreme Court for several days. Today, oral arguments are usually limited to one hour or less, and the Court hears only a very small percentage of the several thousand cases that arise through the expanded lower court system and the increasingly popular appeals procedures. The same type of pressure extends to the single supreme court in many states.

Population growth is one of many contributing factors to the pressures on our system of justice. The evolution of metropolitan communities and the accompanying modern life styles are also related. In urban areas, there is an increase in litigation and other legal actions, perhaps due to increasing numbers of impersonal contacts and frustrations. However, court congestion and legal delays reflect not only population change, but also, and perhaps more importantly, broadened concepts of the kinds of injustices amenable to adjudication and extension of the concepts of due process.

Improvement of our present system for administering justice must have a high priority on the nation's agenda. Population stabilization cannot accomplish that improvement. It can, as an alternative to continued population growth, reduce one of the pressures on the performance of this critical government function.

NATIONAL SECURITY

In considering the impact of population growth on the capacity of the United States to provide for its national security, the Commission consulted numerous experts within the military establishment and the academic community. They all believed that population stabilization would pose no threat to the country's security.

When the nation was young and her independence not very secure, her defense depended upon the number of people bearing arms. Then, experience clearly showed the wisdom of a larger population. More people meant greater military strength and greater national security. Today, our national security is increasingly dependent upon the skillful and intelligent practice of international relations, and our military strength is less dependent upon men and rifles. Recent technology, including nuclear weaponry, has reduced the significance of massive armies. Minor military conflicts in the future are likely to be small, localized, and dependent on conventional weapons and limited manpower. If there are any major wars in the future, the probability is that they would involve nuclear weapons long before troop activity on the scale of World War II was reached.

Because of the expected nature of future military conflicts, experts suggest that a peacetime active duty force of two to three million would be sufficient to ensure national security.[9] The three million people required by the military would be less than six percent of the male population 18 to 45 years old, even if the country's population growth followed the 2-child projection between now and the year 2000. An even smaller percentage of the population would be required if we had a volunteer army, because there would presumably be less turnover, greater skills, and more efficiency. For comparison, we should note that, since 1955, the Armed Services' demand for the nation's manpower resources has averaged nine to 10 percent of the male population 18 to 45 years old. Clearly, the future population would be more than adequate to supply the military with manpower. Thus, we can discern no threat to the nation's security from lesser future growth of total population.

If there is a change in population that would be important to national security, it would relate to the health, education, and productivity, not to the size of the population. The increasingly complex technology of war, and the growing reliance of the military on machines rather than on men, mean that military manpower must be better educated and skilled than in the past. Beyond this, we must consider what proportion of people are active in the social, political, and economic life of the nation. At present, this portion of the population in the United States does not include all adults—in particular, those who are poor, discriminated against, unemployed, unproductive, and counterproductive. The conversion of this fraction into a part of the fully active population would be significant for national security.[10]

THE EFFECTS OF GOVERNMENT PROGRAMS ON POPULATION DISTRIBUTION[11]

Policies and programs designed to influence the migration and distribution of the population are not unknown in this country. The Ordinance of 1785, which opened up the Ohio territories, and the Homestead Law of 1862 were part of a national policy to settle the western frontier. The Resettlement Administration during the Depression was an attempt to slow migration trends from farm areas.

At present, the United States has no explicit overall population distribution policy, nor does it have any programs whose primary intent is to influence major migration trends. However, many public programs, such as economic development of rural and depressed areas, urban renewal of central cities, and open space acquisition, have the modification of settlement trends as a secondary intent. Such programs have had relatively greater impact within metropolitan areas than between regions. Their indifferent success in affecting broad geographic distribution has been attributed to the fact that they were neither designed, administered, nor funded to counteract effectively the strong economic forces of the private sector which induce population trends.

There is a virtually endless list of programs which have unintended consequences for the territorial arrangement of the population. The federal highway program, national parks system, minimum wage laws, import quota system, housing programs, and many others, all have distributional effects which are diverse and often conflicting.

Programs that have a particularly clear impact, stimulating the growth of many areas by attracting migration, are the

Defense Department's procurement and research and development programs, which account for about 10 percent of total federal expenditures. The rapid growth of Texas and southern California reveals the significance of such programs. Other programs give rise to outmigration. For example, recent agricultural policies providing incentives to restrict acreage and increase productivity, may have been partly responsible for heavy migration off the farm.

Perhaps unintended demographic consequences are unavoidable if policy goals other than population distribution have priority. Nevertheless, unintended consequences should at least be anticipated. Although the territorial impact of some government programs is known, there is much to be learned. If the demographic side effects of policies were better understood, then the desirability of their consquences could be evaluated in the policy-making process and plans made to alleviate undesirable aspects.

This society has yet to adopt policies to plan for and influence the distribution of a significant proportion of the population according to any scheme that departs substantially from current trends. Although a majority of the public thinks the government should do something about national distribution patterns, there is little active public interest in or support for the formation of a national distribution policy. And, it may be difficult to persuade elected officials in districts or states that would lose population relative to other areas, that the national interest demands a planned reduction in the population of their constituency—and a consequent reduction in the number of representatives, political influence, and federal funds tied to population size criteria.

FRAGMENTATION OF METROPOLITAN GOVERNMENT[12]

One of the major difficulties in guiding and accommodating population growth is the fragmentation of government in metropolitan areas. Population movements are often unaffected by political boundaries and population-related problems extend across jurisdictions.

Local general-purpose governments—counties and municipalities—were created originally to serve all the people living in their territory. Special governments, such as sanitation districts, conservation districts, and port and transit authorities, were developed to perform limited specific services for special constituencies. As metropolitan growth fills in the countryside adjoining larger cities, not only do these local governments find themselves elbow to elbow, but they also become overlaid with a patchwork quilt of special governments with independent policy-making and revenue-raising powers. Missing is the effective force seeking comprehensive solutions to comprehensive problems from a metropolitan-wide perspective. This territorial and functional fragmentation of governmental responsibility could become an even more serious problem in the year 2000.

In 1967, there were about 16,000 nonschool local governments in metropolitan areas. If recent trends continue, by the year 2000 there are likely to be over 32,000 such governmental units in metropolitan areas. The proliferation of specialized districts will account for half the increase. As metropolitan problems such as air pollution, inadequate housing, crime, and insufficient sewage treatment facilities spread across more and more political boundaries, it becomes increasingly urgent that cooperative metropolitan efforts replace jurisdictional jealousies and narrowly defined self-interests. Although this need for cooperation is gradually becoming recognized, the federal government should increase its efforts to help bring about public understanding of the issue and assist local governments in making the necessary adjustments.

GOVERNMENT PLANNING[13]

The success of government in guiding and accommodating future population change hinges on its ability to plan effectively and comprehensively. This means planning for land use, environmental quality, and the necessary public services. For example, a plan for a sewer line which will encourage residential construction should also be accompanied by plans for adequate sewage treatment, financing a new school, recreational and other community facilities. These plans should be coordinated with development in the neighboring communities.

The federal government has encouraged the development of a technical planning capacity at the local level, but the structure of local government often militates against its effective use. The fragmentation of metropolitan areas into many municipalities, each with power to zone its own land, and each relying on its property tax base for general revenues, effectively prevents the organization or coordination of local zoning changes to implement a strategy for population distribution or development on a metropolitan-wide basis.

Lawrence Christmas, Assistant Director of the Northern Illinois Planning Commission, told us that,

> The primary forces now shaping the [metropolitan] population distribution pattern are comprised of individual decisions by hundreds of suburban governmental units, individual decisions by private developers, and individual decisions by a few large, single-purpose regional and state agencies in Washington.[14]

Tom Bradley, a councilman in Los Angeles, testified that, ". . . cities have failed miserably to plan for orderly growth . . . the cities failed because into the planning vacuum which they left by their inaction, stepped the land developer, FHA, and the highway engineer."[15]

Although the analytical techniques and creative capacities for planning are available in many metropolitan areas today, the absence of adequate mechanisms for coordinating the planning efforts of individual political units means that the resources are rarely used. When they are used, it is to deal with short-term problems imposed by current pressures of population growth.

CONCLUSION

In this chapter, we have argued that slowing down the rate of population growth would ease the problems facing government in the years ahead: Potential demands for many governmental services would be smaller with lower population growth rates; and potential resources to finance governmental activities would be larger as a corollary of higher per capita income.

However, it would be a serious error to read these conclusions as comforting and reassuring. Under the most optimistic assumptions, at least 50 million more people will be added to our population before the end of the century. This growth will add to the demands on governmental services and to the complexity of achieving a participatory political process responsive to contemporary conditions.

More important, these added demands and complexities

will fall on governmental structures and processes already heavily burdened—many of us would say overburdened—by the problems facing the nation. In a time of headlong technological change, economic growth, and continuously rising population, the ability of Americans to deal with environmental pollution, public safety, economic opportunity, racial and ethnic discrimination, and many other urgent issues, is far from assured. Different members of this Commission would assess the present inadequacies of federal, state, and local government in the United States with varying degrees of alarm, but we all agree that fundamental improvements are urgently needed in the effectiveness, speed, and equity with which our various governments deal with vital issues. These issues must be addressed directly, regardless of population change.

Rather than finding reassurance, therefore, in the prospects that lower population growth will ease future governmental problems, we emphasize our concern because even more burdens are going to be added to governments now functioning inadequately.

Two aspects of the matter are of special concern. The first is that the great bulk of the people who will be added to our population over the next few decades will live in metropolitan areas. Coupled with continuing migration from rural to urban areas, this means that the weight of population growth will fall unevenly on governmental units. This will require the greatest response from federal, state, and local governments in dealing with metropolitan problems.

But it is precisely in this field—establishing effective and democratic governmental systems in metropolitan areas—that our existing governments have been most deficient. Archaic governmental boundaries, incongruity between the location of many problems and the location of the financial resources to deal with them, and inequities in the distribution of public services, tax burdens, and the judicial system have been cited as problems. Also the need to accommodate both civil service protection and responsiveness to neighborhood and community demands and an ability to make and execute plans on a metropolitan scale—all these and many other difficulties of metropolitan government are with us now and will be exacerbated by the population growth to come.

The second aspect of government problems of special concern to this Commission is the substantial number of persons in our country who feel that government is not responsive to what they see as the real needs of modern society. Time and again in our public hearings, we were told that groups which feel deprived and discriminated against by current government policies will be skeptical and resistant to new governmental programs such as those needed in the population field. These groups, which feel they are not allowed to participate fairly in governmental processes, will be hard to persuade that the government speaks for them in proposing policies concerning population matters.

These views—which are felt strongly by ethnic and racial minorities but are by no means limited to those groups—were pressed forcefully and persuasively before the Commission not only in public hearings but also by other witnesses, members of the staff, and Commissioners. The Commission believes the conclusion is inescapable: The effectiveness of government in meeting urgent national needs, and in bringing a broader range of our citizens into political participation, will have much to do with the success of the policies and programs we recommend in connection with population.

Population problems cannot be dealt with in isolation. Their solution depends upon understanding and voluntary actions by many of our people, and neither will be forthcoming in adequate degree from those who believe that government does not speak for them and does not respond to their needs.

CHAPTER 7. SOCIAL ASPECTS

In this chapter, we review the relationships between population change and several key aspects of our society. A distinctive feature of a population that is not growing is its relative abundance of old people and its relative scarcity of youth. We explore what further shifts in this direction may imply for the society at large, and the kinds of issues that seem likely to arise with regard to the status of the aged.

Population changes take place through the family and in turn react upon it. As our basic institution, the family's durability may reflect its flexibility in response to transformations in the society around it. We examine recent changes in the family, looking at the connections between family behavior and population change, and what social changes may imply for the responsibilities of family members.

Many expressions of concern over the effects of population growth include references to a sense that life is becoming more crowded and congested. We therefore examine the concept of population density, and how density relates to other factors that influence the character of modern life.

Finally, we show how the status of the socially and economically excluded racial and ethnic minorities in our society is reflected in their fertility and their mortality; and how achieving the goals of social justice and total inclusion into the mainstream for these groups will enhance the American future and will serve the ends of positive population policy as well.

AGE STRUCTURE

Because of a history of relatively high birthrates in the United States, our population has characteristically been "young" compared with that of many European countries. Over time, however, our population has been growing "older" because of the long-term downward trend of the birthrate. Although this trend was interrupted by the postwar baby boom, the decline in the birthrate since then has caused the proportion of the population in the childhood ages to become smaller again. As we have indicated, the effects of the baby boom will be apparent in our age structure throughout this century, as that generation moves into adulthood and

AGE DISTRIBUTIONS, 1970 AND 2000

	Median Age (Years)	Percent at Different Ages			
		Total	Under 18	18-64	65 & Over
1970	28	100	34	56	10
2000 2-child family	33	100	27	62	11
2000 3-child family	27	100	35	56	9
Stabilized Population	37	100	24	60	16

SOURCE: U. S. Bureau of the Census, *Current Population Reports*, Series P-25, No. 470, "Projections of the Population of the United States by Age and Sex: 1970 to 2000."

the working ages, and in the next century when they join the ranks of the older citizens.

The future age structure of our population—the proportion of persons at each age—will be affected by future rates of fertility. The age structure that would result from the 2-child and 3-child levels of fertility can be seen in the table on page 94.

With the 2-child rate of growth throughout the rest of this century, the age structure would show a consistent pattern of becoming older; with the 3-child rate, the age structure would become slightly younger. The age structure that would result from indefinite persistence of a 2-child average— a stabilized population—would have a median age of 37. In such a population, the number and percentage of persons in each group would be roughly the same from birth to age 50

AGE DISTRIBUTION

PERCENT OF TOTAL POPULATION

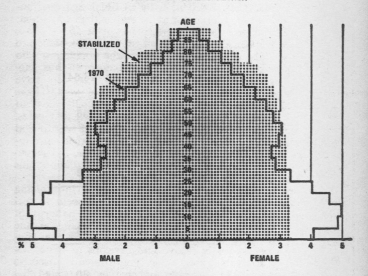

In a stabilized population with low death rates, equal numbers of births and deaths, and no immigration, the number of 50-year-olds would be nearly as large as the number of 5-year-olds.

SOURCE: Ansley J. Coale, "Alternative Paths to a Stationary Population" (prepared for the Commission, 1972).

or 60; there would be nearly as many 50-year olds as five-year olds. Above age 60, the numbers would taper off rapidly because of the high death rates at the older ages. (See chart on page 95.)

What are the implications of an older population? Will changes in our social organization be required? Will the rate of social and technological change diminish? What are the advantages and disadvantages of a population whose age composition is dispersed evenly through the different age levels?

How we define "old" and "young" is always an arbitrary matter determined in large part by custom. Only at the lower and upper age ranges are the functions which people are able to perform clearly related to biological age. For example, it could be argued that a more appropriate delineation of the working age population would be 21 to 70, rather than 18 to 64 years. This would permit a longer period of schooling and training appropriate to the economy's needs. Also, in a population with high longevity, health and vitality can be retained until older ages. Sweden, with an older age distribution than ours, places retirement at 70 rather than 65; India, with a much younger age structure, places it at 55.

One concern often expressed about an older age structure is that there will be a larger proportion of the population who are less adaptable to political and social change, thus suggesting the possibility of "social stagnation."[1] Others have suggested that Sweden and England, both of which have older age structures than ours, are not especially slow to change; but, it is difficult to generalize from particular cases. In any event, other factors, such as accumulated wealth and level of education, obscure the relationship between chronological age and resistance to change. For example, older generations typically grew up in an era of less education; this gap will narrow in the future.

Each new generation is a potential vehicle for introducing new patterns into the society. Younger people seem to feel fewer pressures towards conformity with adult patterns of thought and behavior. However, the extent of change or the direction it will take cannot be predicted. Not all new generations have been equally restive and desirous of major social and political change; and, where youth have been active agents of change, the direction of change advocated has sometimes been oppressive.

Some also speculate that an older population will diminish rapid job advancement because a larger proportion of the labor force will be in the older ages and will retain higher positions longer. In a stabilized population with low mortality, there would be 90 percent as many males and 94 percent as many females at age 50 as at age 20,[2] in contrast to current figures of 63 and 69 percent.[3]

However, a projection of a stabilized age distribution assumes that zero population growth would be maintained with little fluctuation in the birthrate. Although such a population would be older on the average, in reality there could be considerable variation in birthrates around a long-term average yielding population replacement. This would result in age groups of different size and more variation in the age structure than is usually assumed under zero population growth. Indeed, with increasing individual control over fertility, the swings in the annual number of births might well be considerable.

Whether opportunities for individual advancement will in fact diminish will depend obviously on many factors besides age structure. And, in any event, whether a lower rate of occupational mobility is viewed with satisfaction or alarm is largely a matter of values.

Another concern with the changing age composition associated with lower birthrates is the rising proportion of those 65 and over who, many fear, will add to the burden on public funds to care for them. The next section of this report treats this subject more extensively.

In summary, we are led to the conclusion that the age structure of a population is unlikely to be decisive in the forms of social organization which emerge. And, as we have seen, there are many advantages of population stabilization which seem clearly to outweigh any fears of an older population.

THE AGED

In 1970, there were 20 million persons 65 years old and over in the United States. With minor improvements in mortality, and with immigration at current levels, the number expected by the year 2000 is 29 million—a 43-percent increase in the number of these persons. For the remainder of this century and into the third decade of the next, the actual *numbers* in the older ages will be unaffected by future birthrates, for the people now in this group and those who will enter it during this interval are already alive. However,

PERSONS 65 AND OVER

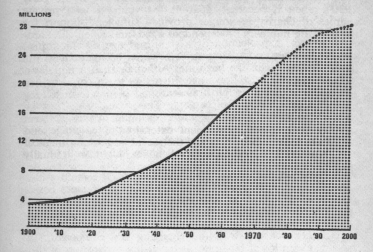

For the remainder of this century, the number of persons age 65 and over will be unaffected by our rate of growth. However, their proportion of the population would be affected by how fast the population grows: In the year 2000 they would be 8.9 percent of the population under the 3-child average, and 10.6 percent of the population under the 2-child average.

SOURCE: U. S. Bureau of the Census.

their *proportion* of the population *will* depend on future birth-rates.

In 1900, about four percent of our population was 65 years of age and older.[4] This proportion has continued to grow steadily during the century, reaching 9.8 percent by 1970. Lower birthrates in the future would further raise the proportion of people in this age group. If the population should grow at the 2-child rate, the proportion 65 and over would reach 10.6 percent by the end of this century. If the 2-child average prevailed until the population ultimately stabilized, the proportion in this age group would level off at approximately 16 percent—a rather considerable increase in this segment of the population. However, if the population grew at the 3-child rate, in the year 2000 the proportion would be 8.9 percent—less than it is now. (See chart above.)

Public concern for the aged has focused largely on problems of money and health. Attention was first drawn to the problems of older people during the 1920's and the early 1930's when it became apparent that families and private sources of charity no longer provided sufficient support for the growing numbers of dependent aged, and when the hardships of the economic depression of the 1930's fell disproportionately upon older workers. Similarly, concern with the health of older people gained momentum during this period, as increasing numbers of people reached the ages at which long-term illness is common, presenting new problems for medical and public health workers.

One consequence was the establishment of our social security system with subsequent extension of coverage and benefits to most aged people and the recent addition of medical care. Numerous public monetary benefits have also gradually been extended to the aged, including special income tax deductions. Also, greater public resources have been devoted to research in the chronic diseases, which primarily afflict people in the older ages, and to extension of services for the chronically ill. Pension plans have become more common, and benefits for those reaching retirement age have been critical bargaining issues for labor unions.

There are compelling reasons for the continued preoccupation of society with the income, employment, and health problems of the aged. Poverty is more prevalent among the elderly—especially among the aged in minority groups—than any other age group.[5] Not all of those now in the older population were covered by the federal Old Age Survivors, Disability, and Health Insurance program (OASDHI) when they were in the work force. Furthermore, the levels of payment under retirement programs have, in many cases, been low and not sufficient to raise recipients above the poverty level.

In the future, the income position of the aged will most likely be improved, because more will be receiving benefits from private retirement funds, will have larger accumulated personal resources, and will be covered by government insurance plans. Much depends, of course, on our ability to control inflation. Some might argue that improving the income position of the disadvantaged before they reach old age would reduce their income deficits in later years. Thus, it may be decided that national priorities should be focused on the disadvantaged; for them, income deficits among the elderly, as among all age groups, are greatest, and improvements have been slowest in coming.

Health needs will continue to figure high on the list of

needs of the older population: Not only will standards of health care increase; there will also be a change in the age composition of the older population. While the entire population 65 years old and over will rise 43 percent between 1970 and the year 2000, persons 75 to 84 will increase by 65 percent, and those 85 years and over by 52 percent. It is among these old people that chronic conditions (including impairments and disease) increase, limitations of activity become more prevalent, and institutionalized care is more often required. Females predominate, for their expectation of life exceeds that of males. As with income, the risks of poor health, limitation of activity, and institutionalization are greater among the disadvantaged segment of the elderly.

The aged are, however, a varied group, and not all have, or perceive themselves as having, severe income or health problems. Although their incomes and total wealth are smaller on the average, the variation in income among the aged is considerable. The elderly probably require less income and most probably expect, and accommodate to, some decline in vigor and health without much difficulty. Even so, the combination of old age with very low income and poor health is devastating.

Two sets of issues are likely to arise with increasing frequency as the number of very elderly grows. First, there are the issues of ethics, personal preference, and allocation of public expenditures connected with prolongation of life. This set of issues, which is just beginning to receive public attention, has not been addressed by this Commission.

The second issue, more widely discussed, is far from resolution. It involves the type of institutional care necessary for the elderly who can no longer be cared for at home. Only a small proportion of the population 65 years and over—five percent in 1970—are institutionalized,[6] but the percentage among those 85 years and over is much larger. This institutionalized population is relatively disadvantaged in terms of health, social ties, and economic resources. To date, the prevailing image of institutional life is largely negative, and older people generally express greater aversion to it than either their relatives or the public at large.

A continuing problem of the aged in our society is finding socially valued roles. What is desirable behavior is less clearly defined for older people than at any other stage in the life cycle. For men, the situation first becomes critical at retirement. Previously, their life courses were more clearly charted. After school came entrance into the labor force; their status in society depended largely on occupational position. After retirement, however, their status, and thus the means for earning social esteem, becomes indeterminate at best.

For women, the loss of status has traditionally appeared earlier in the life cycle, when children left home and family functions diminished. However, a woman's status in society has depended largely on that of her husband, even though she may also have been in the work force for all or part of the time since marriage. Regardless of employment, she typically maintained household and family roles which forestalled her feeling of "uselessness."

Opportunities for the employment of men after age 65 are more favorable for those with higher educational levels, and for those in a few selected occupations. It remains to be seen whether patterns of compulsory retirement would be noticeably altered with slower population growth and smaller numbers of new entrants into the labor market. If the opportunities for advancement diminish in a population with a stabilized age distribution, the bargaining position of the aged would not appear to be strong. Also, increased participation of women in the work force may present additional competition for older workers. Finally, society feels little obligation to provide employment for older people because of income and health supports now established in private retirement programs and in the national social security system.

It is possible, however, that noticeably higher levels of educational attainment, retraining at different stages of life, and a shortened work week (perhaps combined with educational programs) might alter the opportunities for employment—in the aggregate and for older workers as well.

Policies on age at retirement could certainly be made more flexible. Perhaps, however, retirement will be looked upon with more favor once the economic and social supports for the retirement years are more secure. Much depends on the extent to which society legitimates leisure-time activity in comparison with work. If a "leisure ethic" gains greater social acceptance, especially within the younger portion of the work force, people may come to look forward to retirement and the leisure it brings. A man of 65 has an average of 13 years of life remaining, and a woman 16 years,[7] and life expectancy may rise further with advances in medical science. With the increase in the number of older persons and the greater amount of their time available in the future, more consideration should be given to the effective use of volunteers in community agencies. This could contribute materially to both the individuals involved and the welfare of the community.

There are many other questions about the aged to consider

101

—for example, where they will live, their position in the changing family structure, their influence on our political institutions, and so on. We can only speculate about such changes. All we know for certain is that, if the birthrate declines further, the proportion of older people will rise. However, as we have seen, total dependency—the proportion of aged and children together—will decline, because declines in the proportion of children will more than offset the rising proportion of aged. This change will take place gradually, permitting ample time for planning. We are not doing very well now in meeting the problems of the aged—we can certainly do better.

THE FAMILY

We recognize that in opening a discussion of the family we tread on sacred ground, for the family is our most revered institution. As the recognized unit of reproduction and child-rearing, as perhaps the most important socializing agent of oncoming generations, and for its importance in defining the social roles of both men and women in our society, it is central to most of our concerns.

The record attests to the enormous durability of the family as a valued institution, modified in response to changing conditions and to the choices available to different generations. In the United States, most people marry and they marry at an early age. Our population is unusual among industrialized nations in that the proportion ever marrying has always been high for both sexes. Furthermore, this proportion has increased steadily since World War I. Recent generations have shown a greater inclination to marry than any generation in the past century.[8]

Our average age at first marriage is the lowest of any advanced country in the world. The great divide in the orientation to marriage seems to have come in the 1890's, when age at marriage started a long downward movement that lasted, with only minor fluctuations, until the 1960's. In 1959, the median age at first marriage was 22.5 for men and 20.2 for women; by 1970, these averages had reached 23.2 and 20.8 respectively.[9] Thus, in our society, marriage has been almost universal and the age at entry into marriage has been low.

While marriage has been almost universal, divorce has be-

come more frequent. The divorce rate in 1935 was more than twice that in 1900, and the rate in 1970 was more than twice that in 1935.[10] It appears that perhaps as many as one-third of marriages now end in divorce. The increased divorce rate has often been interpreted as an indication that the institution of marriage is disintegrating. However, what appears to be happening is that unsatisfactory marriages are less often tolerated. Part of the increase in divorce is due to the fact that more couples now seek divorce when their marriages fail, instead of remaining separated. Marital dissolution does not mean rejection of the married state. The evidence for this is that, increasingly, the divorced marry again.[11]
an irreversible step. Some evidence supports such a view.

Nearly universal marriage and early marriage in our society would possibly not be so prevalent had not circumstances made marriage less of an economic and social commitment and less of an irreversible step. Some evidence supports such a view.[12] Formerly it was required that the man be able to provide adequate support for the family before marriage. Many men, therefore, had to delay marriage and some had to forego it altogether. Today, however, the proportion of women in the work force has increased markedly; and the willingness of women to work after marriage, with or without children, has encouraged many young people to decide that they could "afford" to marry. Another factor is that, while marriage once led automatically to children, it no longer needs to do so. The increased ease and respectability of divorce and remarriage has likewise reduced the obligation to remain in an unsatisfactory marriage. Finally, still other factors have encouraged earlier and more universal marriage—educational and housing benefits for veterans, federal subsidization of home ownership, college provision of housing services for married students, unemployment compensation, and last, but not least, parental willingness to continue supporting offspring after they are married.

It would appear that the result of these factors has been generally to provide a greater range of choice to men than to women. In quest of a stable relationship, the young woman often does more than perform her normal duties as wife. She often interrupts her own education and takes a dead-end job in order to support the young man while he pursues his education. Increasingly she works after marriage to improve the economic position of the family. It is the woman's responsibilities, and not the man's, which increase if the woman works, for she must carry family as well as job obligations. If divorce occurs, it is easier for the man to remarry, and the woman ordinarily is assigned responsibility for the continuous task of child-rearing, although she may receive financial assistance from the man. With contraception, the wife may have fewer children than before, and be fully occupied with their upbringing for a shorter time after marriage. Thereafter, however, she has the problem of coping with her time and "justifying" her relative inactivity if she does not work. Men, in general, do not face such major role conflicts until retirement.

While marriage is the common bond holding the family unit together, many families are maintained by one parent only, most often the mother. This may be the case for the woman who bears a child out of wedlock and does not put the child up for adoption, or for mothers whose marriages have been dissolved. In most such instances, however, being a single parent is a temporary state, for the person, especially if young, will usually marry or remarry.

Two developments are likely to have an impact on the family. One is the questioning of existing sex mores by young people and open violation of them by some. The other is the women's liberation movement which aims to improve the status of women and to change role relationships within the family.

Changes in sex mores have not occurred all at once; they have been changing for a long time. In many cases, the sex mores were violated by the parental generation, but not so openly. And, overt compliance was achieved at considerable cost, especially in the case of marriages occurring as a result of premarital pregnancy. This is less necessary now with the greater availability of contraception and abortion. Also, many adults are unaware that their own uncertainty and ambivalence has been a factor in the open repudiation of sexual standards by youth.

Some believe that the "sexual rebellion" may be moving in the direction taken in Sweden, where a permissive attitude towards premarital sexual activity is combined with a late age at marriage. However, both these traits are traditional in Sweden; they are not traditional in the United States. Today, many young people live together informally and are experimenting with a greater range of relationships. Whether or not these relationships are enriching depends on the personal responsibility of individuals involved and the attitudes of our society toward these individuals and their life styles. The effects on marriage and family patterns cannot yet be foreseen, and much depends on how the present confusion with respect to premarital relationships gets resolved.

A significant feature of the women's liberation movement is that, although its demands have been made on the basis of equity for women, it has not usually been anti-marriage or anti-children. It has, however, been concerned with changing the role relationships within families and with extending services for children. Its most vocal demand, however, is for equality in the educational and occupational spheres outside the family.

If the movement is successful, many of the role patterns will be dissolved or weakened. We can expect more conflict within marriage as to who will do what, but such conflict has already been apparent in many cases, and many believe that the quality of child-parent and of husband-wife relationships would be improved by more participation of the husband in family life. In those cases where the woman chooses or is required to work, the division of labor within the family will be based less on sex, for the husband also will be expected to assume responsibility for household chores, to share in the responsibility of caring for children, and to accommodate his occupational requirements to the family roles, much as women do.

None of these changes dictates the direction which reproduction within families will take, or whether the responsibility for childbearing and child-rearing will be enhanced, or what will happen to the quality of family life. As more satisfactory alternatives to childbearing and child-rearing become available, that in itself is likely to enhance rational and responsible decisions about reproduction and parenthood.

POPULATION DENSITY AND POPULATION SIZE

More and more Americans live in urbanized areas at densities far exceeding those in rural areas, but urban densities are not increasing. In fact, average density is actually declining, because urban territory is expanding faster than urban population. In 1960, about 96 million people lived in urbanized areas at an average density of 3,800 people per square mile. By 1970, 118 million people lived in urbanized areas, but the density of urban areas had dropped to 3,400.[13]

It is important to distinguish between density and agglomeration. Density, defined as the number of people per unit of area, does not specify the total number of people involved. Population agglomeration refers to large collections of people at an unspecified density. A small town may have a high density if the lots are small and the buildings tall. Many suburban areas have a low density but contain a large population distributed over extensive areas.

We need to understand the effects of urban density itself and the effects of having such large proportions of our people living in areas that include millions of people. What can be said about "crowding" and its effects? To what extent can social problems—high crime rates, mental illness, mass violence—be attributed to density and to the scale at which we live in metropolitan areas? What will be the social effects of near-total urbanization?

What is the meaning, in terms of daily life, of urban densities which can reach as high as 67,000 people per square mile on Manhattan Island in New York City?[14] Without knowing the context in which it is experienced, the fact of high density tells us little about its importance or impact on human behavior.

High density does not necessarily imply crowding, since the type of activity a person is engaged in, its duration, and the person's attitude all shape perception of whether a particular situation is crowded. The high density at a movie theatre does not cause a crowded feeling as long as each person has a seat. The same density at an office where people are active would probably be unbearably crowded. And certainly where a family of eight lives in three or four rooms the situation is undesirably crowded. In this case, high density coupled with poor housing conditions and poor nutrition, can only aggravate an otherwise difficult situation and seriously hinder the development of children. We cannot, however, assume that all high density situations are either crowded or necessarily bad. Some are, some are not.

Other things being equal, we know that increases in density cause increases in air pollution as the natural recycling system is overloaded. Similarly, traffic and other forms of congestion grow with density, as growing numbers of people hinder each other's movement. But, other factors, such as population size, the layout of the city, and its type of transportation system, are also important.

In general, the research on the effects of population density on human behavior is sparse and the findings either inconclusive or negative. Despite popular belief, the evidence is lacking to show that social pathology is associated with density itself. The most judicious conclusion we can reach is that little is known and that conventional measures of density are of little use as single indicators.

Some intriguing research has been conducted on animals

106

which indicates that certain kinds of anti-social behavior result from excessive crowding.[15] Attempts at similar research on humans have only begun, and the results are inconclusive. One study, which placed groups of individuals in rooms of different sizes, showed no effects on the performance of tasks. Men in such groups evidently became more aggressive and competitive, but women became more pleasant and less competitive. With men and women together, all effects of density disappeared.[16]

Urban areas and central cities do have higher rates of crime and mental illness than rural areas, but efforts to implicate population density have been inconclusive. Other factors, such as income and education appear to be more important than density itself.[17]

It is just possible that we may come to look at the decline in urban densities as a mixed blessing. In suburban areas, one can identify undesirable consequences of haphazard development at densities which are low relative to central cities. If continued in the decades ahead, declining densities could produce a serious reduction of available open space where we can occasionally escape from the pace of urban life.

Many of the concerns about the possible effects of density—the differences in the quality of life in small towns versus large cities, the concern about the loss of a sense of community and individual identity, increasing alienation, and similar questions—are more properly matters of the scale of social organization rather than population density. For example, concerns about the individual's impact on political decisions more clearly involve population size and the nature of political organization than population density.

As the individual becomes a smaller fraction of the total aggregate, his identification and commitment to the whole may diminish. But the effect of increasing size on the individual's identity depends on many other factors such as the strength of family, neighborhood, ethnic, religious, and other organizations in the collection of communities comprising the metropolis.

Undoubtedly the description of big city life as impersonal has some validity. In the course of one day, people living in big cities have contact with many individuals, far too many to know or even recognize. Indeed, the opportunity for such contacts is one of the advantages of urban living, since it facilitates communication and exchange. Under these circumstances, anonymity and impersonality are necessary in order to get through a day's work.

In the space of a single lifetime, we have been transformed

from a predominantly rural to a predominantly urban nation. The effects of living at high densities and in large population groups are only two demographic dimensions of this transformation. Others might come from the change in composition of urban population. In the past, our urban places have grown in part through an influx of people originating in rural areas. The differences in childhood experiences that rural people brought with them to the city probably exerted significant influence on our urban society. Today, as rural to urban migration diminishes, the influence of people of rural origin will soon come to an end. Future generations will be created from people who have been city-born and city-bred.

For better or for worse, we are becoming a nation of metropolitan dwellers. The essential point is that the consequences of this are not well known. We ought to be much more concerned than we seem to be about developing some reliable knowledge of the social and psychological consequences of urbanization, and the associated implications of urban densities and the increasing scale and complexity of social organization accompanying metropolitan agglomeration.

RACIAL AND ETHNIC MINORITIES

Any effort to grasp the dynamics of our population on a national scale include a serious effort to understand what is happening among the socially and economically disadvantaged racial and ethnic minorities—blacks, Indians, Spanish-speaking groups, and others—who are struggling to break out of the backwaters of our society. We have met with social scientists, government officials, and spokesmen from these communities. At best, we have been able to develop only a broad outline of the intricate role population plays among the many pressures under which our deprived groups live. However, this much we can say: This nation cannot hope to successfully address the question of future population without also addressing the complex network of unemployment, poor housing, poor health services, and poor education, all of which combine to act upon, and react to, the pressures of population.

At the outset, we must recognize that our population problems cannot be resolved simply by inducing our "have-not" groups to limit the number of children they have. Although the fertility of minority groups is higher than that of the rest of the population, it is not they who bear the primary responsibility for population growth.

Despite their higher fertility rates, minorities—precisely because of their smaller numbers—contribute less to population growth than does the rest of the population. Among all women 35 to 44 years old in 1969, the Spanish-speaking, Indians, and blacks together contributed 30 percent of the childbearing in excess of replacement needs, while the non-Spanish-speaking white majority contributed 70 percent.[18] An estimate for 1967 indicates that well over half of all childbearing in excess of replacement needs was attributable to the nonpoor, non-Spanish, white majority.[19] Looking at it another way, if no babies had been born to black or Spanish-speaking parents throughout the decade of the sixties, our population would be only four percent smaller than it is today. On the other hand, if there had been no births to non-Spanish-speaking whites, our present population would be 13 percent less.[20]

The idea that our population growth is primarily fueled by the poor and the minorities having lots of babies is a myth. There is nonetheless a strong relationship between high fertility and the economic and social problems that afflict the 13 percent of our people who are poor, and we must address it.

In the first place, the link between birthrates and poverty is so tight that family size in general is a good indicator of how far into the mainstream of American life a group has moved. The largest families are among our rural ethnic, low income, and cultural minorities, regardless of race. They include southern Appalachian whites, southern blacks, Mexican-Americans, American Indians, and other groups.

As these groups move into the mainstream, their family size diminishes. For example, blacks with high school diplomas have about the same number of children as their white counterparts; college-educated blacks have even fewer children, on the average, than their white counterparts.[21] Mexican-American fertility also declines in response to increased education.[22]

In the second place, the sordid history of race relations in our nation has left a widely felt legacy of fear and suspicion that will poison any population policy unless it is clear that such a policy is being developed to enhance the quality of life for all Americans, and not to restrict or curtail the gains made by minorities. As Dr. Eugene S. Callender, president of the New York Urban Coalition, told us:

Minority groups must share the generally growing concern for the quality of life available to us as the population increases. However, it must also be kept in mind that minority groups have only recently been allowed to become participants in this system, to receive its benefits and to share in shaping its future. We are even more anxious about our position within the society, since our few gains are, even now, tenuous.[23]

The fragility of these gains, coupled with the record of white America in relation to nonwhite and Spanish-speaking minorities, practically assures, Dr. Callender added, that any governmental efforts in the field of "population" will be viewed with distrust if not outright alarm:

Within this country, Blacks, Indians, Chicanos, Puerto Ricans, and Orientals feel that such [population] control is solely to the advantage of the majority population. Minority groups at this point in history do not feel that they can afford to trust that the "nobler instincts" of the white majority will prohibit the resurgence of subtle and overt forms of racism.

This wariness is reinforced by a belief that population is of particular interest to affluent whites, and is irrelevant to the everyday survival problems faced by blacks and other minority groups. A witness at our Washington hearings told us that many blacks believe that whites who once joined them in battles against discrimination did so more out of the excitement of joining a "cause" than because of opposition to racial and social injustice. As the battles grew more difficult, whites tired of the effort and now have turned to a new cause— ecology—which blacks consider a copout from the real problems blacks face. As one witness at our Washington hearings noted, "what few white liberals which were left after the 'backlash' have gone traipsing off after daisies and low-phosphate detergents." This witness added:

If this [ecology] movement also talks about fewer people, the question of "who gets to survive" is raised. So, to us, it becomes "every man for himself" now, because we have no reason to expect that we won't get the worst of this one too.[24]

This feeling of powerlessness, of exclusion, has led some spokesmen to suggest that the only way to break into the "system" is by growing so large in numbers that they can no longer be ignored. As we learned from a Spanish-speaking witness at our hearings in Los Angeles, the apparent lack of majority responsiveness leads Spanish-speaking people to believe that, ". . . the only way we will get groups like yours to be responsive to our needs is through sheer weight of numbers." It may be, he added, that "what we must do is to encourage large Mexican-American families so that we will eventually be so numerous that the system will either respond or it will be overwhelmed."[25]

The Reverend Jesse Jackson reminded us in Chicago that the basic drives among all people are for food, clothing, shelter, recognition, and security. He added that:

> . . . You have to recognize that the American group that has been subjected to as much harassment as our community has is suspect of any programs that would have the effect of either reducing or levelling off our population growth. Virtually all the security we have is in the number of children we produce.[26]

The political success of blacks in Newark, New Jersey, Gary, Indiana, and elsewhere are cited by Jackson and others to indicate that continued growth in their communities is required to assure not only survival, but political leverage as well.

However, our public opinion survey revealed that most black people believe continued growth is a problem for this nation. Fifty-one percent said population growth is a serious problem, another 35 percent termed it a problem but not so serious, and 10 percent said it was no problem at all.[27]

While excess fertility among blacks and other minorities is not the main source of the problem of national population growth, nonetheless it is clear that many minority families regard excess fertility as a serious *personal* problem. The evidence for this is the response of minority families to family planning services when these are made available in an acceptable manner. Like other groups, minority members seek to limit their family size as a means of achieving a better quality of life for themselves and their children.

Americans, regardless of their racial or ethnic backgrounds, tend to have smaller families as their education, their jobs, and their incomes improve. However, those who have not been able to climb onto the socioeconomic escalator have also not adopted the pattern of smaller family size. Hence, unblocking our minorities and enabling them to get into the

111

mainstream is going to have a significant effect upon future population levels.

Historically, there has been a close link between urbanization and upward social and economic mobility. But this link has broken down for blacks, the Spanish-speaking, Indians, and other "have-not" groups. For whites, the descendants of immigrants or migrants have done better than their parents. The first arrivals may have taken jobs in factories or on the docks, but they had children who finished high school and went into skilled occupations, and grandchildren who finished college and moved into the professional ranks—and out of the central cities into the suburbs.

There is no question that black people who move from farm to city are better off than those who stay on the farm. The city is where they go for jobs and educational opportunities that simply are not available in rural areas. The problem is that subsequent advances have not come to them as they have come to the majority.

Even though blacks are narrowing the education gap, they are not faring as well economically. In fact, the better educated a black becomes, the worse grows the income gap between himself and a comparably educated white.* For example, in 1969, the median income for men with an eighth grade education was $4,300 among blacks and $5,500 among whites—a difference of $1,200. For those with high school diplomas, black men had a median income of $6,100, whites $8,600—a difference of $2,500. Among college graduates, black men earned median incomes of $8,600, which was $3,800 below the $12,400 earned by whites. The black college graduate in 1969 was earning no more than a white with a high school diploma.[28] For men of Spanish origin, the 1970 median income was $6,000 compared with $8,200 for all whites and $5,000 for blacks.[29]

Those minority people who have "made it" into the system have adopted the small-family pattern. The problem is that so few of them have made it. The task is to make the system work for them as it has for the majority.

If the facts of life for blacks and many other minorities are grim—the facts of death are no better. Blacks live, on the average, seven years less than whites, though this is not as bad as the turn of the century when the gap in life expectancy was 15 years.[30] Current differences are due primarily to premature death among black adults between the ages of 20 to

*A separate statement on this point by Commissioner D. Gale Johnson appears on pages 286-287.

60, and, secondarily to higher mortality among black children.[31] The sources of this higher black mortality is found in the social and economic facts we have already noted.

A Houston case study showed that the number of deaths in 1960 among Mexican-Americans was 12 percent higher for males, and 67 percent higher for females than would have been the case if they had been subject to the death rates experienced by non-Spanish whites. The corresponding figures for excess mortality in Houston's black population were 43 percent for males and 87 percent for females.[32] National figures show that total mortality among Indians exceeds white mortality by 50 percent.[33]

The existence of large differences in mortality by socioeconomic level within minority populations suggests that the excess mortality of these groups can be largely reduced with improvements in levels of living.[34]

In Little Rock, Arkansas, a black man confronted us with a more basic issue: Do we, as a society, *want* to improve conditions for the poor and the excluded? He questioned whether we do:

> I suggest to you that many of us who are advantaged have a vested interest in keeping the disadvantaged exactly where they are. Our economic and political strategies are clearly designed to keep a segment of our population poor and powerless. I suggest that many of our social welfare programs have failed and are failing to help the poor and oppressed among us because they were never intended to help them.[35]

The decade 1960 to 1970 saw a doubling of the number of young black men and women aged 15 to 24 in the metropolitan areas of every part of the nation except the south.[36] This increase, twice that for comparable white youth, was the result of higher black fertility to begin with, participation in the post-World War II baby boom, and continued migration away from southern rural poverty. The result has been more and more young black people ill-equipped to cope with the demands of urban life, more likely to wind up unemployed or in dead-end, low-paying jobs, and caught in the vicious wheel of poverty, welfare, degradation, and crime.

The facts we have cited describe a crisis for our society. They add up to a demographic recipe for more turmoil in our cities, more bitterness among our "have-nots," and greater divisiveness among all of our peoples. What we have said here means that unless we address our major domestic social problems in the short run—beginning with racism and poverty—we will not be able to resolve fully the question of population growth. And, unless we can resolve the question of population growth, in the long run it not only will further aggravate our current problems, but may eventually dwarf them.

CHAPTER 8. POPULATION AND
PUBLIC POLICY

We have reviewed population trends in the United States and examined their implications. Now we are ready to talk about the meaning of these trends for policy.

Four things stand out: First, the effects of our past rapid growth are going to be with us a long time. Second, we have to make a choice about our future growth. Third, the choice involves nothing less than the quality of American life. And, fourth, slower population growth provides opportunities to improve the quality of life, but special efforts are required if the opportunities are to be well used.

A LEGACY OF GROWTH

Regardless of what happens to the birthrate from now on, our past growth commits us to substantial additional growth in the future. At a minimum, we will probably add 50 million more Americans by the end of the century, and the figure could easily be much higher than that.

We will be living for a long time with the consequences of the baby boom. Not long ago, that surge of birth caused double sessions, school in trailers, and a teacher shortage. Now it is crowding the colleges and swelling the number of people looking for jobs. As these young people grow older, they will enter the ranks of producers as well as consumers, and they will eventually reenter dependency—the dependency of the aged.

We are going to have to plan for this. Swelling numbers of job applicants put an extra burden on full employment policy, if only because failure in this respect now affects so many more people than it did once. This will continue to be true for many years. People think the "baby boom" ended in the 1950's. Not so. This was only when it reached its peak. The last year when births exceeded four million was 1964, only eight years ago. In fact, today's eight-year-olds are just as numerous as 18-year-olds. So it is not too late to try to do better by the youngest of the baby-boom babies than we did by the oldest.

The baby boom is not over. The babies have merely grown older. It has become a boom in the teens and twenties. In a few decades, it will be turning into a retirement boom. During the second decade of the next century, 30 million people will turn 65, compared with 15 million who had their 65th birthday in the past 10 years. Will the poverty of the aged be with us then? Census Bureau reports disclose that 25 percent of today's aged are in poverty, compared with eight percent of people in the young working ages of 22 to 45. Thirty years from now, will we do better by the swelling numbers of aged than we do by those we have now? Will we develop alternatives to treating the elderly as castoffs? Not if we don't try. Not if we don't plan for it.

We may be through with the past, but the past is not done with us. Our demographic history shapes the future, even though it does not determine it. It sets forth needs as well as opportunities. It challenges us to get ready. While we cannot predict the future, much of it is foreseeable. For this much, at least, we should be prepared.

THE CHOICE ABOUT FUTURE GROWTH

We have to make a choice about our future growth. As a Commission, we have formed a definite judgment about the choice the nation should make. We have examined the effects that future growth alternatives are likely to have on our economy, society, government, resources, and environment, and we have found no convincing argument for continued national population growth. On the contrary, the plusses seem

116

to be on the side of slowing growth and eventually stopping it altogether. Indeed, there might be no reason to fear a decline in population once we are past the period of growth that is in store.

Neither the health of our economy nor the welfare of individual businesses depend on continued population growth. In fact, the average person will be markedly better off in terms of traditional economic values if population growth slows down than if it resumes the pace of growth experienced in the recent past.

With regard to both resources and the environment, the evidence we have assembled shows that slower growth would conserve energy and mineral resources and would be a significant aid in averting problems in the areas of water supply, agricultural land supply, outdoor recreation resources, and environmental pollution.

Slower population growth can contribute to the nation's ability to solve its problems in these areas by providing an opportunity to devote resources to the quality of life rather than its quantity, and by "buying time"—that is, slowing the pace at which problems accumulate so as to provide opportunity for the development of orderly and democratic solutions.

For government, slower population growth offers potential benefits in the form of reduced pressures on educational and other services; and, for the people, it enhances the potential for improved levels of service in these areas. We find no threat to national security from slower growth. While population growth is not by any means the sole cause of governmental problems, it magnifies them and makes their solution more difficult. Slower growth would lessen the increasing rate of strain on our federal system. To that extent it would enhance the likelihood of achieving true justice and more ample well-being for all citizens even as it would preserve more individual freedom.

Each one of the impacts of population growth—on the economy, resources, the environment, government, or society at large—indicates the desirability, in the short run, for a slower rate of growth. And, when we consider these together, contemplate the ever-increasing problems involved in the long run, and recognize the long lead time required to arrest growth, we must conclude that continued population growth —beyond that to which we are already committed by the legacy of the baby boom—is definitely not in the interest of promoting the quality of life in the nation.

THE QUALITY OF AMERICAN LIFE

We are concerned with population trends only as they impede or enhance the realization of those values and goals cherished in, by, and for American society.

What values? Whose goals? As a Commission, we do not set ourselves up as an arbiter of those fundamental questions. Over the decades ahead, the American people themselves will provide the answers, but we have had to judge proposals for action on population-related issues against their contribution to some version of the good life for this society and, for that matter, the world. What we have sought are measures that promise to move demographic trends in the right direction and, at the same time, have favorable direct effects on the quality of life.

We know that problems of quality exist from the variety of indicators that fall short of what is desirable and possible. There are inequalities in the opportunities for life itself evidenced by the high frequency of premature death and the lower life expectancy of the poor. There is a whole range of preventable illness such as the currently high and rising rate of venereal disease. There are a number of congenital deficiencies attributable to inadequate prenatal care and obstetrical services and, in some cases, to genetic origin. Not all such handicaps are preventable, but they occur at rates higher than if childbearing were confined to ages associated with low incidence and if genetic counseling were more widely available.

Innate human potential often has not been fully developed because of the inadequate quality of various educational, social, and environmental factors. Particularly with regard to our ethnic minorities and the female half of the population, there are large numbers of people occupying social roles that do not capitalize on their latent abilities and interest, or elicit a dedicated effort and commitment. There is hunger and malnutrition, particularly damaging to infants and young children, that should not be tolerated in the richest nation the world has ever known. Sensitive observers perceive in our population a certain frustration and alienation that appears to go beyond what is endemic in the human condition; the sources of these feeling should be explored and better understood.

And we can also identify and measure the limiting factors,

118

the inequalities of opportunity, and the environmental hazards that give rise to such limitations in the quality of life—for example, inadequate distribution of and access to health, education, and welfare services; cultural and social constraints on human performance and development associated with race, ethnic origin, sex, and age; barriers to full economic and cultural participation; unequal access to environmental quality; and unequal exposure to environmental hazard.

There are many other problems of quality in American life. Thus, alongside the challenges of population growth and distribution is the challenge of population quality. The goal of all population policy must be to make better the life that is actually lived.

OPPORTUNITY AND CHOICE

While slower population growth provides opportunities, it does not guarantee that they will be well used. It simply opens up a range of choices we would not have otherwise. Much depends on how wisely the choices are made and how well the opportunities are used. For example, slower population growth would enable us to provide a far better education for children at no increase in total costs. We want the opportunity presented by slower growth to be used this way, but we cannot guarantee that it will be. The wise use of opportunities such as this depends on public and private decisions yet to be made.

Slowing population growth can "buy time" for the solution of many problems; but, without the determined, long-range application of technical and political skills, the opportunity will be lost. For example, our economic and political systems reward the exploitation of virgin resources and impose no costs on polluters. The technology exists for solving many of these problems. But proper application of this technology will require the recognition of public interests, the social inventiveness to discover institutional arrangements for channeling private interests without undue government regulation, and the political courage and skill needed to institute the necessary changes.

Slower population growth offers time in which to accomplish these things. But if all we do with breathing time is breathe, the value of the enterprise is lost.

Population change does not take place in a vacuum. Its consequences are produced through its joint action with technology, wealth, and the institutional structures of society. Hence, a study of the American future, insofar as it is influenced by population change, cannot ignore, indeed it must comment upon, the features of the society that make population growth troublesome or not.

Hence, while we are encouraged by the improvement in average income that will be yielded by slower population growth, we are concerned with the persistence of vast differences in the distribution of income, which has remained fixed now for a quarter of a century.

While we are encouraged by the relief that slower population growth offers in terms of pressure on resources and the environment, we are aware of the inadequacy of the nation's general approach to these problems.

We rely largely on private market forces for conducting the daily business of production and consumption. These work well in general and over the short run to reduce costs, husband resources, increase productivity, and provide a higher material standard of living for the individual. But the market mechanism has been ineffective in allocating the social and environmental costs of production and consumption, primarily because public policies and programs have not provided the proper signals nor required that such costs be borne by production and consumption activities. Nor has the market mechanism been able to provide socially acceptable incomes for people who, by virtue of age, incapacity, or injustice, are poorly equipped to participate in the market system for producing and distributing income.

Our economy's use of the earth's finite resources, and the accompanying pollution or deterioration of the quality of water, air, and natural beauty, has neglected some of the fundamental requirements for acceptable survival. Often the time horizon for both public and private decisions affecting the economy has been too short. It seems clear that market forces alone cannot be relied upon to achieve our social and environmental goals, for reasons that make exchange, though the main organizing principle, inadequate without appropriate institutional and legal underpinnings.

In short, even if we achieve the stabilization of population, our economic, environmental, governmental, and social problems will still be with us unless by will and intelligence we develop policies to deal with the other sources of these problems. The fact that such policies have shown little conspicuous success in the past gives rise to the skepticism we have expressed above in our discussion of the relations between government and population growth.

The problem is not so much the impact of population on government as the adequacy of government to respond to the challenge of population and the host of issues that surround it. Long-term planning is necessary to deal with environmental and resource problems, but there are only beginning signs that government is motivated or organized to undertake it. A major commitment is required to bring minorities into the mainstream of American life, but the effort so far is inadequate. It is clear that the "real city" that comprises the metropolis requires a real government to manage its affairs; but the nation is still trying to manage the affairs of complex, interconnected, metropolitan communities with fragmented institutional structures inherited from the 18th century.

Population, then, is clearly not the whole problem. But it is clearly part of the problem, and it is the part given us as the special responsibility of this Commission. How policy in this area should be shaped depends on how we define the objectives of policy in respect to population.

POLICY GOALS

Ideally, we wish to develop recommendations worthwhile in themselves, which at the same time, speak to population issues. These recommendations are consistent with American ethical values in that they aim to enhance individual freedom while simultaneously promoting the common good. It is important to reiterate that our policy recommendations embody goals either intrinsically desirable or worthwhile for reasons other than demographic objectives.

Moreover, some of the policies we recommend are irreversible in a democratic society, in the sense that freedoms once introduced cannot be rescinded lightly. This irreversibility characterizes several of the important policies recommended by this Commission. We are not really certain of the demographic impact of some of the changes implied by our recommendations. One or two could conceivably increase the birthrate by indirectly subsidizing the bearing of children. The rest may depress the birthrate below the level of replacement. We are not concerned with this latter contingency because, if sometime in the future the nation wishes to increase its population growth, there are many possible ways to try this; a nation's growth should not depend on the ignorance and mis-

121

fortune of its citizenry. In any event, it is naive to expect that we can fine-tune such trends.

In the broadest sense, the goals of the population policies we recommend aim at creating social conditions wherein the desired values of individuals, families, and communities can be realized; equalizing social and economic opportunities for women and members of disadvantaged minorities; and enhancing the potential for improving the quality of life.

At the educational level, we wish to increase public awareness and understanding of the implications of population change and simultaneously further our knowledge of the causes and consequences of population change.

In regard to childbearing and child-rearing, the goals of our recommendations are to: (1) maximize information and knowledge about human reproduction and its implications for the family; (2) improve the quality of the setting in which children are raised; (3) neutralize insofar as it is practicable and consistent with other values those legal, social, and institutional pressures that historically have been mainly pronatalist in character; and (4) enable individuals to avoid unwanted childbearing, thereby enhancing their ability to realize their preferences. These particular policies are aimed at facilitating the social, economic, and legal conditions within our society which increase ethical responsibility and the opportunity for unbiased choice in human reproduction and child-rearing. At the same time, by enhancing the individual's opportunity to make a real choice between having few children and having many, between parenthood and childlessness, and between marriage and the single state, these policies together will undoubtedly slow our rate of population growth and accelerate the advent of population stabilization.

In connection with the geographic distribution of population, our objectives are to ease and guide the process of population movement, to facilitate planning for the accommodation of movements, and to increase the freedom of choice in residential locations.

To these ends, therefore, we offer our recommendations in the belief that the American people, collectively and individually, should confront the issues of population growth and reach deliberate informed decisions about the family's and society's size as they affect the achievement of personal and national values.

CHAPTER 9. EDUCATION

One characteristic American response to social issues is to propose educational programs, and this Commission is no exception. The range of educational topics impinging on population is broad and diffuse; somewhat arbitrarily, we have elected to organize the subject into three categories: population education, education for parenthood, and sex education. This is not the only way to organize this material. It is for the individual community, school, or agency to decide what is appropriate and wise for them in preparing such educational programs.

POPULATION EDUCATION

If Americans now and in future generations are to make rational, informed decisions about their own and their descendants' future, they must be provided with far more knowledge about population change and its implications than they now possess.* The amount and accuracy of information currently held by Americans on the subject of population leave much to be desired. Approximately six out of 10 questioned in our 1971 poll either did not know or could not guess the size of the United States population within 50 million persons (205 million in 1970). And among young persons between

* A separate statement by Commissioner Alan Cranston appears on pages 268-269.

16 and 21, many of whom are still in school, the proportion answering correctly rises only a couple of percentage points. The record is even worse with respect to information about the world's population. Only 16 percent know or can guess the size of the world's population within one-half billion persons (3.6 billion in 1970). If information on such elementary facts is missing, one can imagine the state of more advanced knowledge and understanding.[1]

Population education involves more than simply learning the size of different populations. Ideally, it includes some elementary knowledge of the arithmetic of population growth and the growth of metropolitan areas and suburban decentralization. A program of population education should seek to present knowledge about population processes, population characteristics, the causes of population change, and the consequences of such change for the individual and for the society. We believe that population education should not approach population as a "problem" to be solved or as a point of view to be promoted. The goal of population education is to incorporate concepts and materials related to population into the school curriculum in order to educate future generations, enabling them to make more intelligent decisions with regard to population matters.[2]

Although some students are exposed to a smattering of population content in courses such as geography and biology, there is hardly any systematic coverage of the topic.

There is no evidence that anything approaching an adequate population education program now exists in our schools. Very few teachers are trained in the subject and textual materials are scant and inadequate.

Teachers can be trained in the content of the population field and in the methods of population education, through preservice and in-service programs, summer institutes and workshops, the development of mobile teams of specialists, and other special programs. Some beginnings in this direction have already been made.

It is, of course, understandable that schools are under enormous pressure to incorporate in their curriculum many new topics ranging from driver education to drug education. The techniques for incorporating population materials into other courses will have to be explored.

Congress has begun to recognize the need for population education. Population is among the subjects that may be included in programs funded under the Environmental Education Act of 1970. P.L. 91-572, the Family Planning Services and Population Research Act, contains an authorization of $1.25 million in fiscal year 1973 for family planning and population information and education.

However, the Environmental Education Act is seriously underfunded; and population education, which is only a small element of the program, is unlikely ever to receive adequate attention under the present legislation. The Office of Education, which administers the environmental education program, has not been an enthusiastic advocate of population education. This situation might change if adequate authority and funding became available for such a program.

Although Congress authorized funding of population education under P.L. 91-572, in the first two years no funds have been made available under the Act for this purpose. In fiscal year 1973, the Department of Health, Education and Welfare has requested $170,000 for population education. In a paper prepared for the Commission, one expert estimated that federal funds amounting to $25 million over the next three years are needed in this field.

Responsibility for coordinating activities in population education has recently been assigned to the Deputy Assistant Secretary for Population Affairs. This represents an initial step toward establishing quality programs in population education. The Commission suggests that, as activity in the field of population education expands, it may be necessary to review periodically the location of this responsibility.

In view of the important role that education can play in developing an understanding of the causes and consequences of population growth and distribution, the Commission recommends enactment of a Population Education Act to assist school systems in establishing well-planned population education programs so that present and future generations will be better prepared to meet the challenges arising from population change.

To implement such a program, the Commission recommends that federal funds be appropriated for teacher training, for curriculum development and materials preparation, for research and evaluation, for the support of model programs, and for assisting state departments of education to develop competence and leadership in population education.

At the college level, a recent survey of 537 accredited four-year institutions in the United States indicated that nearly

125

half offer a course in demography or population problems. Variation by type of institution was considerable, with only one-fifth of the Catholic schools, but two-thirds of the state or municipal schools offering a population course.[8] In reality, only a small fraction of the college population is exposed to formal coursework in demography. The Commission feels that a useful way to increase this exposure would be to include population in the large introductory social science courses offered by all colleges and universities. Additionally, exhibits, lectures, and programs sponsored by campus groups would serve to increase student awareness of population questions.

EDUCATION FOR PARENTHOOD

Life in the future will depend significantly on the characteristics of our children. The Commission's interest is not limited to the number of children in our population, but extends to a concern for the quality of their development. How adequately are we raising our children, and how can we insure that parents and children are given the opportunity for self-fulfillment?

There is a diversity of styles of family life in America today. It includes the conventional nuclear family (parents and children) along with extended families and experiments in communal living. In addition, a great many of the traditional functions of the family are being assumed by other institutions. Although its functions diminish and its size and form change, the family as a basic social institution shows little sign of obsolescence. The family remains the primary environment for the physical, emotional, social, and intellectual development of children. The home continues to be the focus for learning about parenthood. Children are constantly being educated for their future roles as parents by the examples set for them. The infant shares in the loving environment of his home; the young child learns discipline and the daily activities of family life; the teenager begins to understand the responsibilities involved in the creation of a home.

Since the overwhelming majority of Americans marry and have children, we tend to overlook the fact that we are not all equally suited for parenthood any more than we are for teaching school or playing various sports. Matters of temperament, age, health, and competing interests, to mention just a few, are considerations in determining whether or not to have children. For most people, choosing to remain childless is not a real option. Our society should enlarge its tolerance and accept, without stigma, those individuals who choose not to become parents.

Costs of Children[4]

At the same time, the Commission considers it important for parents and prospective parents to have some understanding of the implications of their reproductive decisions for themselves and their children. The benefits and rewards of children are well known, but not many recognize the emotional and financial costs involved. For many young people, becoming a parent represents a greater change in their lives than does marriage; and they are unprepared for the emotional demands of parenthood or the impact of each additional child on the family unit.

Although many couples have only a vague idea of the financial costs of a child, more and more parents are enlarging their expectations for their children. This change in expectations has meant a change in costs. Parents today, in addition to paying for the birth and rearing of a child, may also bear the costs of a college education. The costs of raising a child from birth through college, without including the costs borne by the public sector, are estimated in the table on page 128. As substantial as these are, the direct cost is only part of the total. With the birth of a child, one parent—usually the woman—will tend to spend more time at home, thereby giving up the income which she otherwise would have earned. Today, with more women better educated and having better jobs, the earnings a woman foregoes due to the birth of a child are often substantial. Depending on her educational background, a woman's loss of earnings over a period of 14 years due to the birth of her first child might be as high as $60,000. Although she will forego less in the way of earnings with subsequent children, the loss of income, combined with the costs of raising a family, may place a heavy financial burden on the parents. Information on the costs to the family of raising a child is an important part of education for parenthood. With some idea of the financial demands of children, parents can plan ahead and be better prepared to provide the kind of life they want for their children.

Another type of cost for many individuals and their children are the disadvantages that result from early childbearing. Infants of young mothers, especially those under 19 years

The Total Cost of a Child, 1969

	Discounted	Undiscounted[a]
Cost of giving birth	$ 1,534	$ 1,534
Cost of raising a child	17,576	32,830
Cost of college education	1,244	5,560
Total direct cost	20,354	39,924
Opportunity costs for the average woman[b]	39,273	58,437
Total costs of a first child	$59,627	$98,361

a Discounted and undiscounted costs—spending $1,000 today costs more than spending $1,000 over a 10-year period because of the nine years of potential interest on the latter. This fact is allowed for in the discounted figures by assuming interest earned annually on money not spent in the first year. True costs are not accurately reflected in the undiscounted estimates, for these are simply accumulations of total outlays without regard to the year in which they must be made.

b Depending on the educational background of the mother, the opportunity costs (earnings foregone by not working) could be higher or lower.

SOURCE: Ritchie H. Reed and Susan McIntosh, "Costs of Children" (prepared for the Commission, 1972).

of age, are subject to higher risks of prematurity, mortality, and serious physical and intellectual impairments than are children of mothers 20 to 35. Despite a downward trend, a quarter of American girls who recently reached their twentieth birthday had already borne a child. Moreover, the mother, father, and child are more likely to be disadvantaged in social and economic terms than are couples who postpone childbearing at least until the mother is in her twenties.[5] In addition, a recent government report indicates that the probability of divorce is considerably higher for couples married when the wife is younger than 20 years old.[6]

Family Life Education

The decision to marry and the decision to bring a child into the world should not be made lightly. Both marriage and parenthood should imply a deep personal commitment and a continuing emotional investment. As a nation, we have a responsibility to provide better preparation for parenthood. At the present time, some school systems throughout the country have included family life courses in their curriculum. The Catholic Church has been in the forefront in family life education and is working to inform children and their parents on issues involved in family living. Programs in home economics similarly provide training for marriage and parenthood. The subject matter of these courses is extremely variable, including topics on the functions of the family in human history and in modern industrial society, nutrition and home management, the physiology of reproduction, the physical and emotional relationships involved in dating and marriage, and the roles of family members, including discussions of the changing status of women and patterns of child-rearing. Supplementary to these school programs are the efforts of community groups, such as the Red Cross, in training and guiding prospective parents. In regard to parent education, the White House Conference on Children concludes:

Where parent education does occur, it is typically presented in vicarious forms through reading and discussion. . . . Excellent preparation for parenthood can be given to school-age children through direct experience under appropriate supervision, in caring for and working with those younger than themselves.[7]

The mass media are a potent educational force in our society. American children and adults spend an estimated average of 27 hours a week watching television.[8] They also spend large amounts of time reading newspapers and magazines, listening to the radio, and going to movies. Family life, as depicted in soap operas, situation comedies, and romantic magazines and films, bears little resemblance to that experienced by most of the population. In our judgment, the media should assume more responsibility in presenting information and education for family living to the public.

In proportion to the number of individuals who are and will become parents, our educational effort is insufficient. The Commission believes that community agencies, especially the school, should become more sensitive to the need for preparation for parenthood and should include appropriate subject matter in their programs. We observe that there is information and expertise in the various aspects of family life scattered throughout the public and private sector. The Commission suggests that the Department of Health, Education and Welfare provide financial support for programs designed to examine and coordinate existing information activities and resources in this field.

If one of our goals is to maximize the opportunities for parents and their children, the concept of education for parenthood goes beyond the provision of courses in family life. The field expands to considerations of maternal and child health, the emotional and physical conditions under which we raise our children, and finally the genetic endowment with which the young will develop. Discussion and recommendations on issues of maternal and child health are found in Chapter 11.

Nutrition[9]

The existence of hunger and malnutrition in the United States is well known. Although it is difficult to separate nutrition from the total physical, social, and biological environment, the Director of the National Nutrition Survey estimates that there may be more than 10 million malnourished Americans among the poor. Of these, approximately 40 percent are children. Of all the children surveyed, 15 percent showed evidence of growth retardation—an anticipated result, since malnutrition is known to inhibit the normal growth process.[10]

Experts have stated that, ". . . if malnutrition persists during the first few years of life, the child is doomed to foreshortened physical and mental development, increased susceptibility to infection and impaired response to his environment.[11]

Malnutrition is not only a threat to growth and development, it endangers life itself. Scientists have shown that malnutrition directly increases the mortality rate of pregnant women and, indirectly, of infants; maternal malnutrition is a major cause of immaturity and prematurity among infants. Between one-half and three-fourths of all children who die in the first four weeks of life are premature. A Norwegian study has demonstrated that improved nutrition resulted in a 50-percent decrease in still births, premature births, and infant mortality.

We urge private and public agencies to combine in establishing programs to prevent malnutrition and its effects. Malnutrition can be prevented by providing the appropriate food to expectant mothers and to children under three years old, particularly those living in poverty.

If any food supplement program is to be successful, food fads and habits must also be changed. Nutrition education is a vital component in any program to prevent and correct malnutrition.

It is not only the poor who are in need of nutrition education. All groups in our society require information to improve their nutritional health. Currently, we are giving a good deal of attention to consumer education, including some nutritional education. We urge that these efforts extend to ensuring fair and honest advertising and labeling of the products we consume.

Environment and Heredity

We have all heard the term "deprived environment" used to describe the handicaps of ghetto children; yet, relatively little attention has been paid to determining the environmental needs of children. More consideration should be given to the physical, intellectual, and emotional environments in which we raise our children. Other groups and commissions are reviewing many of these issues; our concern is that we recognize the need for programs to provide parents with the education, skills, and services to deal effectively with these problems.

The relative importance of heredity and environment in shaping an individual's growth and development remains uncertain. Clearly, it is desirable to reduce the incidence of genetically related disorders in the population. The frequency of such disorders is much higher than formerly suspected. According to experts:

No less than 25 percent of hospital and other institutional beds are estimated to be occupied by patients whose physical or mental illnesses or defects are under full or at least partial genetic control.[12]

Others estimate that one out of 15 children is born with some form of genetic defect, some so severe as to have tremendous implications in the life of the affected person and his family.[13]

The provision of genetic advice to parents and prospective parents can increase the responsibility of their reproductive decisions. With the information provided by genetic screening and counseling, a couple can approach parenthood with some notion of the probability of their child having a genetic disorder. We believe that this increased knowledge and awareness can benefit parents and children alike.

It would be unrealistic at the present time to imagine that we can launch a full-scale program of genetic screening and counseling. For centuries, man has observed that some disorders are found with greater frequency in certain families, and in some social and ethnic groups; it has only been in the last half century that knowledge has accumulated concerning the actual mechanism controlling inheritance. And there remains a great deal to learn regarding the genetic components of many disorders and the precise mode of their inheritance. Furthermore, only recently have we become concerned with the ethical and moral implications of the expanding technology of genetics.

As a Commission, we encourage increased support of: (1) research to identify genetically related disorders; (2) development of new and more refined screening techniques and research aimed at improving the delivery of these services; (3) extension and improvement of the care and treatment of persons suffering from genetically related disorders; and (4) exploration of the ethical and moral implications of genetic technology.

Although the science of genetics is still in its early development, our knowledge and technology are sufficient to begin to develop the educational, screening, and counseling programs to identify and inform couples at risk.

Private and public funds should be made available to develop facilities and train personnel to implement programs in genetic screening and counseling. A small number of such programs are already functioning within groups in the population known to experience a high frequency of certain disorders. For example, bio-chemical evaluation of the fetus is now used to detect the presence of Tay-Sachs disease among members of the Jewish community, and prenatal chromosome analysis can detect Down's syndrome (monogolism), which occurs with a high frequency in older pregnant women. A simple blood test is now available to screen for sickle cell anemia, which affects tens of thousands of black Americans, and to identify those individuals who are carriers of the sickle cell trait.

The Commission believes that genetic education is an important component in any program of education for parenthood. Therefore, we suggest that genetic information be part of the health education services offered in comprehensive programs where patient counseling is involved, such as family planning services, premarital counseling, prenatal clinics, and maternal and child health projects. Moreover, we suggest that material on genetically related diseases be included in the school curriculum. Professional education should be expanded to alert doctors, nurses, and other health workers to recognize genetically related problems and to refer them to available genetic counseling services.

In the United States at present, the one role which most people ultimately assume—parenthood—is given little attention. The Commission urges that parents and prospective parents have access to the information, techniques, and services needed to raise their children to be healthy, creative individuals who are capable of full participation in our society.

SEX EDUCATION[14]

In our society today, many young people appear to be questioning traditional sexual codes and experimenting with new life styles and new moralities. Although there are many manifestations of change, it may be that the fundamental change consists of a greater willingness to submit our sexual attitudes and behavior to public discussion. Traditional and religious constraints on such discussion have receded; psychiatric writing has induced us to accept sexuality as a basic aspect of personality development and interpersonal relationships.

For some, the subject of human sexuality refers to the physiological and emotional responses to sexual stimuli; recent research into the biology of human sexuality reflects this perspective. For others, sexuality consists of learning the guidelines for appropriate sexual behavior. In its broadest sense, sexuality is no less than the fact of being a man or a woman, and how this identity affects personality and human relationships.

Whatever the limits of the subject, there seems to be a lag between the recognition of the importance of sexuality in human relationships and the development of ways to improve this aspect of our lives. One reason for this is the insecurity felt by most people in dealing with human sexuality. The challenge is great and there are few acknowledged experts to guide us. When so basic a system of attitudes and behavior appears to be changing and when there is conflict between traditional sexual mores and contemporary sexual behavior, the task is to educate and inform in this climate of uncertainty.

As a nation, we are reaching a consensus on the need for sex education; and there is widespread support for these programs from the general public. A number of states have passed legislation in support of sex education in public schools. Some local school districts have instituted programs in family life and sex education. Many responsible organizations have indicated their support for sex education programs. In 1969, the president of the National Congress of Parents and Teachers stated that "sound education about sexuality is basic if children are to understand human development, cope with stresses and pressures of adolescence in modern America and become adults capable of successful marriage and responsible adulthood."[15] The *Interfaith Statement on Sex Education,* urges "all (parents, clergy and school) to take a more active role, each in his own area of responsibility and competence, in promoting sound leadership and programs in sex education."[16]

There is a wide range of opinion on the subject of sex education among specialists who are themselves divided on the definition and content of sex education programs. To some degree, the social and cultural backgrounds of the groups with whom the sex educator is most familiar, and his perception of their immediate needs, are reflected in his definition of sex education. The sex educator working in an urban ghetto will have views on the methodology and presentation of sex education which might differ from those of an educator working in a middle-class suburban community. Furthermore, there is a dearth of carefully constructed programs with clearly stated assumptions, values, aims, and mechanisms for evaluation.

Some authorities define the subject from a relatively narrow, pragmatic perspective. They are of the opinion that young people reject the authority of the school as representing "the establishment," thereby making it difficult, if not impossible, for schools to be an effective force in discussing the sensitive relationships involved in human sexuality. These educators feel that students should be taught what they want to know—that is, the specific facts about reproduction, contraception, abortion, and venereal disease. Moreover, students want the opportunity to discuss in the classroom their attitudes toward sexual behavior. This subject matter should be presented in a straightforward manner in existing biology and health courses. And, these school programs should be combined with community efforts sponsored by youth-oriented groups, Planned Parenthood centers, and similar groups.

Others view sex education as a form of preventive medicine,

as an "appreciation of maleness and femaleness in relationship with the same and opposite sex—part of the total personality and health entity of each individual—character education." From this perspective, sex education is not reproduction education or simply the presentation of facts; it is seen as a way of helping people, especially the young, to understand themselves and their sexuality in relation to the human community.

Although no single definition of sex education is accepted by all those working in this field, we find more agreement on the general objectives of sex education programs.

A major goal of sex education is to improve human relationships by helping individuals deal more openly and reasonably with their sexual concerns. In addition, sex education programs aim to increase the individual knowledge and appreciation of human sexuality.

Programs in sex education have the responsiblity to present, in an appropriate manner, factual information on the emotional, physical, and social aspects of sexuality.

Another goal of sex education is to enhance communication between the generations regarding sexual attitudes and behavior. Most would agree that the home should be the source of sound sex education. In fact, informal education about sexuality is constantly provided in the home environment as children are influenced by parental attitudes and behavior. A recent survey conducted for the Commission on Obscenity and Pornography indicates that an overwhelming number of those interviewed reported parents as the preferred source of sex education. However, mothers were an actual source of sex information for 46 percent of the women, and parents served as an actual source for only 25 percent of the men.[17] Unfortunately, large numbers of parents feel factually and emotionally ill-prepared to handle the topic with their own children. Most adults have had no formal sex education, and the characteristic lack of communication about sexuality is a source of great frustration and anxiety for parents and children alike. The community can assist in this difficult task by providing sex education for citizens of all ages; sex is a vital aspect of life for people in every age group, and education in sexuality should be an ongoing process.

The Commission recognizes that there is no best way to define or conduct sex education programs, and that local communities and groups must create programs which coincide with their values, resources, and needs.

Today there is an increasing openness and public presentation of sexual matters. Some take advantage of this situation, presenting sex in a sensational manner. Not enough information about sexuality is presented to the public by responsible sources. For example, we see no justification for a situation where newspapers accept advertisements for X-rated movies, while advertisements for birth control methods are unacceptable.

With an appreciation of the difficulties involved, we feel it is possible to present material from this intensely personal aspect of life in an open and forthright manner, while maintaining respect for the intimate and private nature of the subject. We believe this can best be done through responsible programs of sex education.

Yet there remains a well-organized and vocal minority actively opposing programs of sex education. Some of these groups go so far as to interpret sex education as a politically inspired plot to teach young people how to engage in sexual activity, thereby officially condoning "immorality" and "perversion." We regret that these groups have successfully forestalled sex education programs in 13 states.[18] We call upon all groups to join in the creation of appropriate, high quality programs in sex education. The issue was underscored by the observation of a high-school girl at one of the Commission's public hearings: ". . . the refusal to provide education will not prevent sex, but it certainly will prevent responsible sex."[19]

Ignorance does not serve to prevent sexual activity, but rather promotes the undesirable consequences of sexual behavior—unwanted pregnancy, unwanted maternity, and venereal disease. These problems seem particularly acute for the adolescent segment of our population. Unfortunately, society has been slow to face the fact that, with or without formal sex education, there is a considerable amount of sexual activity among unmarried young people. A recent national study of unmarried teenage girls revealed that 14 percent of 15-year-olds and up to 44 percent of 19-year-olds reported having had sexual relations. Only 20 percent of these girls used contraception regularly. Such a low incidence of contraceptive use is particularly significant when less than half of these girls knew when during the monthly cycle a girl can become pregnant.[20] Rates of out-of-wedlock births to young women ages 15 to 19 increased by two to threefold between 1940 and 1968.[21] (Discussions of teenage pregnancy and contraceptive information and services for teenagers are found in Chapter 11.)

Venereal disease in the United States is considered by public health officials an epidemic of unusual extent and severity. They estimate that 2.3 million cases of infectious venereal disease were treated in the United States last year. The incidence of reported venereal disease is highest among persons under 25.[22]

After a consideration of alternative mechanisms for improving and increasing programs of sex education throughout the nation, the Commission suggests that funds be made available to the National Institute of Mental Health to support the development of a variety of model programs in human sexuality. These programs should include school- and community-based projects in a number of different communities. In the area of sex education there are few carefully designed programs were clearly defined goals and mechanisms for evaluation. The evaluation and testing of different model projects would greatly enhance the field of sex education.

We believe that sex education ideally should be focused in the home and supplemented by schools and other community groups including religious, medical, and service organizations.

To handle this material successfully, those people involved should be individuals who themselves experience no difficulty in being open and direct about sexual matters, and who have the sensitivity and perception to gain the trust of youth. Few of today's teacher training institutions provide adequate education in this field. From a sample of 100 teacher training schools, it was discovered that only 13 percent provide any kind of specific training for teachers of sex education.

The Commission supports those community agencies and educational institutions training professional sex educators, and urges more schools to include such training in their programs. Moreover, we encourage institutions involved in training professionals in the health and welfare fields, such as doctors, clergy, family-planning workers, and social workers, to add courses in human sexuality to their curriculum.

Recognizing the importance of human sexuality, the Commission recommends that sex education be available to all, and that it be presented in a responsible manner through community organizations, the media, and especially the schools.

CHAPTER 10. THE STATUS OF
CHILDREN AND WOMEN

THE CHILDREN

There is no paradox in welcoming the trend toward smaller families and simultaneously viewing children as our most valuable resource. In the past, we have not given children as high a place in our priorities as in our rhetoric. With a renewed trend toward fewer children per family, now is a propitious time to begin.

The total needs of children within our society are addressed in detail in the report of the 1970 White House Conference on Children. There are, however, several issues of special relevance to our task. Among these are child health and development, welfare of pregnant adolescents, rights of children born out of wedlock, and adoption.

Health and Development

We know that the physical, emotional, and intellectual potential of each human being is greatly affected by the health and nutrition of the expectant mother and by the care given to the child in the first few years of life. However, adequate prenatal care is not available to many women, especially the poor who live in inner-city ghettos and in rural areas, pregnant adolescents, and women pregnant out of wedlock. One result is higher rates of death or illness among such mothers and infants. Our nation's infant mortality rate is higher than that of 12 other nations, and it varies within the United States according to location and socioeconomic group. Infant mortality is higher among nonwhites and the poor than among whites and the middle class. The incidence of cerebral palsy and other birth disorders is also higher among the same groups.

Regular health care during the first year of life is a key to preventing or correcting illnesses that may handicap for life; but pediatric services are not sufficiently available to the poor. In addition, very few private health insurance programs pay for well-baby care, and even nonpoor parents may have difficulty in meeting these costs.

Since 1935, the federal government has supported programs to extend and improve health services for mothers and children, especially in rural areas. One of these, the Maternal and Child Health Care program of the Department of Health, Education and Welfare, provided maternity nursing services to over a half million women in the year beginning July 1, 1970. Almost 1.5 million children received preventive health services that included attention to their nutritional and other special needs. Another, the Maternity and Infant Care program, was established in 1963 to help reduce the incidence of mental retardation and other handicapping conditions caused by complications associated with childbearing, and to help reduce infant and maternal mortality by providing health care to high-risk mothers and their infants. As of July 1971, 56 maternity-and infant-care projects admitted 141,000 new maternity patients and over 47,000 infants.[1]

Federal support of these programs is not increasing significantly; and they are unable, as presently constituted, to meet the needs of all low-income women who are not receiving private health care. Moreover, neither program is designed to defray the costs of maternal and infant care for the nonpoor.

The Commission believes that our nation should set a goal of providing comprehensive health care to all mothers and children. This should be a high priority of our health-care system. The costs and methods of developing a complete fertility-related health program are discussed later. Two-thirds of the costs of such a program would be for maternal and infant care.[2] The costs to the nation, over and above current expenditures, are not excessive. The savings, in terms of improved maternal and infant health, would be considerable. Until the time that it becomes fully operational, existing federal maternal and infant care programs, especially those carried out under the authority of Title V of the Social Security Act, should be extended and enlarged.

Child Care

It is essential to recognize the critical significance of the first three years of life for the emotional and intellectual, as well as the physical, development of children.* Information and education on the importance of early cognitive development should be made available to parents. In both the home and in child-care programs, every effort should be made to provide the best possible health, nutritional, emotional, and educational support during this vital period.

Many parents today are looking for assistance in the care and rearing of their children. There are various reasons for this, including the steadily growing employment of women, the declining reliance on relatives, and the increasing realization of the learning potential of pre-school children.

In 1970, almost 2.6 million children under 18 had mothers who worked at least part time; over 5.8 million of these children were under age six.[3] Large numbers of these working mothers were the sole support of their families or supplemented incomes near the poverty level. Many middle-class women are also entering the work force. Changing values, the rising number of divorces, and the increasing costs of children in an urban environment are some of the factors contributing to this new trend.

The child-care arrangements made by working mothers, especially those whose ability to pay is limited, are frequently inadequate. Many children are cared for in their homes by adult relatives or babysitters, but many are cared for by sisters or brothers who are themselves children. Other children receive care outside of the home under various arrangements. Only a small percentage are enrolled in nursery schools or day-care centers, and many of these are of low quality. At least one million young Americans receive no supervision at all—these are the so-called "latch-key" children who wander about after school or remain at home alone when ill.[4] These conditions are unacceptable.

In other societies and in earlier times in our own country, very young children were exposed to a variety of adults and other children. In the so-called extended family, care was often provided by grandparents, aunts, and cousins. In larger families and before universal education, many children depended

* A separate statement by Commissioner John N. Erlenborn appears on page 276.

141

upon other siblings for much of their care. Today, greater mobility, smaller families, and suburban housing patterns have tended to isolate mother and child alone in the home for extended periods of time. As with employment, these trends appear to be increasing. Many families would benefit from versatile part-day as well as full-day child-care programs, or from programs that could provide day and night care in case of a family emergency.

Research has indicated the high learning potential of pre-school children, and many people are beginning to urge that some exposure to formal learning begin before age six. Some have suggested that child-care programs become extensions of the educational system. As the birthrate falls, school systems may find that the desire for earlier entry into the educational system will coincide with available classroom space. However, the needs of a child-care system are such that substantial changes would be required in the present operation of the public school system.

Some of the opposition to the creation of a child-care system in this country is based on the following beliefs: it may be destructive of the family; we cannot afford to undertake something as expensive as good developmental child care; and by reducing the tension between motherhood and other roles, child care will encourage the birth of more children.

We believe that institutional child care, if undertaken on a broad basis, may have some beneficial implications for the family. Economic and educational functions have been separated from the family without destroying it. A "latch-key" child will probably benefit from anything that gets him off the street. The child from a more traditional home may benefit from the companionship of other children. It is unlikely that any child could benefit from a sterile, institutional setting that offers no stimulation. The kind of care a child receives is more important than where he receives it. A child may learn to love or hate in his home, in a neighbor's home, or in a child-care center. What is essential is that children receive love, warmth, continuity of care, and stimulation.

Aside from the quality of care, parents must be able to make the decision whether or not to use child-care services and to what extent. Any form of compulsory child care is unacceptable, including the requirement that mothers place young children in these programs in order to comply with regulations that exact training and employment as a condition for benefiting from assistance programs.

Developmental child care seems preferable to custodial programs; and there is no question that such programs, on a large

142

scale, will involve enormous expense. One source estimates that it would cost $20 billion per year in public funds to pay for the best kind of full-time developmental program for the 18 million children from families with incomes under $7,000.[5] There may be ways to obtain good care for less. Experimentation with a variety of programs and personnel seems essential.

Those who are able to pay for child care should do so. Recent amendments to federal tax law to permit working persons with incomes under $18,000 to deduct up to $4,800 per year in child-care costs should make it possible for many middle-income families to pay for these services.[6] Union and industry programs that provide care for children of members and employees should be expanded. Even so, public funds will be necessary both to stimulate innovative programs and research, and to subsidize services for lower-income families.

Many people concerned with population growth have argued against public subsidization of child-care programs because they believe such programs may encourage childbearing. In the short run, child-care programs may reduce the tension between motherhood and employment, and thus make it possible for some working women to feel they can manage the responsibilities of both employment and children. However, it is also possible that child-care programs will have a negative impact on fertility. Parenthood is an almost universally desired status in our society and most couples want at least one child. The availability of child care is not likely to affect the behavior of the woman who perceives her role as that of wife and mother; nor is it apt to effect the decision to have a first child. After the first or second child, however, the economic opportunities available outside of the home to a woman who wishes to work may affect her desire to have additional children. With child care available, women who want to work will have the opportunity to enter or reenter the labor force much sooner; and the rewards of employment may compete effectively with the satisfactions of additional children. On the other hand, if a woman is unable to seek alternative roles outside the home, perhaps because of an inability to make adequate child-care arrangements, she might channel all her creative energies into her domestic role and might be encouraged to have additional children.

In the long run, therefore, child-care programs may reduce fertility. Faced with no prospects for child care, many women have chosen to foresake career aspirations rather than forego motherhood. If future young women perceive that they may combine both roles, it is likely that more of them will undertake the training and education necessary to pursue careers outside of the home.

We believe that the demand for child-care services will continue to grow. The challenge is to make certain that they enhance the well-being of the child.

The Commission therefore recommends that both public and private forces join together to assure that adequate child-care services, including health, nutritional, and educational components, are available to families who wish to make use of them.

Because child-care programs represent a major innovation in child-rearing in this country, we recommend that continuing research and evaluation be undertaken to determine the benefits and costs to children, parents, and the public of alternative child-care arrangements.

Adolescent Pregnancy and Children Born out of Wedlock

The problem of pregnant adolescents requires special attention by our society. In 1968, just over 600,000 infants, 17 percent of all births in that year, were born to women under 20 years old. Childbearing at any age is a momentous event for a woman; but pregnant teenagers, especially those in the early teens, often experience serious health and social difficulties quite different from those of women over 20.[7]

Their babies have a higher incidence of prematurity and of infant mortality. Girls who marry or have a first child at an early age also tend to bear subsequent children at a rapid rate, so that intervals between births are relatively short. A study of one metropolitan area found that 60 percent of girls who had a child before the age of 16 had another baby while still of school age.[8] Education and employment opportunities may be seriously impaired. In other sections of this report, we stress the necessity of minimizing adolescent pregnancy by making contraceptive information and services available to sexually active young women. When an adolescent does become pregnant, however, she should not be stigmatized and removed from society. In the past, pregnant girls almost always had to leave school as soon as their condition became known. Today, more and more school systems are making efforts to see that the pregnant adolescent does not suffer

144

from lack of educational opportunity. Recently the Commissioner of the Office of Education stated:

> Every girl in the United States has a right to and a need for the education that will help her prepare herself for a career, for family life, and for citizenship. To be married or pregnant is not sufficient cause to deprive her of an education and the opportunity to become a contributing member of society. The U.S. Office of Education strongly urges school systems to provide continuing education for girls who become pregnant.[9]

We support the Commissioner's view, and believe that society will be well-served if all school systems would make certain that pregnant adolescents have the opportunity to continue their education, and that they are aided in gaining access to adequate health, nutritional, and counseling services.

Out-of-wedlock births among young people aged 15 to 19 are increasing in the United States. In 1965, there were 125,000 children born to unwed teenage mothers; in 1968, the figure rose to 160,000. By 1970, the figure is estimated to have risen to 180,000. The proportion of out-of-wedlock births among 15- to 19-year-olds rose from 15 percent in 1960 to 27 percent in 1968.[10]

Unwed mothers are less likely than married mothers to have adequate prenatal care; and children born out of wedlock are more likely to be born prematurely and to die in the first year after birth. Adequate provision of contraceptive information and services, regardless of age, marital status, or number of children, is likely to reduce rates of out-of-wedlock pregnancy.

Our concern is specifically for the child who is born out of wedlock. This child is not only more likely to suffer from a health problem; he is born into a society that traditionally views him as socially, morally, and legally inferior. Under English common law, the child of an unwed mother was the child of no one and had no rights of inheritance. Unfortunately, this tradition has been preserved in many jurisdictions. In many states, children born out of wedlock do not have the same rights to child support or inheritance as children born to married women.[11] In some instances, when a man has a wife and children born in wedlock, there are legal limits on the amount that a father may will to a child born out of wedlock.

The purpose of this legal discrimination was to protect the sanctity of the family and to discourage extramarital sex. That

145

goal has not been fully realized. Furthermore, the assumption that eliminating distinctions between children born in and out of wedlock will somehow undermine the family has itself been undermined by the fact that there has been no apparent increase in the rates of out-of-wedlock births and/or irregular unions in those countries where discrimination against such persons has been abolished.[12] There is a trend within this country to reduce discrimination against these children. Every state now recognizes that a mother has a legal right to the custody of a child born out of wedlock, and some states grant equal custody rights to the father. In states permitting recovery for wrongful deaths, there is a trend toward considering children born out of wedlock the natural progeny of both father and mother for purposes of collecting damages. The 1965 amendments to the Social Security Act[13] made it possible for the child to collect social security and other federal benefits on an equal basis with children born in wedlock. Such cases include those where the father has contributed to the support of the child or has been decreed by a court to be the child's father. Other, more subtle forms of discrimination are also slowly being eliminated. Several states prohibit any statement on a birth certificate as to whether a child is born in or out of wedlock, or as to the marital status of the mother.

There is no justifiable reason to discriminate between children according to the circumstances of their birth. The word "illegitimate" and the stigma attached to it have no place in our society.*

The Commission recommends that all children, regardless of the circumstances of their birth, be accorded fair and equal status socially, morally, and legally.

The Commission urges research and study by the American Bar Association, the American Law Institute, and other interested groups leading to revision of those laws and practices which result in discrimination against out-of-wedlock children. Our end objective should be to accord fair and equal treatment to all children.

Adoption [14]

One consequence of unwanted childbearing, especially out-of-wedlock births, has been an increase in the number of

* A separate statement by Commissioner John N. Erlenborn appears on page 277.

children available for adoption. In 1969, there were 171,000 children adopted, roughly two-thirds of whom were born out of wedlock. However, in the same year, nearly half a million children lived in foster homes, group homes, or child welfare institutions.

It has been asserted that increased adoption might lower the birthrate. Had all the children in foster homes and institutions been adopted, the total number of adoptions in 1969 would have reached over half a million. If each of these children had represented a birth averted, the total reduction in the birthrate might conceivably have reached 18 percent. This would be a one-time effect, however, because the large number represents an accumulation of unadopted children over many years.

The potential annual reduction in the birthrate can be derived from the number of children born and made available for adoption each year. In 1968, there were 339,000 out-of-wedlock births recorded.[15] Had each of those children been adopted by a family which otherwise would have borne a child of its own, the birthrate would have dropped by 11 percent at most. However, this is an extreme upper limit, because many children are not adopted as substitutes for childbirth. Some are adopted for humanitarian reasons; others are adopted by infertile couples. Some out-of-wedlock children are retained by their families; and there are administrative complexities and racial attitudes which prevent other children from being adopted. Thus, the demographic impact of adoption on the birthrate in the United States is minimal.

The value of adoption, however, is not diminished by the lack of demographic significance. It is a practice that holds rewards for children, parents, and society. There appears to be a substantial number of prospective parents interested in adopting children, including couples unable to bear children of their own. Presumably others would become interested in adoption if it became more widely publicized that constraints on adoption were less stringent than frequently believed, and if public subsidies were available to assist adopting parents. For example, about a fifth of our states have recently enacted legislation to make it possible for a public agency to grant subsidies to adopting parents. In addition, there is probably an increasing number who would be willing to adopt rather than bear all of their children. More than half (56 percent) of the respondents to the Commission's public opinion poll indicated that they would consider adopting a child if they already had two children and wanted a larger family.[16] Thus, the symbolic value of adoption as a mode of responsible parenthood may come to outweigh its direct demographic impact.

At the present time, it is not possible to determine reliably the potential number of children available for adoption, or the total number of parents who would adopt children. In this country, adoption placement is shared by public and private agencies. Legislation governing adoption differs among states and within states. There is, therefore, considerable variation in adoption practice and procedure, as well as in the availability of services for prospective adoptive parents and children. Due to provisions, guarding the secrecy of legal proceedings and changes in the child's birth certificate, little information about adoption exists in the public domain. Nor is much known about who assumes the responsibility for rearing children born out of wedlock.

It is our impression that adoption might become a more widespread practice with: (1) changes in legislation; (2) changes in adoption services; and (3) improved education about adoption opportunities.

The Commission recommends changes in attitudes and practices to encourage adoption thereby benefiting children, prospective parents, and society.

To implement this goal, the Commission recommends:

Further subsidization of families qualified to adopt, but unable to assume the full financial cost of a child's care.

A review of current laws, practices, procedures, and regulations which govern the adoptive process.

Such a review could be carried out by the Council of State Governments, the American Law Institute, and the American Bar Association, and should include study of the inadequacy and comparability of laws, the rights of natural parents, the rights of children, the options for foster care and other custodial care as opposed to adoption, and eligibility requirements for adoptive parents, including such criteria as age, race, marital status, religion, socioeconomic status, and labor-force status of prospective mothers.

INSTITUTIONAL PRESSURES

Every human society has various ways of channeling reproductive behavior, both formally through the legal system and informally through social institutions and cultural norms. For most of human history, such influences have been strongly pronatalist as societies sought to ensure survival in the face of high mortality. Today, in the modern technological society, the balance has shifted. But childbearing is so interwoven with other aspects of social life, and affected by laws promulgated for other purposes, that it is not easy to say what would constitute genuine "neutrality" in this respect, or what would be truly "voluntary." Just how close to "neutral" is the present situation, in either the legal or the institutional sphere? Where are the major pressures one way or the other?

A consultant to the Commission concluded:

> . . . our society is already pervaded by time-honored pronatalist constraints. . . . We cannot preserve a choice that does not genuinely exist, and, by the same token, it makes no sense to institute anti-natalist coercions while continuing to support pronatalist ones.[17]

Institutionalized pronatalist pressures include: (1) the socialization of the young into sex-typed roles, with the boys pointed toward jobs and the girls toward home and motherhood; (2) discriminations against the working woman and, even more, the working mother; and (3) restrictions on higher education for women. Such pressures are so pervasive that they are typically perceived as "natural," and not simply cultural prescriptions. They are so powerful that even the current movement for women's liberation has hardly questioned motherhood as one of the goals for the modern woman.

There is no denying the strength of these pressures in today's society, or the psychic punishments employed in their enforcement. However, there are some contrary social trends as well —the limited economic value of children in an urbanized, industrialized society; the substantial liberation that has already occurred in the status of women; the rise of universal education; the increasing ethos of rationality and freedom of choice in reproduction; the decrease in pressure from traditional religious doctrine and, in some cases, direct religious support for more freedom of choice—in short, all of the still emerging social changes associated with the transition from traditional to modern society. Indeed, it is largely this counterbalancing that has resulted in the historical decline of birthrates in the developed countries, as compared with the high birthrates in developing countries where the pronatalist pressures are stronger still.

Similar tendencies, in both directions, are also present in the legal structure and public policy of the United States. Governmental actions that can effect childbearing decisions by individual couples include the laws regulating marital status (age at marriage, divorce, responsibility for child care, status of children born out of wedlock, even homosexuality); laws directly regulating fertility control (contraception and abortion); tax policy on income, property, and inheritance; housing regulations and subsidies, urban renewal programs, and welfare policies; food subsidies; health programs; aid to families with dependent children; fiscal support of formal schooling; allocation of expenditures to "male" or "female" sectors of the economy; even the draft laws. Although our knowledge of these influences is uncertain, three points should probably be made: (1) rarely are such laws adopted on demographic grounds; governmental influence is unintended, the by-product of policies adopted for other reasons; (2) the influence is mixed some pronatalist, some anti-natalist—and not easily balanced; and (3) accordingly, their influence is not likely to be great.

Thus, the informal, institutional pressures would appear to be much stronger than the formal, legal ones. They are probably also more difficult to change, at least over the short run. The objective for American society should be to make the childbearing decision as free of possible of unintended societal pressures: It should not be to "force" people to become parents in order to seem "normal," but to recognize that some people, and perhaps many, are not really suited to parenthood. We should strive for the ideal of diversity in which it would be equally honorable to marry or not, to be childless or not, to have one child or two or, for that matter, more. Our goal is one of less regimentation of reproductive behavior, not more.

Women: Alternatives to Childbearing

Historical Change

Societies have varied widely in their family arrangements and ideal roles for men and women, but the desire for progeny has characterized both agricultural and industrial societies.* Until modern times, high rates of reproduction were necessary

* A separate statement by Commissioner John N. Erlenborn appears on pages 278-280.

to offset high mortality—especially high among infants and children. In agricultural societies, children had an economic value. More hands were an asset in a home-centered economy. Also, before care of the aged became institutionalized, parents had to rely upon their children for care in their old age; and large numbers of children were advantageous. As a result of these factors and of shorter life expectancy, women spent most of their adult lives bearing and rearing the four or five children traditionally expected.

In an earlier time, when economic functions were centered in the home, both men and women shared child-rearing and economic roles. When the industrial revolution shifted economic activities into the marketplace, women were required by the necessities of child-rearing to remain behind in the home. Over the years, this division of labor between the sexes became well-established, and has perhaps reached a new high in parts of this country where the mother tends the children in the suburbs, while the father commutes long distances to work and has only a few hours each day to spend with the family.

Long before the tradition of the large family disappeared, some couples had begun to adopt the small family pattern as individually desirable. With declining mortality rates, diminishing economic value of children, increasing costs of raising a child in an industrialized urban society, and improved methods of fertility control, both the number of children desired and born declined. Today, women marry earlier, have smaller families earlier, and live longer than they did 50 years ago.

One result of reduced fertility and increased longevity has been that, although virtually all American women marry and bear children, they spend less and less of their lives in maternal functions. Most women have completed their childbearing by age 30; and typically, by their mid-30's, the last child is in school. By age 50, the chances are that all children have left home. And the average woman who reaches 50 today can look forward to 28 more years of life after her maternal activities have ceased. Women of all ages have contributed invaluable services to their communities through volunteer activities. At the same time, more and more women are beginning to work, to seek higher education, and to choose roles supplementary to or in place of motherhood. We have not yet fully accommodated these changes in our social, legal, and economic structures.

If we should achieve a stationary population, women will spend even less of their lives in bearing and rearing children

151

since family size, on the average, will be smaller. More women may forego motherhood altogether.

For all of these reasons, it would seem good social policy to recognize and to facilitate the trend toward smaller families by making it possible for women to choose attractive roles in place of or supplementary to motherhood.

Alternative Roles

Although we believe that increasing the freedom of women to seek alternative roles may reduce fertility, this change is not sought on demographic grounds alone. The limitations on the rights and roles of women abridge basic human liberties that should be guaranteed to all, regardless of the future course of population growth.

Here, as in the control of reproduction, our goal is to increase freedom of choice. Just as we oppose coercion in the control of fertility, we oppose any effort—explicitly or implicitly—to penalize childbearing and parenthood. We reject the notion that either motherhood or childlessness is or should be made to seem unfashionable. Instead, we seek a greater range of choice. Women should be able to choose motherhood, work, or other interests. Both men and women should be free to develop as individuals rather than being molded to fit some sexual stereotype.

Maximizing choice will require changes in the way men and women are educated, as well as in certain legal and economic practices. We have come to view certain roles, jobs, school courses, feelings, actions, and reactions as either male or female, and this effectively limits choice.

Building self-images begins within the family. Girls should learn to look upon the wife-mother role as but one among a number of desirable roles. They should be helped to develop a sense of responsibility and confidence; personal achievement and enterprise should become valued traits for them. At the same time, boys should learn to relate to girls as true equals.

Schools are among the most important institutional forces at work in defining male and female roles. Women's horizons are effectively limited in many instances by the courses girls are encouraged to take or not take, and by implications that it is less necessary for them to excel academically or to pursue higher degrees. Textbooks that always show women in stereotypical domestic roles are probably effective image shapers.

It would be desirable to end sex differentiation in school

152

courses, to train guidance counselors to view students as individuals, to channel educational and vocational interests without regard to sex, and to revise school books to show men and women in attractive roles both outside and inside the home.

There is, despite the number of working mothers, considerable ambivalance in our society as to whether women with children should be working outside the home. If the notion is to receive greater social acceptability, some redefinition of the family roles of men and women will be required. Under such conditions, both husband and wife would share more equally in both economic and domestic functions. Women who now work outside the home, often receive little assistance from their husbands in domestic functions. Greater participation of the husband in family matters would probably reduce home-job tensions for the wife. It would also provide fathers more opportunity to participate in the rearing of their children and give children the opportunity to know their fathers better. Many young couples are striving to develop this pattern of family life, but it is difficult to achieve within the present American context. A reworking of family roles would necessarily involve changes in institutional practices— different sets of working hours and provision for some sort of paternity leave, for instance. Certainly, more study of the effects of changing family structures and roles is necessary.

Although it is no longer necessary for all men and all women to marry and have children, virtually all American men and women do. We realize that not everyone is suited for marriage and child-bearing, but those who choose to remain single and childless are viewed with some suspicion in our society. It would be particularly helpful if marriage, child-bearing, and childrearing could come to be viewed as more deliberate and serious commitments rather than as traditional, almost compulsory behavior.

Employment

More and more women are entering the labor market; today 43 percent of all women are in the work force.[18] Some analysts conclude that employment for women has a depressing effect on fertility. Census Bureau data and various studies show that, in the United States, employed women have borne fewer children than economically inactive women.[19] It is difficult, however, to determine the direction of cause and effect in this relationship. Some women may limit family size because they are working, but women with children frequently do not work because they must care for the children.

Given the kinds of jobs usually open to women and the employment patterns of women, claims that employment has reduced fertility should be made with caution. Most women are in low-paying, low status jobs that are unlikely to compete effectively with childbearing. Further, until very recently, most women worked only until they had children, and returned to work after the children left home. This pattern, of course, contributed to the limitations on pay and promotion because women were not in the labor force long enough to secure seniority and higher pay.

There is no question that women have experienced and continue to suffer discrimination in employment. Often, they are paid less than men for the same work, and are barred from certain job positions by protective laws. Generally, they have less chance for advancement even when they remain in the work force for extended periods of time. Minority women have suffered the greatest deprivation in the labor market. Black women are consistently among the lowest paid of all workers and the most likely to live in poverty.[20]

Recent federal and state laws to combat sex discrimination have had some beneficial effect. However, further action is necessary. Women should have equal access to all areas of the labor market, for several reasons. First, despite the generally held opinion that women work only until marriage or for "pin money," there are 12 million women in the labor force who have children under 18.[21] A 1965 Department of Labor report states that about two-thirds of all working women gave economic considerations as their reason for employment.[22] In 1971, 44 percent of working women were the sole support of a family.[23] Many others worked to supplement the low incomes of their husbands. These women must have an equal opportunity to support themselves and others.

Second, we believe that attractive work may effectively compete with childbearing and have the effect of lowering fertility, especially higher-order births. Virtually all American couples want at least one child, but there is some evidence that rewarding employment may compete successfully with childbearing beyond the first child.

Third, even if the number of children desired does not change very much in the future, more women are likely to be entering the labor market. Many will be single and will support themselves and others. Others will work to augment family income. Whatever the reason for working, equity de-

154

mands that all participants in the labor force have equal opportunity to advance as far as their skills and desires permit.

Education

Education is an important key to achievement in employment in this country. Part of the reason women are underrepresented in such fields as law, medicine, and engineering is that they do not have equal access to the higher educational experience required by those fields.

There is abundant evidence that higher educational attainment is associated with smaller families in the United States. The American college graduate tends to marry later and procreate later, and to have fewer children per family or to form more childless families.

While sex differences among whites in the attainment of a high-school education have been minimal over the past 50 years, men have had and continue to have a better chance of achieving a college education. In 1970, 59 percent of college students were men. A woman's chances of going on to advanced degrees are much smaller than a man's. In 1970, 60 percent of all master's degrees and 87 percent of all doctorates were awarded to men. This inequity appears to stem both from institutional discrimination and from traditional expectations that women will spend their lives in the home and therefore have less need for higher education.[24]

In 1970, some eight million Americans were enrolled in vocational education programs.[25] Women in these programs have been enrolled in the traditionally female occupations of health, business and office work, and home economics. In many schools, women are not permitted to take courses traditionally viewed as male oriented—electrical or electronics technology, drafting, data processing, and power machine operation—which usually pay more.

The Commission believes that, as attitudes toward and individual control of family size continue to change and more women seek employment outside of the home, more women will also seek technical training, college, and graduate educations. So that opportunities will be available on an equal basis, institutional discrimination against women in education should be abolished. Enactment of several of the recommendations contained in the Report of the President's Task Force on Women's Rights and Responsibilities would go far toward resolving institutional discrimination.[26] Because sex is not included in federal legislation which prohibits discrimination

155

in federally assisted programs, women have sought a variety of means to gain entrance to the student bodies and teaching staffs of universities. These methods have been only partially successful in achieving integration of the sexes. Since virtually all schools receive some federal aid, extending federal law to include sex discrimination, while exempting presently existing one-sex schools, would go far toward increasing opportunities in a more orderly fashion.

Equal Rights

As we have learned in the struggle for equal rights for minorities, an end to legal descrimination does not guarantee equality.* However, equality cannot begin to exist until all legal barriers have been abolished. Women in the United States occupy a separate and unequal status under the law. Under common law, women were afforded few rights, and our Constitution was drafted on the assumption that women did not exist as legal persons. The legal status of women has improved in the past century with the adoption of the Nineteenth Amendment, alteration of some common law rules, and passage of some positive legislation. But equal rights and responsibilities are still denied women in our legal system. We believe this should be remedied. The right to be free from discrimination based on race, color, or creed is written into our fundamental document of government. We believe the right to be free from discrimination based on sex should also be written into that document.

The Commission therefore recommends that the Congress and the states approve the proposed Equal Rights Amendment and that federal, state, and local governments undertake positive programs to ensure freedom from discrimination based on sex.

Tax Policy and Public Expenditures

The costs to parents of bearing and raising children were discussed in an earlier chapter. Those costs, however, represent only a portion of the true costs of children. A research paper prepared for the Commission reached the tentative con-

* A separate statement by Commissioner Howard D. Samuel appears on page 311.

156

clusion that public funds—through tax benefits or expenditure programs—subsidize an additional large portion of the costs of shelter, health, education, and welfare, thereby benefiting couples with children more than those without children. All citizens, regardless of whether or not they have children, pay for the public costs of children.[27]

None of the tax policies or expenditure programs which benefit children was instituted with the expressed intention of encouraging childbearing. They all resulted from other perceived needs within our society. Despite the fact that none of these programs was intended to be pronatalist, many believe this has been the result. They maintain that social welfare programs which benefit children have the effect of encouraging population growth.

An examination of the effects of these laws in that respect is worthwhile. Some programs may be said to encourage growth because they are supportive of physical well-being. For instance, food and health programs have improved the chances of successful outcome of pregnancy and have helped to reduce infant mortality.

Other programs have both benefited some families with children while burdening others—housing programs are an excellent example. Middle- and upper-class families, with and without children, are more likely to purchase homes and, therefore, have benefited from tax deductions on interest paid on home mortgages. They have also benefited from such programs as Federal Housing Authority and Veterans Administration loan guarantees, Federal National Mortgage Association and Government National Mortgage Association mortgage purchase authority, and Farmers Home Administration subsidized housing. On the other hand, some housing programs have had the effect of burdening families with two or more children, especially among the poor. The public housing program, often described as pronatalist, has in fact rarely benefited the larger family. Until adoption of the 1968 Housing Act, the emphasis in public housing was on smaller units. In that year, one-third of all families moving into projects were elderly. One-third had one or two children, one-fifth had three or four, and only one-tenth had over four. At the same time, through urban renewal and clearance for public housing and federal highway programs, the federal government destroyed more low-income housing units than it constructed in the 1960's. It can be said that the overall effect of federal housing programs has been to benefit middle- and upper-class families with children, but to make it more difficult for low-income families with children to find suitable housing.

157

Some programs have obviously benefited families with children, but there is no proof they have encouraged the birth of additional children. For instance, tax exemptions for children benefit parents; but the amount of the deduction is so small in contrast to the cost of child-rearing, that it is difficult to imagine that anyone would have additional children in order to secure additional exemptions.

Public assistance programs, especially aid to families with dependent children, are frequently cited as encouraging reproduction among the poor. This cannot be demonstrated except insofar as assistance payments make it possible for these families to be better fed and cared for, thereby strengthening their reproductive capacities. For years, the argument has been that, because assistance payments are based upon the number of children in the family, welfare mothers have more children in order to increase their monthly payment. Welfare payments and standards vary widely. In November 1971, the average payment per family in New Jersey was $250; in Mississippi, it was $55. Neither is large enough to support a family of any size well. In addition, most state standards of need are set in such a manner that progressively less is paid for each child; and 20 states have set maximum payments for each family regardless of the number of children.[28]

Many people believe that welfare families are much larger than families in general. They are, in fact, half a child larger on the average. Between the years 1967 and 1969, when welfare payments were increasing, the average family size of welfare recipients was declining.[29] In New York City where, according to the pronatalist view, steadily increasing payments and program utilization in the years 1959 to 1970 should have encouraged more births, the percentage of welfare mothers bearing children each year dropped from 18.9 percent in 1959, to 11.3 percent in 1970.[30]

This brief review of programs that benefit and/or burden reproduction indicates how scant our knowledge is of the demographic effects of tax and expenditure programs. We feel it would be valuable to undertake studies to provide more information in this area, and to determine at what point reproductive behavior is measurably affected by these programs.

While we are unable to find evidence that present tax policies and public expenditures promote the birth of additional children, it is conceivable that the reverse might be true. As concern about overpopulation has grown, some individuals and groups have proposed consideration of tax policies or other programs that would penalize childbearing.[31] Three types of policies have been proposed. The first would require parents

158

to assume all or a greater portion of the costs of their children. For instance, public education and health and welfare programs would either be abolished or substantially reduced, and tax deductions for children eliminated or cut back. The second type of policy would penalize or levy a fee for childbearing. The third type of policy would provide direct financial rewards for not having children, or in some cases, a bonus for undergoing sterilization. Since it is generally assumed that it is not childbearing per se but excessive childbearing that is to be avoided, all of these proposals have variants in which penalties or rewards would go into effect for any child after a certain number. For example, public education would be available for the first two children but not the third child; a fee would be levied for the third child or a reward paid for each year in which a third child was not born.

Many problems arise in regard to these proposals. First, disincentive programs that penalize childbearing, withdraw public subsidies of children, or limit public benefits to a certain number of children in each family, have the effect of penalizing the child and his siblings. For instance, if public education were limited to two children and a third child were born, the family would have the option of not educating the third child or of depriving the children of some benefits in order to support the cost of private education for that third child. The penalty, of course, falls most heavily upon the poor. To penalize children in order to motivate their parents is not justifiable.

Second, the type of program that offers direct financial rewards for limiting childbearing would almost certainly offer greater inducement to the poor. A flat rate of perhaps $300 for not bearing children is more likely to affect the behavior of the poor than of the middle class, since the $300 has a relatively higher value to the poor. A graduated bonus, increased according to income, might still be more likely to affect the behavior of the poor, depending upon the increase, since the subjective need for money is not the same at all levels. The need for a bonus of $300 to pay for next month's food and shelter is unlike the need for $3,000 to purchase a new car. If, as some have proposed, a bonus is to be offered for sterilization, the question of financial inducement becomes even more difficult so long as the procedure is substantially irreversible. Childbearing is very highly valued in our society, and sterilization should never be undertaken without serious prior thought and knowledge of the ramifications. Since a poor person would be especially vulnerable to financial inducements, important ethical and moral questions arise. Bonus payments would serve to discourage childbearing only among the relatively few who are poorest. Therefore, it would not affect our overall growth substantially, and would weigh unevenly upon decisions about childbearing in a manner we find unacceptable.

Third, not only would these policies have more effect on the poor, but actual proposals to carry them out have, almost without exception, been directed specifically toward one group —welfare recipients. Bills to penalize childbearing by welfare mothers have been introduced in a number of states. Coercive proposals in regard to welfare recipients have included mandatory sterilization after a specific number of out-of-wedlock births. Most of the proposals have been framed in terms of "voluntary action": The woman may choose to practice birth control or lose custody of her children; the woman may choose to be sterilized or go to jail; the woman may choose to be sterilized or lose her welfare benefits. In 1971, the last proposal was approved by a committee of the Tennessee state legislature. In Connecticut last year, the state legislature considered a proposal to pay a bonus of $300 to every welfare mother who chose to be sterilized. This Commission has made clear the value it places upon voluntary fertility control, including sterilization. We wish to make equally clear our opposition to any program that singles out any group and attempts to control their reproduction as the price for receiving aid for their children, for maintaining custody of their children, or for retaining their own freedom.

Clearly, no proposal to penalize childbearing or reward nonchildbearing can be acceptable in a situation in which fertility control is not completely reliable and large numbers of unwanted births occur.

Finally, past attempts to accomplish specific nonrevenue goals through taxation have often been unsuccessful or have led to unexpected side effects that overshadowed the original goal. Some have suggested that one conceivable way to end the argument over the anti- or pronatalist effects of tax policies would be to undertake a fundamental revision of the tax system to eliminate all deductions, exemptions, and loopholes. This would remove any possible special inducements to childbearing. It would also broaden the tax base and reduce the rate of the tax levy.

Quite apart from the issue of using fiscal policy to affect childbearing is the question of whether it is equitable to require taxpayers who do not have children to pay for the programs that make it less expensive for others to have and rear their children. Present tax policies and expenditure programs have the effect of distributing the costs of children throughout the society and of redistributing income in a manner that benefits parents over nonparents. If parents were required to bear the costs of their children, governmental expenditures and taxes would be lower. Or alternatively, nonparents could be taxed at lower rates if the tax structure were arranged so that the costs of programs benefiting children fell only upon parents.

If parents and children are viewed as a single unit and anything which benefits the child is viewed as a benefit to the parent, then some inequity is unquestionably involved. However, if the child is viewed separately from his or her parents and raising the next generation is viewed as the responsibility of society as a whole, the question of equity in supporting children ceases to exist. All children require some minimum amounts of food, shelter, protection, and education; and the general good of society is served by insuring that they receive it. Nonparents certainly have an interest in seeing that all children are inoculated and that epidemics are avoided. Nonparents certainly benefit from the scientific and cultural advances that result from the education of young people. The only reason to alter present policies which are supportive of children would be if an even higher goal were to be served. We cannot foresee any goal with a higher priority than insuring the welfare of future generations. We believe the public support of children, at least at the present level, is justifiable. In fact, some of the Commission's proposals would have the effect of increasing that support for reasons which we also believe are justifiable.

CHAPTER 11. HUMAN REPRODUCTION

Contemporary American couples are planning to have an average of be ween two and three children. Given the fact of youthful marriage, far-from-perfect means of fertility control, and varying motivation, many of these couples will have children before they want them and a significant fraction will ultimately exceed the number they want.

Recent research[1] has disclosed a substantial incidence of such unplanned pregnancies and unwanted births in the United States. According to estimates developed in the 1970 National Fertility Study conducted by the Office of Population Research at Princeton University, 44 percent of all births to currently married women during the five years between 1966 and 1970 were unplanned; 15 percent were reported by the parents as having never been wanted. (See table on page 164.) Only one percent of first births were never wanted, but nearly two-thirds of all sixth or higher order births were so reported. In theory, this incidence of unwanted births implies that 2.65 million births occurring in that five-year period would never have occurred had the complete availability of perfect fertility control permi ted couples to realize their preferences. And these estimates are all conservative.

Unwanted fertility is highest among those whose levels of education and income are lowest. For example, in 1970, women with no high-school education reported that 31 percent of their births in the preceding five years were unwanted at the time they were conceived; the figure for women college graduates was seven percent. Mainly because of differences in education and income—and a general exclusion from the

Unwanted Fertility in the United States, 1970[a]

Race and Education	Most Likely Number of Births per Woman	Percent of Births 1966-70 Unwanted	Percent of Births 1966-70 Unplanned[b]	Theoretical Births per Woman without Unwanted Births
All Women	3.0	15	44	2.7
College 4+	2.5	7	32	2.4
College 1-3	2.8	11	39	2.6
High School 4	2.8	14	44	2.6
High School 1-3	3.4	20	48	2.9
Less	3.9	31	56	3.0
White Women	2.9	13	42	2.6
College 4+	2.5	7	32	2.4
College 1-3	2.8	10	39	2.6
High School 4	2.8	13	42	2.6
High School 1-3	3.2	18	44	2.8
Less	3.5	25	53	2.9
Black Women	3.7	27	61	2.9
College 4+	2.3	3	21	2.2
College 1-3	2.6	21	46	2.3
High School 4	3.3	19	62	2.8
High School 1-3	4.2	31	66	3.2
Less	5.2	55	68	3.1

[a] Based on data from the 1970 National Fertility Study for currently married women under 45 years of age.

[b] Unplanned births include unwanted births.

socioeconomic mainstream—unwanted fertility weighs most heavily on certain minority groups in our population. We have relevant data for blacks only, but this is probably true for Mexican-Americans, Puerto Ricans, Indians, and others as well.

For example, if blacks could have the number of children they want and no more, their fertility and that of the majority white population would be very similar. These figures about our black population illustrate the inequality of access of our minority populations to the various means of fertility control, as well as to the education and income which is so closely connected with that access.

Not all unwanted births become unwanted children. Many, perhaps most, are eventually accepted and loved indistinguishably from earlier births that were deliberately planned. But many are not; and the costs to them, to their siblings and parents, and to society at large are considerable, though not easy to measure.

And the costs are not only financial. The social, health, and psychological costs must be enormous. Despite the incidence of unwanted fertility—an incidence which in terms of ordinary public health criteria would qualify as of epidemic proportion—there is little hard evidence on which to assess its impact. There was one study in Sweden[2] in which a sample of children born to women whose applications for abortion were denied, was compared over a 20-year period with a control group of other children born at the same time in the same hospital. They turned out to have been registered more often with psychiatric services, engaged in more antisocial and criminal behavior, and have been more dependent on public assistance.

The psychological burdens carried by children who are literally rejected by their parents and given over to institutional care cannot be measured easily. But they must be considerable, and we do know that the costs to society of providing for the care of abandoned infants are significant.

Most of the costs of unwanted fertility are not visible in the dramatic instances of abandonment or child abuse, but rather in the more prosaic problems of everyday family life. Family budgets can be seriously strained by the unexpected and unwanted birth of a child. And those who can least afford such additional burdens most often experience them. The incidence of unwanted births is twice as great among couples whose annual incomes fall below $4,000 as it is among those with incomes of $10,000 and higher. Since most unwanted births experienced by married couples occur late in the childbearing years, the woman who had been waiting for her youngest child to be in school before returning to work can find her plans abruptly frustrated.

There are also health costs involved. As President Nixon observed:

. . . involuntary childbearing often results in poor physical and emotional health for all members of the family. It is one of the factors which contributes to our distressingly high infant mortality, the unacceptable level of malnutrition . . .[3]

These health problems result, in part, from the fact that most unwanted births occur to women in the later years of childbearing. And these are the ages at which there are considerably greater risks to maternity. For example, although maternal mortality has declined by 94 percent over the past 30 years to a rate of 24 maternal deaths per 100,000 live births, the risks increase sharply at the older ages. Compared

165

with the rate at age 20 to 24 when the risk is lowest, the rate is four times greater at ages 35 to 39, almost eight times greater at ages 40 to 44, and nearly 20 times greater at older ages.[4]

The risk to the infant's life is also associated with the mother's age; the infant mortality rate runs almost one-third higher among women 35 years of age and over, than among women aged 20 to 24.[5]

Because of the strong association between maternal age and the appearance of certain hereditary diseases, the prevention of births to women over 35 would reduce the incidence of such diseases. For example, the incidence of Down's syndrome, which accounts for 95 percent of mongolism, would be reduced significantly by the avoidance of childbearing in the older ages.

How far down the road toward population stabilization would the prevention of unwanted births take us? Since fertility has been changing so rapidly in recent years, such an estimate is difficult to make. The record of women who are approaching the end of their childbearing, those 35 to 44 years old in 1970, indicates that 27 percent had at least one unwanted birth, a total of one in every six births. The prevention of the unwanted births in this group would have carried them about three-fifths of the way to the replacement level. But women in those age groups were the main participants in the post-war baby boom and have had the highest fertility of any women in modern time. And there has been a signifiant change downward in the family-size expectations of young couples.

We conclude that there are many "costs" associated with unwanted fertility, not only financial, but health, social, psychological, and demographic costs as well.

The Commission believes that all Americans, regardless of age, marital status, or income, should be enabled to avoid unwanted births. Major efforts should be made to enlarge and improve the opportunity for individuals to control their own fertility, aiming toward the development of a basic ethical principle that only wanted children are brought into the world.

In order to implement this policy, the Commission has formulated the following recommendations that are developed in detail in the remainder of this chapter:

The elimination of legal restrictions on access to contraceptive information and services, and the development by the states of affirmative legislation to permit minors to receive such information and services.

The elimination of administrative restrictions on access to voluntary contraceptive sterilization.

The liberalization of state abortion laws along the lines of the New York State statute.

Greater investments in research and development of improved methods of contraception.

Full support of all health services related to fertility, programs to improve training for and delivery of these services, an extension of government family planning project grant programs, and the development of a program of family planning education.

CONTRACEPTION AND THE LAW[6]

After almost a century of innumerable efforts on the part of many individuals and agencies, Congress finally, on January 8, 1971, repealed the 1873 Comstock Act—a broad gauge obscenity law which had prohibited in its omnibus sweep the importation, transportation in interstate commerce, and mailing of "any article whatever for the prevention of conception." Thus, the anti-contraception law of the federal government is now substantially limited to unsolicited contraceptives and unsolicited contraceptive advertising.

The states, too, have considerably modified their "little Comstock laws," so that today contraception is legal for adults in all states (with the possible exception of Massachusetts and Wisconsin, which specify that the adults must be married). However, more than half the states retain, in effect, statutes which prohibit or restrict the sale, distribution, advertising, and display of contraceptives.

Approximately 22 states prohibit the sale of all or some contraceptives; but all states, either by statute or common law, allow exceptions for doctors, pharmacists, or other licensed firms or individuals. Roughly 23 states prohibit commercial advertising of contraceptives, but most of these states make exceptions for medical and pharmaceutical journals.

The same 23 states also condemn the display of contraceptives and of information about them, but, with a few possible exceptions, explicitly permit such display under certain circumstances. At least 27 states, either expressly or inferentially, prohibit the sale of contraceptives through vending machines.

Literal interpretations of these anti-birth control laws are often unreliable; their enforcement is uneven, and in some instances, there are conflicting interpretations. In several states, court decisions have modified or even nullified the letter of the statute.

Some attacks on the statutes have been successful, but court decisions are much less visible than statutes. Clearly, the statutes themselves should be clarified or, better still, repealed.

One way or another, these laws inhibit family planning programs, and/or impinge on the ready availability of methods of contraception to the public. By prohibiting commercial sales, advertising displays, and the use of vending machines for nonprescription contraceptives, they sacrifice accessibility, education, and individual rights in the interest of some undefined purpose. Whatever the original justification for these laws, their result is to prevent contraceptive information and supplies from being easily obtainable in general and, in some instances, make them unobtainable.

Merely removing such laws will not automatically ensure freedom of access and choice. More is needed in the way of affirmative programs to distribute such information and supplies to all who may wish to use them. Nonetheless, it is desirable and important that laws not operate as impediments.

The Commission thus recommends that: (1) states eliminate existing legal inhibitions and restrictions on access to contraceptive information, procedures, and supplies; and (2) states develop statutes affirming the desirability that all persons have ready and practicable access to contraceptive information, procedures, and supplies.

Legal Impediments for Minors

It seems clear that the law also plays a role in the inadequate access of teenagers to contraceptive information and services.* The laws here are not so much the laws on contraception, but the inchoate and never universally applicable common law rule which has been considered to bar medical treatment and examination of minors without parental consent. Although it has been assumed that this was the rule at

* Separate statements by Commissioners Paul B. Cornely, M.D. (pp. 263-264), Alan Cranston (p. 269), and John N. Erlenborn (pp. 280-281) appear on the indicated pages.

common law, the fact is that there were always many exceptions recognized by the same common law, some of which seem to sanction contraceptive services to teenagers—for example, in emergencies or when the minor was married or otherwise "emancipated." Recently, the courts, including the United States Supreme Court, have held that minors are not second class citizens and that they are entitled to constitutional rights of many kinds. Arguably, one of these rights is the right to decide whether or not to have a child.

In addition, some state courts have declared the existence of a further exception to the common law rule which has since become known as the "mature minor rule." In essence, it provides that a minor may consent to medical treatment for himself if he understands the nature of the treatment and it is for his benefit.

Notwithstanding the fact that there appears to be no case on record of a successful suit against a doctor or a health agency for rendering any kind of medical service to a minor over 15 without parental consent, the uncertainty and ambiguity in the general law governing medical services to minors has inevitably restricted access to contraceptive services. Many physicians are reluctant to prescribe contraceptives even for sexually active minors who have been, or who clearly will be, exposed to the risks of pregnancy. Despite the absence of prosecutions and civil suits, physicians continue to fear that action will be taken against them.

Faced with this reluctance on the part of the medical and related professions, an ever-increasing number of states have enacted new laws to permit minors to consent to medical services in general, or in such areas as birth control, venereal disease, and drugs. Nevertheless, it is clear that many of the new statutes do not cover thousands of single minors—those who are not yet parents, who want to postpone becoming such, who are living with their families, who prefer to stay in school, or who are not managing their own financial affairs. Even some of those state laws which authorize family planning programs impose, specifically or in practice, such ineligibility requirements as parenthood or marriage, 18 years of age and married, or marriage or parental consent.

Medical and agency practices tend to be restrictive and discriminatory against minors in the absence of a clear mandate for full availability from the legislature. A number of major United States medical organizations have made recommendations approaching the recent statement of the Executive Board of the American College of Obstetricians and Gynecologists which declared:

169

The never married, never pregnant, sexually-involved female has not yet been reached with effective contraception. The laws of some states indirectly prohibit this service to minors and thereby prevent the gynecologists from serving them or place the physician in legal jeopardy if he does so.[7]

The Board went on to state that "the unmarried female of any age should have access to the most effective methods of contraception," and urged that legal barriers which restrict the physician's freedom should be removed "even in the case of the unemancipated minor who refuses to involve her parents."

Because of the serious social and health consequences involved in teenage pregnancy and the high rates of teenage out-of-wedlock pregnancy and venereal disease, the Commission urges the elimination of legal restrictions on access to contraceptive and prophylactic information and services by young people.

We recommend that states adopt affirmative legislation which will permit minors to receive contraceptive and prophylactic information and services in appropriate settings sensitive to their needs and concerns.

To implement this policy, the Commission urges that organizations, such as the Council on State Governments, the American Law Institute, and the American Bar Association, formulate appropriate model statutes.

VOLUNTARY STERILIZATION[8]

Given the difficulties experienced by many women with the pill and the intrauterine device, and the high failure rates of many other methods of contraception currently used, an increasing proportion of persons are turning to surgical sterilization. According to the 1970 National Fertility Study, sterilization has become a very popular method of preventing conception. Almost three million wives under the age of 45, or their husbands, had elected sterilization for contraceptive reasons. This amounts to nearly one in every five couples able to bear children who do not intend to have any more.

About half of such operations are elected by women and half by men. Between 1966 and 1970, the typical case was a woman of 32 or a man of 35 with an average of nearly four children.

The average fecund woman, after the birth of her last wanted child, has some 10 or 15 years of exposure to the risk of an unwanted conception before the onset of menopause, and current patterns of contraceptive use offer little confidence. Elective sterilization—tubal ligation for females and vasectomy for males—offers many couples secure protection against involuntary pregnancy. The former requires a 15-minute operation in which the fallopian tubes are tied off and several days hospitalization; the vasectomy, typically performed in a doctor's office in a few minutes, involves cutting and tying the *vas deferens* tubes which carry the sperm, a procedure which, contrary to some misunderstanding, has no significance for sexual behavior. A new procedure for women —laproscopic/culdoscopic sterilization—has also been developed. This procedure requires no hospitalization. And research on reversibility of male and female sterilization is under way. New developments in the male procedure offer the possibility of substantially increasing the probability of reversal; and the existence of sperm banks greatly modifies the major concern about possible changes of mind in the future.

The legal situation with respect to voluntary sterilization is quite different than with contraception or abortion. There is no general federal law governing voluntary sterilization, and the few existing state laws, by and large, present no insuperable problems. Rather, the lack of any specific law in many states often leaves physicians in a climate of uncertainty where many fear civil or criminal liability for performing voluntary sterilizations, even though, under well-settled principles of law, what is not prohibited is permitted.

Apart from the vagueness of the statutory situation, many hospitals impose various requirements for voluntary sterilization which greatly cut down on its availability. Such requirements include limiting the procedure to persons of specified age and number of children, or permitting only therapeutic as opposed to contraceptive sterilizations.

In order to permit freedom of choice, the Commission recommends that all administrative restrictions on access to voluntary contraceptive sterilization be eliminated so that the decision be made solely by physician and patient.

171

To implement this policy, we recommend that national hospital and medical associations, and their state chapters, promote the removal of existing restrictions.

ABORTION

The Law[9]

Prior to the second quarter of the 19th century, the law applicable to abortion in the American colonies, and subsequently in the expanding United States, was the Common Law of England. Under that law, women were free to have abortions at least until "quickening"—the first perception of fetal movement by the pregnant woman, which usually occurs between the 16th and 20th week.

In the second quarter of the 19th century, restrictive laws were enacted in 12 states. The only known contemporary authoritative texts explaining the reason for the enactment of these prohibitions of abortion before "quickening" relate to New York and New Jersey. Both point to the life and health of the pregnant woman as the objective. Before the introduction of ether anesthesia (1846) and antisepsis (1867), any surgery was likely to cause death from shock or infection. Actually, at the time New York State adopted such restrictive laws in 1829, serious consideration was given to banning all surgical operations except when necessary for the preservation of life. Thus, in the drafting of such legislation, the concern of the law-makers was medical rather than moral. It was in the latter half of the century that the sensationalism of Anthony Comstock inspired a moral fervor which resulted in moral considerations becoming the dominant element in highly stringent laws against abortion.

Currently, in over two-thirds of the states, abortion is a crime except to preserve the life of the mother; 12 states have changed their abortion statutes consistent with the American Law Institute Model Penal Code provision on abortion which prohibits abortion except in cases where the mother's life or her mental or physical health is in danger, or to prevent the birth of defective offspring, or in cases of rape or incest. In 1970, abortion laws in Alaska, Hawaii, and New York were liberalized by law and in the state of Washington by popular referendum. Currently, abortion is being reviewed in the courts in over half of the states.

At its 1972 meeting, the House of Delegates of the American Bar Association approved a Uniform Abortion Act recommended by the Commissioners on Uniform State Laws stating that abortion may be performed by a duly licensed physician upon request.

The Moral Question [10]

The Commission recognizes that abortion is a complex issue requiring a thoughtful balancing of moral, personal, and social values. As the Commission moves toward a population policy for the United States, our principal objective is the enrichment of life, not its restriction. We share with our fellow citizens an abiding concern for the sanctity of all human life. Thus, we appreciate the moral decisions involved in abortion, as well as the possible insensitivity to all human life implied in the practice of abortion. It is from this perspective that we have approached three moral issues concerning abortion which we believe to be of foremost importance.

The first issue relates to the fetus, both as to the termination of potential life and determining when that life actually begins. The second relates to bringing into the world an unwanted child, particularly when the child's prospects for a life of dignity and self-fulfillment are limited. Third, there is the question of the woman who in desperation seeks an abortion. Our society faces a difficult decision when the woman believes her well-being is threatened and she sees no other way out but an illegal abortion with all its attendant dangers.

The Commission believes that a wise and sound decision in regard to the abortion question requires a careful balancing of the moral problems relating to the woman and the child along with those concerning the fetus.

In the development of western culture, the tendency has been toward a greater protection of life. At the same time, there is a deep commitment in our moral tradition to individual freedom and social justice. The Commission believes that the various prohibitions against abortion throughout the United States stand as obstacles to the exercise of individual freedom: the freedom of women to make difficult moral choices based on their personal values, the freedom of women to control their own fertility, and finally, freedom from the burdens of unwanted childbearing. Restrictive statutes also violate social justice, for when abortion is prohibited, women

173

resort to illegal abortions to prevent unwanted births. Medically safe abortions have always been available to the wealthy, to those who could afford the high costs of physicians and trips abroad; but the poor woman has been forced to risk her life and health with folk remedies and disreputable practitioners.

Public Health[11]

Abortion is not new; it has been an alternative to an unwanted birth for large numbers of American women (estimates ranged from 200,000 to 1,200,000 illegal abortions per year in the United States). The Commission regards the issue of illegal abortion with great concern and supports measures to bring this medical procedure from the backrooms to the hospitals and clinics of this country. It is becoming increasingly clear that, where abortion is available on request, one result is a reduction in the number of illegal abortions. Deaths as a consequence of illegal abortion have dropped sharply in New York since the enactment of a liberal abortion statute. The number of women admitted to New York City hospitals with incomplete abortions has also declined. The experience in California is comparable; the number of maternal deaths has decreased as the number of therapeutic abortions has increased. Comparative data from Czechoslovakia, Hungary, and Poland also indicate that, after liberalization of abortion laws in the 1950's, hospital admissions for "other" abortions declined.

A reduction in the number of illegal abortions has an important impact on maternal mortality. Maternal mortality ratios (including the 12 deaths out of 278,122 abortions performed under legal auspices) in New York City dropped by two-thirds the year after abortion became available on request. For 1971, New York City experienced the lowest ratio of maternal deaths ever recorded. Judging from the experience in other countries, there is reason to suspect that the maternal death ratio will continue to decline. The most important variables in mortality from abortion are the length of gestation and the technique involved. The greatest number of complications occur after the 14th week of gestation. In New York, abortions performed before 12 weeks have a complication rate of 4.6 per 1,000 abortions; for those after 12 weeks, the rate is 26.8 per 1,000. The safety record will undoubtedly improve as physicians and institutions gain more experience with the procedure, and as the proportion of first trimester abortions increases. The choice of the technique for performing an abortion is largely determined by the period of gestation. As the number of early abortions increase so will the use of the safest known technique—suction curettage.

In his testimony before the Commission, Gordon Chase, New York City Health Services Administrator, reviewed the impact of abortion on request on infant mortality:

> For example, infant mortality, which has been dropping in the City, has apparently been further reduced by abortion "on demand." This is because the procedure is now broadly available to those women who are at greatest risk of giving birth to infants who may die: namely, very young women, unwed mothers, who generally get poorer pre-natal care, and women who have had many previous births and pregnancies, as well as women with medical handicaps. For 1969, infant mortality was 24.4 per 1,000 live births; it was down to 21.6 for 1970; and down still further to 20.7 in 1971, the first year in which the law would have had an impact. Neo-natal mortality—deaths occurring in the first 28 days of life—shows a more striking decline: from 18.1 to 16.2 to 14.9 in the past three years.[12]

What is the effect of abortion on out-of-wedlock births? The best information comes from New York, where out-of-wedlock births have been on the rise since they were first recorded in 1954. Statistics for the first eight months of 1971 indicate that, for the first time, the rate is declining. Moreover, the New York City programs for unmarried pregnant girls have reported a sharp decline in the number of applicants this year.

In summary, we are impressed that the availability of abortion on request causes a reduction in the number of illegal abortions, maternal and infant deaths, and out-of-wedlock births, thereby greatly improving the health of women and children.

Family Planning

The Commission affirms that contraception is the method of choice for preventing an unwanted birth. We believe that abortion should not be considered a substitute for birth control, but rather as one element in a comprehensive system of maternal and infant health care. For many, the very need for abortion is evidence of a social and personal failure in the

175

provision and use of birth control. In the year beginning July 1, 1970, an estimated 505,000 legal abortions and an unknown number of illegal abortions were performed in the United States.[13] Far too many Americans must resort to abortion to prevent an unwanted birth. It is our belief that the responsible use of birth control can be achieved only when sex counseling and contraceptive information and services are easily accessible to all citizens.

The Commission expects that, with the increasing availability of contraceptives and improvements in contraceptive technology, the need for abortion will diminish. It is encouraging to learn that there has been a marked increase in recent attendance in family planning programs in New York City.

The Demographic Context

In reviewing the abortion issue, one central concern has been an evaluation of the demographic impact of abortion. We appreciate the historic importance of placing recommendations on abortion in a demographic context.

At the present time, it is difficult to make precise quantitative statements concerning the demographic impact of abortion. We are unable to estimate the effect on the birthrate of an unknown number of illegal abortions. There is little doubt, however, that legal and illegal abortions exert a downward influence on the United States birthrate. Support for this general conclusion is found in the preliminary data from New York and the experiences of some other nations with liberal abortion policies, notably Japan and the Eastern European countries.[14] However, caution must be exercised in generalizing from the experience of other countries to the impact of abortion on United States population growth. The United States differs from these other nations socially, politically, economically, and most importantly, in the level of contraceptive practice.

Only limited data on the demographic consequences of abortion are available from New York. Our best estimate of the probable impact if the entire country were to follow the New York law would be a decline of 1.5 per 1,000 in the birthrate in the first year after restrictions were removed.[15]

Public Opinion

Public opinion on abortion is changing, tending recently to grow more liberal. Some 14 to 20 percent more women in 1970 than in 1965 approve of abortion for various reasons, according to interview data collected in the 1965 and 1970 National Fertility Studies.[16] The public opinion survey conducted in 1971 for the Commission indicates that half of all Americans believe that abortion should be a matter decided solely between individuals and their physicians; an additional 41 percent would permit abortion under certain circumstances, and six percent flatly oppose abortions under any circumstances. Estimates of the current state of attitudes on abortion doubtless depend very much on the phrasing of the question and the interpretation of the respondent.

In general, support for increasing the availability of legal abortions is strongest among non-Catholics and among those who are well-educated. Among the general public, 38 percent feel that the government should help make abortion available to all women who want it.[17]

Recommendations

The abortion issue raises a great number of moral, legal, public health, and demographic concerns. As a group, the Commission has carefully considered these issues, and based on their personal views, individual members of the Commission have resolved these questions differently.*

A few members of the Commission** are opposed to abortion. These Commissioners consider abortion a remedial measure, and choose to emphasize society's responsibility for improving and enriching the lives of all citizens.

Some Commissioners*** approve of abortion only under the specific conditions set forth in the American Law Institute model abortion statute. These Commissioners believe that no woman should be forced to bear a child, thereby endangering her physical or mental health. Their concern is that abortion be available only on a limited basis and that it be considered as a last resort to protect life or health.

The majority of the Commission believes that women should be free to determine their own fertility, that the matter of abortion should be left to the conscience of the individual

* Separate statements by Commissioner Alan Cranston (pages 264–265) and Commissioner John N. Erlenborn (pages 281-282) appears on the indicated pages.
** Separate statements by Commissioners Paul B. Cornely, M.D. (pages 264-265) and Grace Olivarez (page 291) appear on the indicated pages.
*** A separate statement by Commissioner Marilyn Brant Chandler appears on pages 261-262.

concerned, in consultation with her physician, and that states should be encouraged to enact affirmative statutes creating a clear and positive framework for the practice of abortion on request.

Therefore, with the admonition that abortion not be considered a primary means of fertility control, the Commission recommends that present state laws restricting abortion be liberalized along the lines of the New York State statute, such abortions to be performed on request by duly licensed physicians under conditions of medical safety.

In carrying out this policy, the Commission recommends:

That federal, state, and local governments make funds available to support abortion services in states with liberalized statutes.

That abortion be specifically included in comprehensive health insurance benefits, both public and private.

METHODS OF FERTILITY CONTROL

Although current knowledge, if applied systematically, could bring about considerable progress toward reducing unwanted fertility, the successful control of reproduction depends greatly on the availability of efficient methods for regulation of fertility.*

The development of the pill and the intrauterine device represent major innovations in contraceptive technology, but they are far from perfect solutions to the problem of control of reproduction. We must have contraceptives and other methods of fertility control that are safe and free of any adverse reactions; effective, acceptable, coitus independent, and accessible commercially rather than medically; and inexpensive, easy to use, and reversible. This goal will be reached only if research efforts equal the magnitude of the task.

Currently, some new approaches to fertility control are in experimental trial; other possibilities are under laboratory investigation.[18] The list of potentialities includes daily pills for

---

* Separate statements by Commissioners John N. Erlenborn (page 283) and George D. Woods (page 312) appear on the indicated pages.

women that would be safer than those now available; weekly or monthly pills for men or women; a small plastic implant to be placed under the skin of men or women that could last for years; sophisticated devices or procedures that would make voluntary sterilization of either men or women safer, simpler, and more reversible; modern forms of intrauterine or intravaginal devices that women could use safely in a variety of ways depending on their own preferences; natural substances that could regularize menstrual cycles and improve the rhythm method; and natural substances for post-coital use which interfere with the development of pregnancy. Thus, prospects exist for developing new methods of fertility control which could have advantages over those currently available. However, none of these contain all of the elements of the "perfect" contraceptive.

Until a dozen years ago, all major methods of contraception were based on the simple principle of preventing the sperm and egg from meeting in the fallopian tube, where fertilization occurs. The rhythm method of contraception was the first attempt at fertility control based on the understanding of the endocrinological aspects of the ovarian cycle and the limited duration of egg survival. The pill and the intrauterine device further exploited this knowledge and represented significant breakthroughs in a field which has been largely neglected by science for most of human history. However, in terms of the potential technology which should be feasible as a result of today's sophisticated scientific capabilities, the contraceptive methods currently available are fairly primitive.

Other methods of fertility control are far from perfect. Voluntary sterilization is increasing in popularity; and new procedures are being tried, but progress is slow. There is widespread resort to abortion in the United States and throughout the world. In the last decade, new techniques have emerged which are simpler and less traumatic; but they are expensive and need further refinement.

Methods of fertility regulation remain limited because our knowledge of basic reproductive biology is inadequate. We do not fully understand what governs ovulation, how long an ovum can survive, what governs sperm production, how long sperm survive, what governs a menstrual cycle, or how long it lasts. Such knowledge is essential for the practice of "rhythm" as well as for effective chemical or mechanical contraception. Unwanted and accidental pregnancies are only one consequence of our ignorance. Many couples avoid pregnancy only through use of methods that are cumbersome and produce a great deal of anxiety. Others who desperately want children

179

cannot conceive. A large number of married couples suffer from problems of infertility; the ability to help them is sorely limited by the same lack of information concerning basic reproductive processes that inhibits effective contraception.

This knowledge is essential, not just for regulating fertility, but also for improving the outcome of pregnancy. Today, many mothers suffer the risk of serious injury, ill health or even death in pregnancy and childbirth. Too many children are born with physical and mental handicaps. We spend billions in therapy, remedial treatment, custodial care, and repair of damage that might have been prevented by a more complete understanding of the factors governing reproduction.

Whether the interest is in conception or contraception, in chemical or mechanical contraception or in rhythm, in genetic counseling or mental retardation or cerebral palsy, the basic knowledge necessary is largely the same. There must be an understanding of the role and functioning of the ovary and the testes, of the egg and the sperm, of the process of fertilization itself, and the normal course of gestation. This is knowledge we do not have and must attain.

Any overall strategy for the development of new agents or methods of fertility control must include not only basic research in the biology of reproduction, but also clinical trials, and related toxicological investigations, the development of new products and techniques, and the continuing evaluation of new methods with regard to both effectiveness and short-term and long-term safety. It is essential, too, that extensive critical evaluation be made of the total effects of existing methods of contraception.

The limited amount of usable knowledge of human reproduction and fertility control is the result of the lack of interest we have had in this by comparison with other scientific and technological fields. As Secretary Richardson acknowledged in the Department of Health, Education and Welfare Five-Year Plan for Family Planning Services and Population Research:

. . . in spite of its transcendent importance to human existance, reproduction has received relatively little scientific attention. Even with today's concern for the population problem, the most talented among young investigators all too frequently seek other subjects.[19]

It is not difficult to understand why this has been the case. Career choices are largely shaped by the priorities that public and private institutions set when they allocate their resources.

During the past two decades, as government support for science has mushroomed, the role of government in setting scientific priorities has become decisive. Our scientists have been responsive to these priorities, creating entirely new scientific subcommunities, where none previously existed—in defense, space, and favored areas of medical research.

Beginning a quarter of a century ago with the formation of a committee on human reproduction by the National Research Council, there have been several efforts to stimulate greater interest in fertility research. This issue has been placed before the nation by scientists and citizens with impeccable credentials. The results of these efforts have not come close to the commitment required.

For too long, fertility control was viewed as an unacceptable subject for public concern; private resources were required to lead the way in supporting research in this field. Pharmaceutical companies have supported a large portion of contraceptive research. One incomplete survey showed that their cumulative expenditure from 1965 through 1969 amounted to $68 million.[20] It is unrealistic to rely primarily upon those companies to do the necessary research in this field. Pharmaceutical companies cannot be expected to continue to invest heavily in research unless they can expect a profit from it. Some of the kinds of contraceptives needed may not offer prospects of profits.

A few private foundations have contributed a large share of the money spent in reproductive research, providing over 60 percent of all of nonindustry funds expended in 1969. However, only five percent of all private funds spent on medical research went to the population field, and it is unlikely that the foundation investment will increase substantially.[21]

Presidents Kennedy, Johnson, and Nixon all expressed support for increased governmental funding of fertility-related research. The Congress has authorized up to $93 million for population research in fiscal year 1973.[22] Both President Johnson's Committee on Population and Family Planning, and a committee of experts appointed to advise the Secretary of Health, Education and Welfare on the scope of research needs, urged federal expenditures of at least $100 million; and the latter group recommended that the total federal expenditure rise to $250 million by fiscal year 1974.[23] The Five-Year Plan for Family Planning Services and Population Research, drawn up by the Department of Health, Education and Welfare, is based upon a federal expenditure in fiscal year 1973 of $75 million.[24] These amounts are modest in terms of society's total research expenditures. They are modest in terms of the federal government's research expenditures, but they are far above the total amounts requested and approved for population research. The budget for fiscal year 1973 includes only $44.8 million for this purpose—less than half of the amount authorized and only $5.5 million more than in the previous fiscal year. This amount is far too small for a task which is crucial both in dealing with the population problem and in improving the outcome of pregnancy for women and children. It is essential to increase support for both biomedical and behavioral research related to fertility.

Support for research and training in the basic science of reproduction alone requires at least $100 million in federal funds annually. An additional $100 million annually is required for developmental work on methods of fertility control.[25] Although a larger component of support may be expected from nongovernmental sources for some aspects of product development, the federal government must still provide the major portion of the funding. In addition, at least $50 million a year in federal funds are needed for behavioral and operational research which is discussed further in Chapter 15.

An important step in helping people throughout the world to control their fertility more successfully is the development of better methods of fertility control. The need is urgent, and we would like to see all of the required funds for research in this field become available immediately. However, it seems clear that the capacity does not currently exist within the federal government to administer effectively such an expansion. We believe this capacity should be developed as soon as possible; we speak to this issue in some detail in our organizational recommendations in Chapter 16.

The Commission recommends that this nation give the highest priority to research in reproductive biology and to the search for improved methods by which individuals can control their own fertility.

In order to carry out this research, the Commission recommends that the full $93 million authorized for this purpose in fiscal year 1973 be appropriated and allocated; that federal expenditures for these purposes rise to a minimum of $150 million by 1975; and that private organizations continue and expand their work in this field.

FERTILITY-RELATED SERVICES

The justification for a national policy and program to reduce unwanted pregnancy is independent of its demographic significance.* From both individual and societal viewpoints, the reduction of unwanted fertility is a highly desirable goal for many other reasons. We have seen that unwanted and accidental pregnancies are associated with serious health, social, and economic consequences. Many couples have learned to cope with these consequences, but they hardly contribute to an improved quality of life for them or their children.

Couples in all socioeconomic groups experience unwanted pregnancies, but they occur most often and have the most serious consequences among low-income couples. Middle-income groups have generally relied upon private physicians for family planning services. Access to these services among lower-income persons, who do not have private physicians, has been severely limited. Until very recently; only private organizations, such as Planned Parenthood, and a few local and state health departments, attempted to provide these services to low-income individuals. However, recognizing the personal, economic, and health benefits of reducing unwanted pregnancy, the federal government, since 1967, has been striving to increase the availability of family planning through a program of subsidized services. The response to the federal family planning program has borne out the contention that there is a need for family planning methods among many low-income people, that this need is perceived, and that individuals will voluntarily use fertility control services if these are offered in a manner and setting that are dignified and humane.

The project grant programs, carried out by the National Center for Family Planning Services of the Department of Health, Education and Welfare and the Office of Economic Opportunity, have been the principal components of the increased federal effort. With a relatively modest federal investment, organized family planning programs have succeeded in introducing modern family planning services to nearly 40 percent of low-income persons in need.[26] The majority of those in need remain unserved, however, and the number of

* Separate statements by Commissioners John N. Erlenborn (pp. 284-285) and George D. Woods (p. 312) appear on the indicated pages.

hospitals, health departments, and voluntary agencies not providing services remains substantial. No organized services have been reported in half of all counties in the country. While P.L. 91-572, the Family Planning Services and Population Research Act, has increased the federal authorization for support of family planning services, existing authorizations account for less than half of the funds required. The five-year plan, prepared in accordance with P.L. 91-572, makes clear that the delivery of services to those who need and want them is feasible and within the capabilities of our existing health system.[27] The achievement of this objective will clearly require additional federal authorizations and appropriations as well as increased support for these programs from state and local governments, and from private philanthropy. It is essential that the current federal program be expanded, strengthened, and provided with the resources necessary to complete its mission.

If family planning services are maximally to assist couples in avoiding the dependency caused by unwanted fertility, the program cannot be limited only to those persons already classified as poor. We are therefore puzzled—and concerned—that the definition of low income embodied in the regulations proposed for the present federal family planning program is set at $4,200 per annum.[28] Public health programs have traditionally been designed to serve all persons who choose to avail themselves of these services; to select family planning services as a major departure from this policy has grave implications. We urge that no means test be applied in the administration of these programs. Their purpose must be to enlarge personal freedom for all, not to restrict its benefits only to the poorest of the poor.

While the current family planning program, which provides services to low-income persons, is justified on the basis of acute need within this group, unwanted pregnancies occur in all segments of our society; there are many nonpoor individuals who need but who do not receive adequate fertility control services.

Fertility-Related Health Services

Most Americans secure their health services through private physicians. Yet studies show that most physicians do not perceive it to be their function to actively provide fertility control services.

In part, this is because of the taboos that have historically surrounded fertility control. But it is also a result of the fact that our medical system primarily emphasizes curative medicine and acute, catastrophic care rather than preventive medicine. For this reason, it is not just fertility-control services that are inadequately provided, but the whole range of fertility-related services including maternity and infant care.

Very few current private or public health financing mechanisms pay for such items as office visits, drugs, and laboratory tests—the principal elements of contraceptive services. One insurance company declined to pay for the cost of inserting an intrauterine device on the grounds that such a procedure does not "represent necessary medical care and treatment." Costs of surgical procedures such as abortion and sterilization are covered inadequately, if at all.

With our growing recognition of the vital importance of adequate prenatal and infant care, it is regrettable that only a fraction of the costs of these services are defrayed by health financing mechanisms. Future generations of Americans should be born wanted by their parents, brought into the world with the best skills that modern medicine can offer, and provided with the love and care necessary for a healthy and productive life.

The Commission recommends a national policy and voluntary program to reduce unwanted fertility, to improve the outcome of pregnancy, and to improve the health of children.

In order to carry out such a program, public and private health financing mechanisms should begin paying the full cost of all health services related to fertility, including contraceptive, prenatal, delivery, and postpartum services; pediatric care for the first year of life; voluntary sterilization; safe termination of unwanted pregnancy; and medical treatment of infertility.

Estimates have been made of the costs to American society of such a program.[29] At current fees and institutional charges, the entire gamut of services for all who would require them, regardless of age, marital status, or income, is estimated to cost from $6.7 to $8.1 billion annually in the next five years. More than 70 percent of this cost would cover maternity and pediatric care, while the balance constitutes the total cost of voluntary fertility control. Individuals, public and private third-party mechanisms, and public health programs already finance

185

all but about $1 billion of this total cost. But many persons do not receive all or some of these critical fertility-related health services as a result of inadequate insurance coverage, lack of income, differential access to medical resources, and inadequate public and private programs.

To place this concept in perspective, it is useful to note that total United States health expenditures in fiscal year 1971 are estimated at $75 billion, and our gross national product at more than $1 trillion. The cost to our society of paying for all necessary modern medical care related to the bearing of healthy, wanted children thus would constitute nine percent of our national health bill, and less than 0.7 percent of GNP. On a per capita basis, the total annual cost of such a comprehensive program would be $32 to $34. In fiscal year 1971, per capita health expenditures of all types totaled $358.

These estimates do not, in fact, represent a true "cost" to our society. The expenditure of these sums for adequate fertility-related medical care would, in all probability, be more than offset by the benefits to individuals and society of the delivery of healthy children and the prevention of unwanted pregnancies. One-fourth of the expenditures for the fertility-control services (as distinguished from maternity and pediatric care) would, in fact, be quickly offset by the elimination of the costs of prenatal, delivery, and postnatal care resulting from unwanted pregnancies and births.

The financing of all health services related to fertility control could easily be integrated into current publicly administered health financing systems, and made part of a new comprehensive national health insurance system. Congress should include this coverage in any health insurance system it adopts.

We wish to point out, however, that its initiation is not dependent upon the adoption of a comprehensive national health system. The same type of coverage could be built into existing private insurance programs. This process could be considerably expedited if federal, state, and local governments would undertake responsibility for stimulating the inclusion of such coverage in private insurance.

Service Delivery and Personal Training

The achievement of such a financing concept would remove the economic deterrent to medical care related to childbearing. Removal of the economic barriers would go a long way toward making services available. However, experience in other health financing programs has demonstrated that it would not, by

186

itself, remedy the present inequities in the distribution of medical services. It would not create physicians in communities which currently have none or too few, nor build adequate health facilities to replace obsolete ones. It would not guarantee the availability of the necessary trained manpower, nor provide the means whereby individuals would receive the full range of information necessary for them to choose wisely the services which best fit their needs.

These problems can only be remedied if, at the same time that the basic costs are assured through comprehensive health financing mechanisms, systematic attention is paid to the organization and delivery of fertility-related health services. The development of health maintenance organizations and group practice modes of delivery may help in this process. The Commission believes that special attention will have to be directed to the specific problems of fertility-related health services.

We therefore recommend creation of programs to (1) train doctors, nurses, and paraprofessionals, including indigenous personnel, in the provision of all fertility-related health services; (2) develop new patterns for the utilization of professional and paraprofessional personnel; and (3) evaluate improved methods of organizing the delivery of these services.

Family Planning Services

At the same time, federal leadership is necessary to insure that our comprehensive health planning program undertakes responsibility for monitoring the extent to which health services related to fertility are actually provided through our health system, and to initiate changes in practices and programs which are needed to insure that services are actually available and accessible to all.

Until the time that private and public health mechanisms have been altered to include adequate coverage and provision of fertility-related services, the present federal programs that provide family planning services and maternal and child care must be continued and expanded.

The five-year plan for family planning services projects the total fiscal requirements over the next five years at between $392 and $434 million. While state and local governments and private philanthropy can and should increase their commitment to this national effort, most experts agree that by 1975, not more than $50 million can be supplied from these sources.[30] The bulk of family planning funds must come from the federal government.

Present specific statutory authorizations for family planning services are not sufficient to meet the level of funding required. Medicaid cannot be expected to provide much assistance.

The Commission therefore recommends: (1) new legislation extending the current family planning project grant program for five years beyond fiscal year 1973 and providing additional authorizations to reach a federal funding level of $225 million in fiscal year 1973, $275 million in fiscal year 1974, $325 million in fiscal year 1975, and $400 million thereafter; (2) extension of the family planning project grant authority of Title V of the Social Security Act beyond 1972, and maintenance of the level of funding at approximately $30 million annually; and (3) maintenance of the Title II OEO program at current levels of authorization.

The program elements thus far recommended would create both a long-term basic financing mechanism for fertility-related health services and an interim program effort to build the needed additional capacity to provide family planning services. To complete the system of fertility-related services, it is necessary to have an adequate information and education program; it is not sufficient just to have services available. People must know that they are available and must have a full range of knowledge about methods of fertility control. The task of informing and educating Americans in this area is too important to be left exclusively to voluntary organizations and sporadic private efforts. It should be the responsibility of society's full range of information and education channels.

Services for Teenagers

As a society, we have been reluctant to acknowledge that there is a considerable amount of sexual activity among unmarried young people. The national study which disclosed that 27 percent of unmarried girls 15 to 19 years old had had sexual relations, further revealed that girls have a considerable acquaintance with contraceptive methods; over 95 percent of all girls 15 to 19, for example, know about the pill. Contraceptive practice, however, contrasts sharply with this picture. Although many young women who have had intercourse have used a contraceptive at some time, this age group is characterized by a great deal of "chance taking." The majority of these young women have either never used or, at best, have sometimes used birth control methods.[31]

We deplore the various consequences of teenage pregnancy, including the recent report from New York that teenagers account for about one-quarter of the abortions performed under their new statute during its first year.[32] Adolescent pregnancy offers a generally bleak picture of serious physical, psychological, and social implications for the teenager and the child. Once a teenager becomes pregnant, her chances of enjoying a rewarding, satisfying life are diminished. Pregnancy is the number one cause for school drop-out among females in the United States. The psychological effects of adolescent pregnancy are indicated by a recent study that estimated that teenage mothers have a suicide attempt rate 10 times that of the general population.[33]

The Commission is not addressing the moral questions involved in teenage sexual behavior. However, we are concerned with the complex issue of teenage pregnancy. Therefore, the Commission believes that young people must be given access to contraceptive information and services.

Toward the goal of reducing unwanted pregnancies and childbearing among the young, the Commission recommends that birth control information and services be made available to teenagers in appropriate facilities sensitive to their needs and concerns.

The Commission recognizes that the availability of contraceptive services alone is insufficient. It has recently been reported that among teenagers, the single most important reason given for not using contraceptives was the belief that, for various reasons, they could not become pregnant. Our survey reveals that nearly two-thirds of our citizens are in favor of high schools offering information on ways to avoid pregnancy.[34]

Young people whose family-building years lie in the future and whose options will depend on their understanding of fertility control and services available to them, must have accurate information about these matters.

The Commission therefore recommends the development and implementation of an adequately financed program to develop appropriate family planning materials, to conduct training courses for teachers and school administrators, and to assist states and local communities in integrating information about family planning into school courses such as hygiene and sex education.

CHAPTER 12. POPULATION STABILIZATION

THE COMMISSION'S PERSPECTIVE

Soon after the Commission's first meeting in June 1970, it became evident that the question of population stabilization would be a principal issue in its deliberations. A population has stabilized when the number of births has come into balance with the number of deaths, with the result that, the effects of immigration aside, the size of the population remains relatively constant. We recognize that stabilization will only be possible on an average over a period of time, as the annual numbers of births and deaths fluctuate. The Commission further recognizes that to attain a stablized population would take a number of decades, primarily because such a high proportion of our population today is now entering the ages of marriage and reproduction.

As our work proceeded and we received the results of studies comparing the likely effects of continued growth with the effects of stabilization, it became increasingly evident that no substantial benefits would result from continued growth of the nation's population. This is one of the basic conclusions we have drawn from our inquiry. From the accumulated evidence, we further concluded that the stabilization of our population would contribute significantly to the nation's ability to solve its problems. It was evident that moving toward stabilization would provide an opportunity to devote resources to problems and needs relating to the quality of life rather than its quantity. Stabilization would "buy time" by slowing

191

the pace at which growth-related problems accumulate and enhancing opportunities for the orderly and democratic working out of solutions.

The Commission recognizes that the demographic implications of most of our recommended policies concerning childbearing are quite consistent with a goal of population stabilization. In this sense, achievement of population stabilization would be primarily the result of measures aimed at creating conditions in which individuals, regardless of sex, age, or minority status, can exercise genuine free choice. This means that we must strive to eliminate those social barriers, laws, and cultural pressures that interfere with the exercise of free choice and that governmental programs in the future must be sensitized to demographic effects.*

Recognizing that our population cannot grow indefinitely, and appreciating the advantages of moving now toward the stabilization of population, the Commission recommends that the nation welcome and plan for a stabilized population.

There remain a number of questions which must be answered as the nation follows a course toward population stabilization. How can stabilization be reached? Is there any particular size at which the population should level off, and when should that occur? What "costs" would be imposed by the various paths to stabilization, and what costs are worth paying?

CRITERIA FOR PATHS TO STABILIZATION[1]

An important group in our society, composed predominantly of young people, has been much concerned about population growth in recent years. Their concern emerged quite rapidly as the mounting pollution problem received widespread attention, and their goal became "zero population growth." By this, they meant in fact sterilization—bringing births into balance with deaths. To attain their objective, they called for the 2-child family. They recognize, of course, that many people do not marry and that some who do marry either

---

* A separate statement by Commissioner Paul B. Cornely, M.D., appears on pages 265-266.

are not able to have or do not want to have children, permitting wide latitude in family size and attainment of the 2-child average.

Some called for zero growth immediately. But this would not be possible without considerable disruption to society. While there are a variety of paths to ultimate stabilization, none of the feasible paths would reach it immediately. Our past rapid growth has given us so many young couples that, even if they merely replaced themselves, the number of births would still rise for several years before leveling off. To produce the number of births consistent with immediate zero growth, they would have to limit their childbearing to an average of only about one child. In a few years, there would be only half as many children as there are now. This would have disruptive effects on the school system and subsequently on the number of persons entering the labor force. Thereafter, a constant total population could be maintained only if this small generation in turn had two children and their grandchildren had nearly three children on the average. And then the process would again have to reverse, so that the overall effect for many years would be that of an accordion-like continuous expansion and contraction.[2]

From considerations such as this, we can begin to develop criteria for paths toward population stabilization. It is highly desirable to avoid another baby boom. Births, which averaged 3.0 million annually in the early 1920's, fell to a 2.4 million average in the 1930's, rose to a 4.2 million average in the late 1950's and early 1960's, and fell to 3.6 million in 1971.[3] These boom and bust cycles have caused disruption in elementary and high schools and subsequently in the colleges and in the labor market. And the damage to the long-run career aspirations of the baby-boom generation is only beginning to be felt.

The assimilation of the baby-boom generation has been called "population peristalsis," comparing it to the process in which a python digests a pig. As it moves along the digestive tract, the pig makes a big bulge in the python. While the imagery suggests the appearance of the baby-boom generation as it moves up the age scale and through the phases of the life cycle, there is reason to believe that the python has an easier time with the pig than our nation is having providing training, jobs, and opportunity for the generation of the baby boom.

Thus, we would prefer that the path to stabilization involve a minimum of fluctuations from period to period in the number of births. For the near future, these considerations recommend a course toward population stabilization which

193

would reduce the echo expected from the baby-boom generation as it moves through the childbearing ages and bears children of its own.

Our evidence also indicates that it would be preferable for the population to stabilize at a lower rather than a higher level. Our population will continue to grow for decades more before stabilizing, even if those now entering the ages of reproduction merely replace themselves. The population will grow as the very large groups now eight to 25 years of age—the products of the postwar baby boom—grow older and succeed their less numerous predecessors. How much growth there will be depends on the oncoming generations of young parents.

Some moderate changes in patterns of marriage and childbearing are necessary for any move toward stabilization. There are obvious advantages to a path which minimizes the change required and provides a reasonable amount of time for such change to occur.

Population stabilization under modern conditions of mortality means that, on the average, each pair of adults will give birth to two children. This average can be achieved in many ways. For example, it can be achieved by varying combinations of nonmarriage or childlessness coexisting in a population with substantial percentages of couples who have more than two children. On several grounds, it is desirable that stabilization develop in a way which encourages variety and choice rather than uniformity.

We prefer, then, a course toward population stabilization which minimizes fluctuations in the number of births; minimizes further growth of population; minimizes the change required in reproductive habits and provides adequate time for such changes to be adopted; and maximizes variety and choice in life styles, while minimizing pressures for conformity.

AN ILLUSTRATION OF AN OPTIMAL PATH[4]

Our research indicates that there are some paths to stabilization that are clearly preferable. These offer less additional population growth, involve negligible fluctuations in births, provide for a wide range of family sizes within the population, and exact moderate "costs"—that is, changes in marriage and

194

childbearing habits, which are in the same direction as current trends.

A course such as the following satisfies these criteria quite well. (The calculations exclude immigration; the demographic role of immigration is reviewed in the next chapter.)

In this illustration, childbearing would decline to a replacement level in 20 years. This would result if: (1) the proportion of women becoming mothers declined from 88 to 80 percent; (2) the proportion of parents with three or more children declined from 50 to 41 percent; and (3) the proportion of parents with one or two children rose from 50 to 59 percent. Also in this illustration, the average age of mothers when their first child is born would rise by two years, and the average interval between births would rise by less than six months. The results of these changes would be that the United States population would gradually grow until it stabilizes, in approximately 50 years, at a level of 278 million (plus the contribution from the net inflow of immigrants). Periodic fluctuations in the number of births would be negligible.

The size of the population in the year 2000 will depend both on how fast future births occur as well as on the ultimate number of children people have over a lifetime. Over the next 10 to 15 years especially, we must expect a large number of births from the increasing numbers of potential parents, unless these young people offset the effect of their numbers by waiting somewhat before having their children. Postponement and stretching-out of childbearing, accompanied by a gradual decline in the number of children that people have over a lifetime, can effectively reduce the growth we shall otherwise experience.

Beyond this, there are persuasive health and personal reasons for encouraging postponement of childbearing and better spacing of births. Infants of teenage mothers are subject to higher risks of premature birth, infant death, and lifetime physical and mental disability than children of mothers in their twenties.[5] If the 17 percent of all births occurring to teenage mothers were postponed to later ages, we would see a distinct improvement in the survival, health, and ability of these children.

It is obvious that the population cannot be fine-tuned to conform to any specific path. The changes might occur sooner or later than in this illustration. If they took place over 30 years instead of 20 we should expect nine million more people in the ultimate stabilized population—or 287 million rather than 278 million. Or if the average age at childbearing rose

195

only one year instead of two, we would end up with 10 million more people than otherwise.

On the other hand, suppose we drifted toward a replacement level of fertility in 50 years instead of 20, and none of the other factors changed. In that case, the population would stabilize at 330 million. In other words, following this route would result in 50 million more Americans than the one illustrated above.

THE LIKELIHOOD OF POPULATION STABILIZATION

Many developments—some old and some recent—enhance the likelihood that something close to an optimal path can be realized, especially if the Commission's recommendations bearing on population growth are adopted quickly.

1. The trend of average family size has been downward—from seven or eight children per family in colonial times to less than three children in recent years—interrupted, however, by the baby boom.

2. The birthrate has declined over the past decade and showed an unexpected further decline in 1971.

3. The increasing employment of women, and the movement to expand women's options as to occupational and family roles and life styles, promise to increase alternatives to the conventional role of wife-homemaker-mother.

4. Concern over the effects of population growth has been mounting. Two-thirds of the general public interviewed in the Commission's survey in 1971 felt that the growth of the United States population is a serious problem. Half or more expressed concern over the impact of population growth on the use of natural resources, on air and water pollution, and on social unrest and dissatisfaction.[6]

5. Youthful marriage is becoming less common than it was a few years ago. While 20 percent of women now in their thirties married before age 18, only 13 percent of the young women are doing so now.[7] It remains to be seen whether this represents a postponement of marriage or a reversal of the trend toward nearly universal marriage.

6. The family-size preferences of young people now entering the childbearing ages are significantly lower than the preferences reported by their elders at the same stage in life.

7. The technical quality of contraceptives has increased

196

greatly in the past 10 years, although irregular and ineffective use still results in many unplanned and unwanted births.

8. The legalization of abortion in a few states has resulted in major increases in the number of legal abortions. The evidence so far indicates that legalized abortion is being used by many women who would otherwise have had to resort to illegal and unsafe abortions. The magnitude of its effect on the birthrate is not yet clear.[8]

9. The experience of many other countries indicates the feasibility of sustained replacement levels of reproduction.[9] Within the past half century, Japan, England and Wales, France, Denmark, Norway, West Germany, Hungary, Sweden, and Switzerland have all experienced periods of replacement or near-replacement fertility lasting a decade or more. Additional countries have had shorter periods at or near replacement levels. While much of this experience occurred during the Depression of the 1930's, much of it also occurred since then. Furthermore, during that period, contraceptive technology was primitive compared to what is available today.

On the basis of these facts, the nation might ask, "why worry," and decide to wait and see what happens. Our judgment is that we should not wait. Acting now, we encourage a desirable trend. Acting later, we may find ourselves in a position of trying to reverse an undesirable trend. We should take advantage of the opportunity the moment presents rather than wait for what the unknown future holds.

The potential for a repeat of the baby boom is still here. In 1975, there will be six million more people in the prime childbearing ages of 20 to 29 than there were in 1970. By 1985, the figure will have jumped still another five million. Unless we achieve some postponement of childbearing or reduction in average family size, this is going to mean substantial further increases in the number of births.[10]

Furthermore, although we discern many favorable elements in recent trends, there are also unfavorable elements which threaten the achievement of stabilization.

1. For historical reasons which no longer apply, this nation has an ideological addiction to growth.

2. Our social institutions, including many of our laws, often exert a pronatalist effect, even if inadvertent.[11] This includes the images of family life and women's roles projected in television programs; the child-saves-marriage theme in women's magazines;[12] the restrictions on the availability of contraception, sex education, and abortion; and many others.

3. There is an unsatisfactory level of understanding of the

197

role of sex in human life and of the reproductive process and its control.

4. While the white middle-class majority bears the primary numerical responsibility for population growth, it is also true that the failure of our society to bring racial minorities and the poor into the mainstream of American life has impaired their ability to implement small-family goals.

5. If it should happen that, in the next few years, our rate of reproduction falls to replacement levels or below, we could experience a strong counterreaction. In the United States in the 1930's, and in several foreign countries, the response to subreplacement fertility has been a cry of anxiety over the national prosperity, security, and virility. Individual countries have found it hard to come to terms with replacement-level fertility rates.[13] About 40 years ago during the Depression, there was great concern about "race suicide" when birthrates fell in Western Europe and in this country. Today, several countries approaching stabilization have expressed concerns about possible future labor shortages. The growth ethic seems to be so imprinted in human consciousness that it takes a deliberate effort of rationality and will to overcome it, but that effort is now desirable.

One purpose of this report and the programs it recommends is to prepare the American people to welcome a replacement level of reproduction and some periods of reproduction below replacement. The nation must face the fact that achieving population stabilization sooner rather than later would require a period of time during which annual fertility was below replacement. During the transition to stabilization, the postponement of childbearing would result in annual fertility rates dropping below replacement, even though, over a lifetime, the childbearing of the parents would reach a replacement level.

In the long-run future, we should understand that a stabilized population means an *average* of zero growth, and there would be times when the size of the population declines. Indeed, zero growth can only be achieved realistically with fluctuations in both directions. We should prepare ourselves not to react with alarm, as some other countries have done recently, when the distant possibility of population decline appears.

CHAPTER 13. IMMIGRATION

Because population growth has rarely been a concern of immigration policy makers, it is especially important to study immigration from the perspective of population policy. In the years 1861 to 1910, the average annual immigration rate per 1,000 total population of the United States was 7.5; the rate for the period 1911 to 1970 dropped to 1.8. The rate for the recent period reflects a rise from the 1930's, when there was a net outflow of migrants, to the 1960's when the rate was 2.2.[1]

Historically, immigration has contributed profoundly to the growth and development of this country. In fact, we pride ourselves on being a nation of immigrants. Traditionally, because of the desire to settle advancing frontiers and the demand for labor in the expanding industries, there were few restrictions on immigration. However, a changing situation early in this century became reflected in new immigration policies. The situation is now changing again, and it is appropriate that the Commission review the role of immigration.

THE PAST

Our nation's history repeatedly reveals the outstanding contributions of immigrants. They provided much of the manpower and initiative that settled the colonies and opened the west. They helped build the railroads, worked in the factories, organized labor, succeeded at the highest levels of business and government, and have left an indelible mark on American arts and scholarship. Immigrants today are contributing in

199

equally significant ways, and there is every reason to expect such benefits from immigration in the future. Our society has been shaped by the many identities of its citizens.

In response to the needs of the economically, religiously, and politically oppressed around the world and to our needs as a new and growing nation, there were no significant restrictions on immigration until after the Civil War. In 1882, Chinese immigrants were excluded. Later, other narrowly selective requirements were imposed for health and public welfare reasons. After World War I, there were strong social and political pressures to impose tight restrictions on immigration. The Immigration Act of 1924 defined special categories of immigrants (close relatives, refugees) not subject to numerical limits and set a quota of about 150,000 for all others. The legislation was based on complicated formulas to restrict immigrants from certain countries in order to retain the racial and ethnic composition of the United States population. This system was replaced by the Immigration Act of 1965.

The 1965 legislation shifted the restrictions from national origins to priorities based on family reunification, asylum for refugees, and needed skills and professions. Because of past restrictions, backlogs of demand, and the 1965 change in policy, there has been a dramatic shift in the geographic origins of our immigrants. From 1945 to 1965, 43 percent of immigrants came from Europe. But, from 1966 to 1970, only one-third of the immigrants were European, while one-third were Canadian and Latin American, and the remaining third were West Indian, Asian, and African.[2] This geographic change has also affected the racial composition of immigrants, increasing the number of nonwhites. Because of earlier changes in composition, women now outnumber male immigrants, and there are more families with dependents.[3] During the sixties, the flow of aliens arriving for permanent residence averaged about 332,000 per year. There were about 100,000 more such persons entering the country in 1970 than was the case in 1960.[4] Because the 1965 changes in immigration policies are so recent, it is not entirely clear whether these adjustments will develop into long-range trends.

THE DEMOGRAPHIC IMPLICATIONS[5]

Immigrants are now entering the United States at a rate of almost 400,000 per year. The relative importance of immigration as a component of population growth has increased significantly as declining birthrates diminish the level of natural increase. However, the proportion of the population which is foreign-born (about five percent) is not changing much. Between 1960 and 1970, about 16 percent of the total population growth was due to net immigration (the difference between the number of people entering the country and the number leaving). However, the increasing relative significance of immigration can be misleading for, if native births and deaths were balanced, immigration would account for 100 percent of population growth.

If net immigration were to remain at about 400,000 per year and all families were to have an average of two children, then immigrants arriving between 1970 and the year 2000, plus their descendants born here, would number 15 million at the end of the century. This would account for almost a quarter of the total population increase during that period.[6]

One should ask not only how much immigration contributes to population growth, but also how seriously immigration affects the advent of population stabilization. If immigration were to continue at the rate of about 400,000 per year, a rate of 2.0 rather than 2.1 children per woman would eventually stabilize the population, though at a later date. And the size of the population would ultimately be about eight percent larger than if there were no international migration whatsoever.[7]

If the flow of residents leaving this country were as large as the flow of immigrants, they would balance each other and have no impact on the growth rate. Unfortunately, no records are kept of people permanently leaving the country; emigration statistics must rely on indirect estimates. Indications are that emigration has been increasing recently from about 23,000 in 1965 to 37,000 in 1970. The most popular destinations are Canada, Israel, and Australia, and these may possibly account for more than half the emigrants. Emigration now is probably only about one-tenth the volume of immigration, but it has been proportionately larger in other periods of history. Of course, it is possible that it may increase again in the future.

Immigration affects not only the growth of the population, but also its distribution. It is not surprising that the settlement patterns of immigrants reflect the distribution trends of the native population, since most immigrants come to this country either to join their relatives or obtain a job. In fact, immigrants tend to prefer metropolitan areas and are concentrated in a few of the largest cities. Immigrants will contribute about 23 percent of the population growth which is projected to occur within fixed metropolitan boundaries between 1970 and 2000, assuming the 2-child growth rate.[8] Not only do immigrants tend to be highly metropolitan, they are also concentrated in a few states. Two-thirds of the recent immigrants intended to settle in six states—New York, California, New Jersey, Illinois, Texas, and Massachusetts.[9]

ILLEGAL ALIENS

A major and growing problem associated with immigration is that of illegal immigrants.* It is impossible to estimate precisely how many escape detection; but, during 1971, over 420,-000 deportable aliens were located. This figure is larger than the number of immigrants who entered legally during the same period. Estimates place the number of illegal aliens currently in the United States between one and two million. Most are men seeking employment. Because the number of illegal aliens apprehended has risen dramatically (from less than 71,000 in 1960 to over 400,000 in 1971), the number of aliens in illegal status has probably been increasing significantly. Also, the problem has been spreading from the southwest, along the Mexican border, to all the major metropolitan areas across the country.[10]

The economic problems exacerbated by illegal aliens are manifold and affect the labor market and social services. It is often profitable for employers to hire illegal aliens for low wages and under poor working conditions; these workers will not risk discovery of their unlawful status by complaining or organizing. Thus, illegal aliens (who usually take unskilled or low-skilled positions) not only deprive citizens and permanent resident aliens of jobs, but also depress the wage scale and working conditions in areas where they are heavily concentrated. Although many aliens enter the United States in order to work and send much of their earnings back to their families and homeland, others are not as fortunate in finding jobs and can be a drain on public welfare and social services. Because of the illegal and precarious nature of their status, these aliens are ready prey for unscrupulous lawyers, landlords, and employers.

* A separate statement by Commissioner Alan Cranston appears on page 271.

Eight out of 10 illegal aliens found are Mexicans. Most of the others are Canadians and West Indians, although there are also sizeable groups of Portuguese, Greeks, Italians, Chinese, and Filipinos. Their countries were affected by immigration policy changes in the 1965 Act, and there is considerable demand and pressure for immigrant visas. The flow of illegal immigrants could probably be reduced if the numbers of permanent residence visas were increased, the economic incentives for hiring illegal aliens were eliminated, and/or the economic advantages of obtaining a job in this country were reduced. In any case, an aggressive enforcement program must be developed along all borders and ports of entry. Any enforcement programs against illegal entry and possible laws against employment of illegal aliens must take special care not to infringe upon the civil rights of Mexicans, Mexican-Americans, and others who are legally residing here and working or seeking work.

COMPETITION FOR WORK

In addition to the adverse economic pressures caused by *illegal* aliens, it is possible that *legal* immigration could have a negative impact if not regulated carefully. It is the purpose of the labor certification program to ensure that immigrants do not compete with indigenous labor, particularly in periods and geographic areas of unemployment. But, only a small percent of immigrants are actually required to be certified. Since immigrants often have relatively high education and skills, there is an economic incentive for employers and institutions to favor them. This can work to the disadvantage of the native-born, particularly members of minority groups and women, who have traditionally been discriminated against and denied opportunities to upgrade their skills.

A flow of highly trained immigrants can mask the need for developing and promoting domestic talents—for example, in the medical field. Although medical schools have recently been expanding enrollments, a significant proportion of the demand for doctors is being met by immigrants trained abroad. It appears that, without the availability of these foreign doctors, the medical schools would be under greater pressure to increase their enrollment and to provide more educational opportunities for all Americans—particularly minorities and women. The fact that there are more registered Filipino doctors (about

7,000 [11]) than black doctors (about 6,000 [12]) practicing in the United States shows the inequities that can arise.

If immigrants are also favored in the unskilled and semi-skilled occupations, the discrimination should be attacked directly. Obviously, such discrimination may have other important sources which may not be affected by immigration policy. Thus, it is important to watch occupational trends, particularly in metropolitan areas, to ensure employment and development opportunities to racial and ethnic minorities. Traditionally, regardless of their ethnic origins, immigrants have started employment at the lowest levels and worked their way up to gain a measure of affluence. For various reasons, blacks have not benefited equally. Special attention to career advancement programs and promotion practices, as well as hiring, is needed to permit blacks to travel the same economic path and have the same opportunities as immigrants.

RECOMMENDATIONS

The Commission believes that it is imperative for this country to address itself, first, to the problems of its own disadvantaged and poor. The flow of immigrants should be closely regulated until this country can provide adequate social and economic opportunities for all its present members, particularly those traditionally discriminated against because of race, ethnicity, or sex.

Thus, the Commission believes that an effectively implemented and flexible labor certification program is necessary to ensure that immigrants do not compete with residents for work. Immigration policies must react quickly to changes in domestic unemployment rates and in occupational and geographic shifts in the labor force. Also, national manpower planners and immigration officials ought to be aware of the more subtle form of discrimination related to immigration. A readily available source of trained professionals from other countries may slow the development of domestic talents and the expansion of training facilities. While this importation of talent may be economical for the United States, it is not fair either to the foreign countries that educate the professionals or to our own citizens—particularly those minority groups and women whose access to professional training and economic advancement has been limited.

In order for Congress and immigration officials to consider

these economic problems, apply appropriate regulations, and expect the economic conflicts to be alleviated, they must also eliminate the flow of illegal immigrants. As has been shown, the economic and social problems associated with illegal immigrants have reached significant proportions.

The Commission recommends that Congress immediately consider the serious situation of illegal immigration and pass legislation which will impose civil and criminal sanctions on employers of illegal border-crossers or aliens in an immigration status in which employment is not authorized.

To implement this policy, the Commission recommends provision of increased and strengthened resources consistent with an effective enforcement program in appropriate agencies.

While the elimination of illegal aliens will alleviate the acute problems associated with immigration, there is still the question of the legal immigrants and their demographic impact. The Commission recognizes the importance of the compassionate nature of our immigration policy. We believe deeply that this country should be a haven for the oppressed. It is important that we be in a flexible position to take part in international cooperative efforts to find homes for refugees in special circumstances. In addition, we should continue to welcome members of families who desire to join close relatives here. Our humanitarian responsibilities to the international community require consideration of matters beyond national demographic questions.

Because the immigration issue involves complex moral, economic, and political considerations, as well as demographic concerns, there was a division of opinion within the Commission about policies regarding the number of immigrants. Some Commissioners felt that the number of immigrants should be gradually decreased, about 10 percent a year for five years. This group was concerned with the inconsistency of planning for population stabilization for our country and at the same time accepting large numbers of immigrants each year. They were concerned that the filling of many jobs in this country each year by immigrants would have an increasingly unfavorable impact on our own disadvantaged, particularly when unemployment is substantial. Finally, they were concerned because they believe that immigration does have a considerable impact on United States population growth, thus making the stabilization objective much more difficult.

The majority felt that the present level of immigration should be maintained because of the humanitarian aspects; because of the contribution which immigrants have made and continue to make to our society; and because of the importance of the role of the United States in international migration.

The Commission recommends that immigration levels not be increased and that immigration policy be reviewed periodically to reflect demographic conditions and considerations.

To implement this policy, the Commission recommends that Congress require the Bureau of the Census, in coordination with the Immigration and Naturalization Service, to report biennially to the Congress on the impact of immigration on the nation's demographic situation.

CHAPTER 14. NATIONAL DISTRIBUTION
AND MIGRATION POLICIES

Reducing national population growth is a long-term process, the benefits of which will be experienced over many years. As the growth of the nation as a whole slows, so will local growth. Unquestionably, then, many of the problems often attributed to distribution—congestion in central cities, air pollution, aesthetically unattractive suburban growth—will be alleviated by national population stabilization. But until stabilization is achieved, we must cope with the difficult problem of where the growth occurring in the interim will be located. And even after the national population stabilizes, problems associated with distribution and mobility will continue to affect the quality of life.

Prominent among traditional American values is freedom of movement, yet blacks and other minorities are restricted in their mobility, especially from city to suburb. Access to high quality education is considered a right of all Americans, yet many rural poor living in depressed regions have inadequate skills. Environmental quality is a national goal, yet high pollution levels are common in large metropolitan areas and in some smaller urban and rural places as well.

Ameliorating these and other problems related to population movement and distribution will require a new approach to policy—one that questions the belief that local population growth is necessarily good, just as it questions the growth ethic for the nation as a whole; one that examines where population growth may appropriately be encouraged as well as where it may not; one that places new emphasis on helping people directly, in addition to aiding the places where they live; and one that gives new importance to social and environmental objectives in the establishment of public policy.

AN APPROACH TO POLICY

Our traditional approach to population distribution policy and local growth has been governed by the ethic that development and growth are inherently good. This is a heritage from the age of a nearly empty continent. But now we need to recognize that continued local or regional growth in some areas may have many undesirable consequences—possibly even threatening the integrity of the human community or the ecosystem.

For many of the same reasons that the nation as a whole should welcome population stabilization, communities and regions should begin to consider seriously whether substantial further population growth is desirable. Several are already doing so. While some areas may secure important gains through an increase in population size, others have little to gain from growth per se. In fact, it is increasingly clear that social and environmental problems are often aggravated by the continued growth of large population concentrations.

At the same time, communities across the country will have to accommodate additional growth in the coming decades; the national population will grow whether or not we eventually achieve population stabilization. It would be just as irresponsible for communities to arbitrarily erect barriers to future growth as it would be to encourage growth for growth's sake. This is not to say that all communities must accept unrestricted growth. But, the accommodation of future population is a public responsibility which must be shared by all communities and dealt with on a broad scale.

Partly as a consequence of traditional beliefs that growth is good, the focus of regional development policy has been to promote the prosperity of places. The approach is based on the philosophy that the way to ensure individual prosperity is through place prosperity. From this perspective, the best strategy to help the unemployed of a small town is to revitalize the town through better development planning and capital investment which will attract new jobs. The fortune of the individual, then, depends on the fortune of the place where he lives.

A second approach would be to emphasize helping people directly. If individuals can be helped to upgrade their skills, then one might both make "their place" more attractive for developmental investments and make the individuals themselves more mobile. With this policy approach, the individual's future is not tied so inextricably to the future of his community. Rather, through geographic and occupational mobility, he may benefit from prosperity at home or elsewhere.

These two policies are potentially complementary. Experience has shown that training people without having appropriate job opportunities available leads to frustration and disappointment. The two policies suggest, on the one hand, attracting jobs to where people live and, on the other, equipping people to fill jobs wherever they may be located, and thus enabling them to participate in a national job market with its vastly greater range of job opportunities. The policy emphasis in the past has been on the development of places. A balanced program for the future would call for greater emphasis on the development of people. Since the adequacy of a national job market is far more readily assured than on a community-by-community basis, such a shift in policy emphasis would facilitate the task of matching jobs and people.

Economic concerns have traditionally been paramount in determining distribution patterns. They had to be, given the need to raise levels of per capita income. But in our attempts to maximize material well-being, we generally ignored other factors that contribute to well-being.

In particular, social and environmental aspects of distribution were not major considerations in either private location decisions or public policy. For example, the traditional economic evaluation of the advantages and disadvantages of life in metropolitan areas often has neglected many important social costs. Today, it has become increasingly clear that, in considering the desirability of moderating population trends or exploring new ways to improve our living environments, social and environmental factors must be given much more importance in policy decisions.

THE MEANING OF A METROPOLITAN FUTURE

The United States is today experiencing three important shifts in population: (1) migration from low-income, rural, and economically depressed areas toward metropolitan areas; (2) a movement of metropolitan population from older, and often somewhat climatically less hospitable centers in the northeast and midwest, toward the newer, climatically favored centers of the south and west; and (3) an outward dispersion of residents from the cores to the peripheries of the metropolitan areas. The combination of these population movements and the continuing increase in our total population has resulted in the development of large metropolitan areas and urban regions—indeed, the emergence of an almost totally urban society.

Although comments about excessive urban size or concentration are so common as to be clichés, the "anthill" image of the "megalopolis" is a misleading guide for policy making. We have seen that, while the percent of the population living in large places is rising, much of this shift is due to natural increase. Furthermore, the average densities of urbanized areas are declining, not rising. We have suggested that the appropriate scale at which to grasp emerging settlement patterns includes the metropolitan area, but goes beyond it to the urban region—a constellation of urban centers dispersing outward. Basically, the urban region is an adaptation of adjacent urban centers to underlying economic change and to most Americans' desire for dispersed suburban living. The easy communication among urban places in urban regions permits the smaller metropolitan areas to benefit from the economic advantages of agglomeration, while avoiding some of the penalties of excessive size and density. Future problems of both urban regions and the metropolis will stem, in large part, from unresolved issues of territorial and governmental structure and restrictions on residential location, not from size or density.

The transition to a metropolitan society in many ways has been beneficial, at least in terms of raising living standards and enhancing personal opportunity. Productivity and average income are higher and inequalities among residents are less pronounced in these areas than elsewhere. Some of the benefits are a result of the absolute size of a metropolitan area. Other benefits are associated with *relative* size. For example, the largest urban center of a region—whether it has 500,000 or 5,000,000 people—usually has the best cultural and health facilities in the region. For whatever reasons, compared to their counterparts in rural areas and small towns, the residents of larger metropolitan centers on the average have access to better health and education facilities, higher income, a wider range of employment and cultural opportunities, and broader avenues of economic improvement for disadvantaged members of the population.

While these benefits accompany metropolitan living, many urban Americans, though more prosperous than they would be in small towns, seem unhappy with the conditions under which they live. They are sensitive to the liabilities which have accompanied metropolitan growth, even if these liabilities have not always been caused by such growth.

As part of living in large metropolitan areas, the average resident is subjected to high levels of pollution and crime, congestion of all sorts, and inadequate access to the outdoors. Moreover, the scale of many metropolises promotes larger slums and ghettos. This scale effect almost inherently increases the separation created by all forms of segregation. Less definable, but no less real to many people, is a feeling of loneliness, impersonality, alienation, and helplessness fostered by being an insignificant one of millions.

Finally, total urbanization and the dominance of metropolitan areas can involve the loss of certain social and community values associated with small-town living. It may carry with it some loss of diversity in living environments—a diversity that is valuable in itself and as an indicator of freedom of residential choice.

A DUAL STRATEGY

How one balances out these considerations is necessarily a subjective matter. The evolution of the United States into a metropolitan society with many large urban areas presents both opportunities and liabilities.

Nevertheless, the Commission believes that the losses resulting from a continuation of current trends in population distribution are sufficiently serious that we should attempt to moderate them. We believe that encouraging the growth of selected urban centers in economically depressed regions in the United States might well enhance opportunities significantly for the residents of those regions. We have seen that the cultivation of growth in smaller centers might assist in the decongestion of settlement in urban regions. Furthermore, creating opportunities in these smaller centers might aid in providing a greater variety of alternative living environments.

However, on the evidence presented to us, we also recognize

211

that powerful economic and demographic trends are not easily modified. Previous government efforts to this end, both in the United States and abroad, have not been marked by conspicuous success. Whatever future success we may have in moderating current trends, most of our population now and in the future will live in metropolitan areas, and serious population distribution problems exist in these areas. Accordingly, we also believe that new and better efforts must be made to plan for and guide metropolitan growth.

Cities, suburbs, small towns, and farms have all provided congenial environments for Americans. But, it may not be possible to accommodate every combination of tastes; it would obviously be impossible, for example, to combine Manhattan's high-density working environment with single-family suburban homes for all who now work there. Nevertheless, in the process of guiding population movement, we should seek to enhance choices of living environments for all members of society to the extent that is possible.

However, promotion of congenial environments and places of opportunity might well be meaningless for disadvantaged people who, because of physical remoteness and immobility, are often denied access to opportunities. A man in an isolated rural town finds it very difficult, if not impossible, to take advantage of a thriving job market in a city several hours away. Similarly, suburban jobs are often too many bus hours away for the central-city black to commute on a daily basis. Whether consciously imposed, or a side effect of a shift in the locations of employment opportunities, these physical barriers create socially destructive situations which need to be remedied. Whereas mobility often provides an avenue to personal welfare, immobility or restricted access denies opportunity. The Commission thus views the reduction of involuntary immobility and restricted choice of residential location as an important goal of any population distribution policy.

A dual strategy—of attenuating and simultaneously better accommodating current trends in distribution—would therefore have several goals:

To promote high quality urban development in a manner and location consistent with the integrity of the environment and a sense of community.

To promote a variety of life style options.

To ease the problems created by population movement within the country.

212

To increase freedom in choice of residential location.

To further these goals, the Commission recommends that:

*The federal government develop a set of national popula-
tion distribution guidelines to serve as a framework for
regional, state, and local plans and development.*

*Regional, state, and metropolitan-wide governmental au-
thorities take the initiative in cooperation with local governments, to conduct needed comprehensive planning and action
programs to achieve a higher quality of urban development.*

*The process of population movement be eased and guided
in order to improve access to opportunities now restricted by
physical remoteness, immobility, and inadequate skills, information, and experience.*

*Action be taken to increase freedom in choice of resi-
dential location through the elimination of current patterns
of racial and economic segregation and their attendant
injustices.*

In what follows, we describe the direction that we believe
distribution guidelines should take and specific actions to
carry out the above recommendations. Fuller and more refined
goals, policies, and strategies must be generated over time,
as we learn—through experimentation with alternative measures, through further research, and through continuous monitoring of trends—how best to influence the pattern that population redistribution takes.

GUIDING URBAN EXPANSION

The emergence of large regions of urban settlement requires that considerations about our environment and quality
of life be reconciled with the forces that propel urban growth.
How can we achieve more desirable patterns of growth than
previously enjoyed, secure ecological balance, enhance the

213

quality of life, and promote the ability of the poor and minorities to enjoy the opportunities of metropolitan areas?

In the 1960's, about 75 percent of national growth occurred within the boundaries of metropolitan areas as defined in 1960; most of that growth was suburban. In the future, regardless of public policy, an even larger portion of national growth is likely to be metropolitan. Accommodating future national growth, then, is primarily a job of accommodating future suburban growth and of sensibly guiding the transformation of currently rural territory to urban uses as metropolitan areas physically expand. How the character and form of the next generation of suburbs develops will play a large role in determining the quality of life of the vast numbers of Americans living in these areas across the country. Will their residents have access to open space, jobs, and community facilities? Will they live in an uncongested clean, environment? Will they be more satisfied in the new settlements than they are in the present suburbs?

The problems and possible solutions for promoting orderly urban growth are not new. Not long ago, the Douglas Commission on Urban Problems explored these questions in detail. Our Commission deals with these issues in recognition of the fact that the major portion of future growth will be metropolitan. As the scale of metropolitan areas increases, the importance of effective planning becomes even greater. While recognition of this need is not new, our findings suggest a degree of urgency not understood before. The territory of urban regions is expected to double between 1960 and 1980, and to grow at a slower rate after that. This means that the land we occupy in the year 2000 is largely being settled now. If we settle it badly now, we shall endure the consequences then.

To achieve effective planning and community development, we need not only more knowledge of how things might be made better, for much is known in this area, but also a new commitment on the part of government and the private sector to do things differently. Moreover, if we are going to achieve a high quality urban environment, marginal changes will not be sufficient. Local governments should broaden their interests and responsibilities beyond local parochial concerns and be responsive to metropolitan and regional objectives. Where necessary, the power of planning and implementation will have to be transferred to a regional or metropolitan-wide authority or government. The logical level from which to guide urban growth is the regional or metropolitan scale.

The interdependence of different aspects of metropolitan

214

areas is evident. The transportation system influences land-use patterns, which in turn influence housing patterns, which in turn influence transportation patterns, and so forth. The system of financing public services influences the quality of education which influences where people seek to live. The expanding employment in the suburbs affects employment patterns in the central city. Yet most local governments within metropolitan areas traditionally have planned with little regard for the effect of their actions on neighboring communities. Where a comprehensive approach has been taken by metropolitan or regional planning agencies, the results have largely been limited because of a lack of both funds and authority to establish priorities and enforce planning decisions. The increased complexity and scale make the continued fragmentary approaches to metropolitan planning and development progressively more costly and wasteful. This suggests that the basic responsibilities for planning settlement patterns, new public facilities, and public services should be at the metropolitan level. To encourage this comprehensive approach and local cooperation, the major portion of federal funds to support planning activities in metropolitan areas should go to the appropriate multi-purpose area-wide planning agency. These agencies, in turn, can support planning efforts for individual jurisdictions within the metropolitan area.

To anticipate and guide future urban growth, the Commission recommends comprehensive land-use and public-facility planning on an overall metropolitan and regional scale.

The quality of life in an urban area depends largely on how its land is used—the location and character of housing, the amount and accessibility of open space, the compatibility of adjacent land uses, the transportation system. Land-use regulations, principally zoning and subdivision regulations, are the chief government tools to influence local land-use patterns and the character of development.

In the past, these controls have been used by local governments largely to prevent undesired uses of land and to protect its market value. This approach has sometimes resulted in the exploitation of land for private gain instead of public benefit. Public objectives such as provision of open space or adequate low-income housing have often been secondary.

In addition, governments have had little control over the

timing of development. This has produced a haphazard pattern of development where land is jumped over when it is to the economic advantage of the developer, but not necessarily in the public interest. Land is wasted and the public provision of sewers, waterlines, and electricity becomes more expensive.

In order to promote environmental, social, and economic objectives, governments must begin to ask what the best use of land would be. New development should satisfy such public needs as ample open space and efficient and equitable transportation. It should not violate the environmental integrity or the social viability of the community. For example, developers should not be permitted to cut down valuable trees indiscriminately or skim off topsoil simply to reduce building costs. New concern for the relationship of land use to environmental quality suggests that this change in attitude has already begun. But, we still have a long way to go.

The Commission recommends that governments exercise greater control over land-use planning and development.

This could be achieved through: (1) early public acquisition of land in the path of future development to be used subsequently as part of a transportation system or for open space; (2) establishment of taxes and easements to influence the use of land and timing of development; (3) establishment of a state zoning function to oversee the use of the land; and (4) establishment of special zoning to control the development of land bordering public facilities such as highways and airports.

Suburban development need not have the sprawling, aesthetically monotonous character of many suburbs built during the 1950's and 1960's. The many amenities and public services now found in suburbia could be improved. This could be done at lower costs, while producing a more pleasing environment than would result if traditional practices were followed. With sensitive planning and development, new suburbs could encourage the sense of community now often lacking. Moreover, in an attempt to satisfy a diversity of preferences, a variety of living environments could be built, from low to high density, small town to cosmopolitan setting.

Although the conventional forms of suburban growth have been fostered by a variety of factors, the role of local zoning is prominent. Through lot-by-lot zoning, even those developers wishing to build comprehensive and imaginative developments encounter difficulty under the constraints of local zoning regulations and subdivision ordinances which designate

216

lot sizes, street frontage, house placement, and even the floor space of a house.

In contrast to the usual fragmented process of urban development, a large-scale approach presents more opportunity for experimentation and innovation in site design and the building of community facilities. Unless current zoning and subdivision regulations are changed, however, the potential opportunities offered by large-scale development will not be realized. Controls must be more flexible to permit new approaches to community development, such as substituting general development guidelines for specific zoning regulations. There is no guarantee that large-scale development will result in high quality. That will require cooperation between developers and government to ensure the promotion of public objectives. But large-scale development offers an opportunity to achieve a high quality living environment.

We are already seeing some of this in planned unit developments and new towns. Designers of planned unit developments are permitted greater flexibility in site design and freedom to combine building types. In return for freedom to disregard lot-by-lot zoning regulations, developers must satisfy requirements for the entire project, and proposed plans receive discretionary public review.

A more comprehensive and larger type of development is the new town or community. These larger developments can theoretically include all the facilities and activities of a city—including shops and offices, entertainment, and health centers. New towns usually are located either within the central city as a new town in-town, or at the periphery of a metropolitan area as a satellite city. They present the opportunity not only for comprehensive planning, but also for subsequent control of the location, timing, and sequence of land development.

However, innovation, even in planned unit developments and new communities, will be limited unless the federal and state governments provide some form of financial assistance to support experimentation. Though the form of assistance would have to be carefully determined, substantial support of experimentation, particularly when the techniques developed could be transferred to other areas, would seem very desirable.

Racial Minorities and the Poor

Historically, the cities of the United States have provided both social and economic advancement to the deprived. Disadvantaged immigrant groups have traditionally shed many of their problems by moving to the city. They have become part of the political, social, and economic life of the country. By and large, however, this process has not worked well for the blacks. Institutional racism has been more pervasive and persistent than earlier forms of ethnic discrimination, and serious inequities remain in education, housing, and employment. These inequities are continuing sources of social conflict, polarization, and isolation. As racial cleavages attain a geographic character, they can only aggravate existing social and economic distinctions. Until the restrictions on the movement of nonwhites to areas of opportunity—geographic as well as economic and social—are eliminated, their participation in society as full citizens will be incomplete.

Four years ago the National Advisory Commission on Civil Disorders said: "Our nation is moving toward two societies, one black, one white—separate and unequal." It added that "white society is deeply implicated in the ghetto." In the intervening years, little if any progress has been made to diminish the isolation of the disadvantaged. If there is any hope for a future where all people can realize common opportunities, the behavior, if not the attitudes, of whites and their institutions needs to be changed so they will no longer support racism.

Resistance to a geographically open society may not be as universal as newspaper headlines imply. According to the Commission's survey, only 26 percent of Americans believe that racial integration in the suburbs is proceeding "too fast," and 60 percent thought it was "too slow" or "just right." Furthermore, in a survey conducted for the Commission on Civil Disorders, nearly half of the black respondents preferred to live in a mixed neighborhood, another third did not care, and only 13 percent preferred all black or mostly black neighborhoods. These results can be viewed as a broad commitment of the black population to mixed neighborhoods.

To help dissolve the territorial basis of racial polarization, the Commission recommends vigorous and concerted steps to promote free choice of housing within metropolitan areas.

Even without further legislation, federal agencies could do much to promote housing integration simply by changing administrative practices. This would require that the federal government become more alert to local housing practices and establish an active program to guarantee local compliance with housing laws. An additional means for pursuing these objectives might be the establishment of institutions which could buy housing in white suburbs and subsequently rent or sell them to ethnic and racial minorities. Where such programs are already operating effectively, they should be expanded and strengthened.

The disparity between white and black incomes has obviously been caused by many factors operating over the years, not the least of which is discrimination. But perhaps because of discrimination, there are other contributing factors, such as differences in education and health, which would put blacks and other minorities at an occupational disadvantage even without racial discrimination in the labor markets.

To remove the occupational sources of racial polarization, the Commission recommends the development of more extensive human capital programs to equip black and other deprived minorities for fuller participation in economic life.

This will require a coordinated set of programs including education, health, vocational development, and job counseling. Greater communication and cooperation are needed among the various organizations—public, nonprofit, corporate —involved in these programs to make them effective.

Racial discrimination, inadequate training, and poor public services are only three of a variety of conditions which help perpetuate poverty in urban areas. An additional factor is specifically related to the location and types of jobs and housing available to blacks and the poor. Access to employment, particularly jobs offering opportunities for advancement, is often restricted not only by the inability of the poor to satisfy job requirements, but also the physical inaccessibility of many jobs. Blacks and the poor are, in part, locked out of jobs because they cannot get to the suburbs where opportunities open up. Reverse commuting can be expensive, time consuming, and difficult. Suburban housing, while closer to job opportunities, is often too expensive or simply unavailable because of racial discrimination.

While the absence in the suburbs of an adequate supply of low- and moderate-income housing available to all races is certainly not the sole or even the primary cause of unemployment or underemployment in the central city, it is a contributing factor which needs to be remedied.

To reduce restrictions on the entry of low- and moderate-income people to the suburbs, the Commission recom-

mends that federal and state governments ensure provision of more suburban housing for low- and moderate-income families.

At least two approaches could be used to increase the supply of suburban housing within the financial reach of low- and moderate-income families. First, ways could be found to lower the cost of some new or renovated suburban housing and still meet the requirements of standard quality housing. Second, families could be given some type of financial assistance to supplement the amount of money they can afford to pay for housing. But neither approach will succeed unless suburbs accept some responsibility to ensure that an appropriate amount of their housing stock is accessible to low- and moderate-income families. One would hope that this would be voluntary, and there are some signs that this is beginning to occur. But acceptance of this responsibility should be encouraged by federal, state, and local governments. For example, federal and state funds and grants could be made dependent on whether the locality fulfilled requirements relating to the amount of land or numbers of housing units designated for low- and moderate-income housing. Whatever methods are used, the increased supply of housing should be scattered throughout the suburbs to avoid a repetition of the economic and racial residential segregation now found in most metropolitan areas.

We must distinguish sharply the long-run national policy of eliminating the ghetto from a short-run need to make the ghetto a more satisfactory place to live. It is clear that improving conditions in the ghetto does not constitute an acceptable long-run solution to the racial discrimination which created the ghetto. But if we wait for the long-run solution, we shall bypass the present need for better schools, housing, public transportation, recreational facilities, parks, and shopping facilities.

These needs illustrate the imbalances between demands on government and resources available to meet them, which accompany the fragmentation of local government within metropolitan areas. These imbalances arise in large part because local public services depend so heavily on locally raised revenues produced by locally applied taxes (principally, of course, the property tax). The present situation invites, in fact encourages, income and racial segregtion between local communities—the flight of the well-to-do from cities to suburbs to which access is limited by zoning. It should not be surprising that people move with an eye to their economic

220

self-interest. A major part of the problem lies in a system that induces people—acting in their own self-interest—to act in such ways as to produce the collective consequences that we see when we examine the levels of segregation and disparities between needs and resources within metropolitan areas.

> *To promote a more racially and economically integrated society, the Commission recommends that actions be taken to reduce the dependence of local jurisdictions on locally collected property taxes.*

We recognize the complexity of trying to determine the best means of carrying out this objective and are not in a position to recommend one best alternative. However, any kind of tax program adopted should be progressive in nature and should provide for the distribution of revenues among jurisdictions according to need.

DEPRESSED RURAL AREAS

Rural-to-urban migration has left behind undereducated underskilled persons in locales that have fallen into economic and social decline.* This is not to suggest that all rural places are suffering from economic obsolescence. On the contrary, many small communities are viable and prosperous. But the economic development of the United States can be traced through the impact it has had on the distribution of population in this country. The decline of Appalachia and the growth of Texas reflect in part the shift from coal to gas and oil as sources of fuel. The shift from rural areas of the mid-continent and the south to metropolitan areas and the coasts reflect increases in the productivity of agriculture and the new dominance of distinctively urban occupations. Accompanying the ascendance of highway and air transport, we have seen the decline of the railroad town. In the process, many places have simply outlived their economic function. Their remaining residents are often ill-equipped to migrate or to cope with increasingly difficult conditions where they now live.

In chronically depressed areas, it may sometimes be true that the prudent course is to make the process of decline more

* A separate statement by Commissioner Alan Cranston appears on pages 272-273.

orderly and less costly—for those who decide to remain in such areas as well as for those who leave. This would hold true if economic analysis discloses that no reasonable amount of future investment could forestall the necessity for population decline as an adjustment to the decline in job opportunities. In that event, the purpose of future investment in such areas should be to make the decline easier to bear rather than to reverse it. In the process, we should ensure that communities that are losing population are still able to provide such basic social services as adequate education and health facilities. The educational needs of a community losing population, for example, may be no less than those in more favored communities. In fact, children growing up in declining communities may be faced with more difficult problems than children elsewhere, since many will choose to move to a new and unfamiliar area. Rural to urban migration of southern blacks might well have been more successful had they received quality education, training, and other vital services before leaving rural areas.

To improve the quality and mobility potential of individuals, the Commission recommends that future programs for declining and chronically depressed rural areas emphasize human resource development.

To enhance the effectiveness of migration, the Commission recommends that programs be developed to provide worker-relocation counseling and assistance to enable an individual to relocate with a minimum of risk and disruption.

Such programs should be designed to match an unemployed worker who is unable to find work locally with job opportunities elsewhere for which he is or can become qualified. Relocation counseling and assistance should not be designed to accelerate migration; rather, it should offer alternatives and facilitate the choice between remaining in a socially congenial and familiar location and moving to an economically healthier, if less familiar, place.

The program should include: (1) information about job opportunities in nearby urban centers; (2) pre-relocation supportive services, such as personal and family counseling; (3) employment interviews in potential destination areas; (4) coordination and assistance in the solution of problems involved in moving; and (5) post-relocation supportive services such as legal, financial, and personal counseling, and assistance to individuals and families in finding housing, schools and day-care facilities, and additional training opportunities.

In general, migration from declining areas is frequently ill-directed. It often involves a lengthy move to a distant city, with all the difficulties of adjustment. A superior approach may be to create new jobs nearer to or within the declining rural areas.

> *To promote the expansion of job opportunities in urban places located within or near declining areas and having a demonstrated potential for future growth, the Commission recommends the development of a growth center strategy.*

This strategy could be reinforced by assisted migration programs that would encourage relocation to growth centers as an alternative to the traditional paths to big cities. Growth centers could also provide many of those who are unemployed and underemployed in declining areas with an opportunity to commute to new or better jobs. In such circumstances, more effective employment could be achieved without altering the living environment. Equally important, such growth centers would provide alternative destinations for urban migrants preferring small town or city living.

The types of growth centers envisioned are expanding cities in the 25,000 to 350,000 population range whose anticipated growth may bring them to 50,000 to 500,000. Somewhat lower and higher limits should be considered for the sake of flexibility. Not every rapidly-growing city within this range should be eligible. Only those cities that could be expected to benefit a significant number of persons from declining regions, as well as the unemployed within the center, should be eligible. Thus, growth centers should be selected on the basis of commuting and migration data, as well as data on unemployment and job opportunities, and physical and environmental potential for absorbing more growth.

Some industries are already relocating in smaller communities which might be good growth centers. The reasons for this new trend in plant location are varied. Some firms are looking for a location removed from the problems of the big city, but which still has good access to a national market through the interstate highway system. Others may seek the type of labor force found in small towns as opposed to the central city. Whatever the reasons, the development has both positive and negative aspects. It usually means new jobs and prosperity for the small town. But by virtue of relocating, a company

223

may leave behind scores of former employees who are at least temporarily unemployed. Recognizing the inadequacy of existing knowledge about this trend and its potential importance for policy, the Commission believes that a thorough examination of this trend should be an important part of future research in regional development policy.

Implementation of a growth center program will not be easy. In recent years, the federal government has pursued, with only limited success, a growth center strategy through programs administered by the Economic Development Administration, the Appalachian Regional Commission, and a number of other regional commissions. Both economic and political constraints have seriously hampered program effectiveness. Further research, substantial increases in funding, and better focusing of investment are clearly needed for such a policy to succeed. Many questions concerning the criteria for selecting growth centers and the most efficient tools to stimulate growth are yet to be answered. A difficult problem will be to avoid unnecessary subsidies for places whose future growth requires no additional stimulus. Moreover, the policy must avoid catering to the industries and interests that profit from growth per se, as distinct from the region-wide interest in building a sound and diversified urban economy. Care must also be taken to avoid simply relocating industries from one area to another, and thereby possibly aggravating the problems of some areas while mitigating those of others. A growth center policy, misdirected, could inadvertently produce overurbanization, or merely represent a transfer, not a reduction, of national problems.

It will be some time before the effectiveness of a growth center policy is known. In the meantime, this policy seems to be a promising way to improve the quality of life for residents of declining and depressed areas. Moreover, this policy can be made consistent with a goal of providing migrants with alternative destinations to large metropolitan areas. In doing so, a growth center policy will also help improve the quality of life in larger metropolitan areas by reducing the migrant-generated pressures on them.

INSTITUTIONAL RESPONSES

These policy guidelines and recommendations chart broad directions for new initiatives. Their specific features should be developed on a regional and local basis, because the problems and possibilities differ for each urban region or metropolitan area. Attempts to take such initiatives, however, are inhibited by the absence of adequate guidelines for translating them into forceful and coordinated action. The necessary first steps are to determine the appropriate role each level of government should have in facilitating and guiding population movement and distribution, and to create an institutional framework to develop and carry out these policies.

Federal

Formulation of overall policies relating to the distribution of population and economic activity must be carried on at the federal level. Indeed, this responsibility was clearly enunciated in Title VII of the Housing and Urban Development Act of 1970. Title VII provides for the development, at the federal level, of a national urban growth policy to encourage desirable patterns of urbanization, economic growth and development of all types of communities. Congress further stated:

> ... better patterns of urban development and revitalization are essential to accommodate future population growth; to prevent further deterioration of the Nation's physical and social environment; and to make positive contributions to improving the overall quality of life within the Nation.

In the Act, Congress calls this policy a national urban growth policy. We believe the policy should be a coordinated set of guidelines to serve as a framework for regional, state, and local plans and development. They should not be restricted to either urban- or growth-related issues, but instead, should apply to the full range of population distribution issues relating to rural and urban people and areas, and conditions of population decline and stabilization, as well as growth. With this in mind, a more appropriate designation would be national population distribution guidelines.

The recent completion of the first *Report on Urban Growth*, as required under Title VII, can only be considered the initial step in developing national population distribution guidelines. It will be some time before these guidelines are well enunciated. And it is likely that they will be continually evolving as conditions change and understanding of the redistribution process grows.

In the meatnime, the federal government should establish a continuing effort to learn more about population movement and distribution and to begin to shape national population distribution guidelines.

Among the important functions which should be a part of this continuing effort are:

To develop goals, objectives, and criteria for shaping national population distribution guidelines.

To anticipate, monitor, and appraise the distribution and migration effects of governmental activities that influence urban growth—defense procurement, housing and transportation programs, zoning and tax laws, and so forth.

To develop a national land-use policy which would establish criteria for the proper use of land consistent with national population distribution objectives and guidelines.

To provide technical and financial assistance to regional, state, metropolitan, and local governmental agencies concerned with planning and development.

To coordinate the development and implementation of a growth center policy.

The delegation of these functions to specific federal organizations is discussed in Chapter 16.

State

At the state level, planning and development agencies should take an active role in the development and implementation of policies to facilitate orderly and high quality urban development. State government is close enough to metropolitan and other urban areas to be aware of their problems. In addition, the power of zoning and other land-use regulations resides with the state. State government, then, is in a strategic position to develop policy guidelines for future development and to coordinate local and metropolitan plans with state development plans. This suggests the need for effective state planning offices.

In addition to better and more active planning at the state level, state development agencies may be desirable to implement development plans on a broad geographical basis. To function effectively in such a role, these agencies must have broad powers to acquire land, to override local ordinances, and actually to carry out development plans.

While the need for such organizations is gradually being recognized, only New York State has actually established one. In its first years of operation, the Urban Development Corporation showed that it can be an effective mechanism, particularly for improving housing opportunities for low- and moderate-income families. It is also committed to actively promoting orderly urban development and is currently involved in the development of several new communities throughout the state. The early success of the Urban Development Corporation, and its promise for effectively guiding orderly urban development, suggests that it would be a good model for other states.

The Commission recommends the establishment of state or regional development corporations which would have the responsibility and the necessary powers to implement comprehensive development plans either as a developer itself or as a catalyst for private development.

Local

A Commission concerned with the impact of population growth must comment upon those features of society which make growth troublesome or not. The point applies as well to population distribution as to growth. And the point is nowhere better illustrated than in the effects of metropolitan growth and expansion, occurring in the context of a fragmented structure of local government. It is obvious that this structure makes regional problems—relating to land use, transportation, the environment, and so forth—extremely difficult to manage, and that, for this reason, reorganization of government in metropolitan areas is long overdue. Moreover, given the heavy reliance of local jurisdictions on locally collected property taxes, the very structure of local government in metropolitan areas influences the way population is distributed. It provides incentives for people and activities to segregate themselves, which produces disparities between local resources, requirements, and levels of service, which in turn invite further segregation.

Perhaps the most important institutional response needed to achieve the objectives and recommendations suggested above is some restructuring of local governments. The number of overlapping jurisdictions with limited functions and the fragmentation of multi-purpose jurisdictions need to be reduced. The responsibility and power to serve the various needs of the metropolitan population should be assigned to the most appropriate level of government. Governmental organization will vary in different locales depending upon existing governmental structures, social and political traditions, urban problems, and specific objectives to be accomplished by reorganization. In some areas, a single metropolitan-wide government might be most appropriate. In others, a two-tier system—such as the one in Toronto, Canada—might be most effective. There are many ways to assign specific governmental functions, services, and taxing powers within a metropolitan area. Functions such as transportation planning and air pollution control belong at the metropolitan level; others, such as the operation of neighborhood health centers, may require closer community accountability, best accomplished within smaller jurisdictions.

The need for reorganizing local governments has been recognized for some time, and there are signs that it is beginning to occur. Increasing awareness of the metropolitan implications of urban problems is leading to more cooperative efforts to achieve area-wide coordination of governmental activities. The federal government has initiated some efforts to encourage this change, but change is slow in coming.

The Commission urges that federal and state governments take action to rationalize the structure of local government. This could be done through encouraging metropolitan areas to examine the effect of their current governmental structure and to determine ways that it might be improved. In addition, federal and state governments could establish requirements or incentives to encourage existing metropolitan-wide agencies, such as councils of governments, to expand their scope of activities, powers, and responsibilities. Or, metropolitan areas could be required to adopt new jurisdictional arrangements as a prerequisite for receipt of funds.

Apart from their stated objectives, governmental activities at all levels often have unintended and contradictory effects on population distribution. Whether building highways, guaranteeing mortgages, or modifying zoning and tax laws, government policies and actions affect population distribution and movement and alter the intricate system of incentives that attracts the private sector. The absence of deliberate policies

228

merely invites hidden ones whose effects may or may not be desirable. Indeed, a 20th century de Tocqueville reviewing these activities could easily mistake inadvertence for perverse design.

It is imperative that public policy take serious and deliberate account of population distribution—the way distribution is affected by policy, and the way it affects policy outcomes.

CHAPTER 15. POPULATION STATISTICS AND RESEARCH

The content of a population policy cannot be immutable, but will need to be adjusted over time in the light of emerging developments, increased knowledge, and changing attitudes of both government and the general public. Thus, the Commission sees national population policy as an evolving rather than a static instrumentality, whose development and implementation are continuing processes. A nation must observe changes in the number and distribution of its population, evaluate these changes, attempt to affect them in ways that will be useful, measure the impact of steps taken, and adapt and redefine the issues to fit the course of the future that it seeks.

Viewed in this fashion, a policy program represents a course of conduct that requires a continuing feedback of information and appraisal to produce an intelligent and responsive program as experience grows. Statistics provide the descriptive element of the universe of policy concerns; research provides the analytical insight into causal relationships and consequences of the phenomena that statistics reveal and measure. Both statistics and research must underlie the formulation of policy and the design and evaluation of programs.

Public policy in regard to population cannot be intelligently conducted in the absence of timely statistics of high quality on a broad range of subjects. This Commission has received excellent cooperation from the federal statistical agencies, but all too often what they could offer was inadequate to the task.

We have reviewed the principal shortcomings in population statistics for the United States. In doing this, we have sought to anticipate statistical needs for the evolution and modification of public policy in the field of population. We believe our recommendations—building on the considerable strengths of our present statistical system noted in the recent report of the President's Commission on Federal Statistics—will provide a sound information base for public policy in the population field.

Our statement of information needs is conditioned by the fact that national population policy touches every sector of the population—geographic, ethnic, social, and economic. Since the total effect can be obtained in many different detailed ways, it is upon the details, rather than just upon the net result, that the process must be appraised. The overall result is, of course, important. It matters whether the nation's population grows rapidly or not; but it matters, perhaps even more, what the components of that growth are—whether changing fertility, mortality, or migration—and where and in what groups the changes are occurring.

The fund of information needed for such appraisal is large, and not cheap to obtain. However, it is basically the same fund that is essential if the entire array of government programs—local, state, and national—are to be well-designed and well-administered. Such programs involve the commitment of almost unbelievably large sums in the fields of health, welfare, education, housing, urban planning, transportation, and the whole gamut of economic planning. Small gains in the efficiency with which such funds are ultilized would quickly more than repay the costs of collecting and analyzing the needed information.

Thanks to this larger significance of the nation's information base, we have no reluctance in recommending strongly the enrichment of our knowledge on the social and economic side of demographic questions as we have done elsewhere on the biomedical side. In both statistical and research programs, we put a high priority on observance of the respondent's privacy, on the use of sampling where it can be substituted for complete enumeration, and on the timeliness, comprehensiveness, and reliability of the data.

The Commission recommends that the federal government move promptly and boldly to strengthen the basic statistics and research upon which all sound demographic, social, and economic policy must ultimately depend, by implementing the following specific improvements in these programs.

VITAL STATISTICS DATA

At present, there is a minimum two-year delay in the publication of final and detailed data on births and deaths. In spring 1972, the most recent detailed vital statistics available were for 1968. This delay has done much to reduce the value of the information collected because all major analyses of trends in fertility and mortality at the national and local, socioeconomic and racial levels are dependent on these detailed tabulations. Moreover, the detailed tabulations furnish indispensable raw materials for the construction of intercensal estimates of the changing population of regions and localities.

Also needed is the modernization of both birth and death certificates to improve the identification of the social, economic, and medical situations of individuals and families and, in the case of births, to improve the analysis of their timing by collecting information about the intervals between births.

For marriage and divorce, only the number of total events is collected from all of the states. The registration system which provides details about the location and characteristics of the individuals involved covers only 40 states and the District of Columbia in the case of marriage, and 29 states in the case of divorce. On these subjects, we have about the poorest statistics of any advanced country.

The Commission recommends that the National Center for Health Statistics improve the timeliness and the quality of data collected with respect to birth, death, marriage, and divorce.

More particularly, the National Center for Health Statistics should:

1. Aggressively pursue its "catch-up" program for the processing of birth and death registration statistics, aiming at the earliest practicable date to achieve reporting of detailed data for each year within six months following the close of that year, and move toward quarterly processing and reporting of these data on a flow basis. Eventually, the same goals should be sought for the reporting of marriage and divorce.

2. Explore the development of a system for priority sampling of birth certificates on a current flow basis that would permit the calculation and reporting of fertility rates specific

for age and other characteristics more promptly than is permitted by even the best possible system for processing the entire mass of data.

3. Undertake a crash program to qualify all states to participate in the marriage and divorce registration area; to institute follow-back surveys for samples of marriages and divorces, such as the present natality and mortality follow-back surveys; to develop information sources on family formation and dissolution, and the fertility and other demographic consequences of family dynamics.

4. Enrich our data about the social, economic, and ethnic factors related to births, deaths, marriages, and divorces.

5. Modernize the birth and death certificates.

ENUMERATION OF SPECIAL GROUPS

Population counts are the subject of considerable controversy about the correct number of blacks and persons of Spanish origin in the population. Incomplete enumeration not only hampers the analysis of our changing demographic situation, it also reduces the claims, especially of our poorest populations, for the many local, state, and federal programs to which funds are allocated on the basis of population counts.

The Commission recommends that the federal government support, even more strongly, the Census Bureau's efforts to improve the completeness of our census enumeration, especially of minority groups, ghetto populations, and all unattached adults, especially males, who are the least well counted.

INTERNATIONAL MIGRATION

Immigrants now contribute one-fifth of our annual population growth. Yet when this Commission tried to find out what becomes of immigrants after they arrive, what kinds of communities and neighborhoods they go to, the jobs they get, the incomes they earn, their marriage and childbearing patterns and subsequent mortality—in other words, how immigrants are fitting into our society and what kind of impact they have—

we could learn very little. Nor could we obtain any but the crudest estimates of the number of Americans emigrating from this country, or the coming and going of civilian citizens. And usable figures on illegal immigration are nonexistent.

The Commission recommends that a task force be designated under the leadership of the Office of Management and Budget to devise a program for the development of comprehensive immigration and emigration statistics, and to recommend ways in which the records of the periodic alien registrations should be processed to provide information on the distribution and characteristics of aliens in the United States.

A mid-decade census containing information on year of immigration has a potentially large contribution to make in this connection.

THE CURRENT POPULATION SURVEY

Jointly sponsored by the Bureau of the Census and the Bureau of Labor Statistics and administered since the late 1930's by the Census Bureau, the monthly Current Population Survey has developed into the nation's principal instrument for providing information about changes in the characteristics of the nation's population between the censuses. By reaching a sample of some 45 to 50 thousand dwellings, it provides precise national estimates, not only of the labor force and employment status, but also information about the socioeconomic characteristics of households and individuals. It also provides usable estimates for geographic divisions and for the larger states and metropolitan regions.

Procedures should be developed to provide more precise information on geographic location, both for the current residence of those interviewed and for the prior residence of persons who have moved. It should be possible to distinguish with reasonable precision such categories as urban versus rural, inside versus outside the central city, and residence inside versus outside incorporated places.

A program of supplementary surveys, including occasional selective supplementation of sample size, should be generated to provide socioeconomic and other data for special groups of the population, such as Spanish-Americans, and for special types of communities whose characteristics make them important for questions of population distribution. The survey should also be liberally employed to ascertain trends in fertility rates and internal migration.

The Commission recommends that the government provide substantial additional support to the Current Population Survey to improve the area identification of those interviewed and to permit special studies, utilizing enlarged samples, of demographic trends in special groups of the population.

STATISTICAL REPORTING OF FAMILY PLANNING SERVICES

The public investment in and commitment to family planning services require the earliest possible development of a comprehensive program of family planning statistics. As a first step in this direction, the National Center for Health Statistics initiated, in January 1972, a national reporting system for family planning services provided in clinics. Coverage includes patients receiving services supported through the family planning project grants funded by the Department of Health, Education and Welfare and the Office of Economic Opportunity, and the nonfederally funded Planned Parenthood programs.

The national reporting system could potentially include all patients to whom family planning services are provided. Accordingly, all government statistical programs on health services which could provide statistics on family planning services should do so. Only when all patient contacts are included can truly national statistics be developed.

The National Center for Health Statistics should take the leadership in the development of uniform statistical definitions and standards for a coordinated federal-state-local system.

The Commission recommends the rapid development of comprehensive statistics on family planning services.

NATIONAL SURVEY OF FAMILY GROWTH

Achieving a policy on population growth and implementing the nation's commitment to family planning assistance will require a flow of data regularly available, at comparatively brief intervals, on factors influencing fertility, such as desired family size, birth-spacing intentions, family planning practices, and the home, neighborhood, and socioeconomic environment of family growth and family-growth decisions. The feasibility of such work has been demonstrated in a series of surveys undertaken since 1955 by private organizations. The National Center for Health Statistics now proposes a biennial survey of family growth for a substantially enlarged household sample to improve the accuracy and scope of national estimates. Funding for preparatory work has been approved, and the National Center for Health Statistics plans to undertake the initial survey of family growth in late 1972.

The Commission recommends program support and continued adequate financial support for the Family Growth Survey as almost the first condition for evaluating the effectiveness of national population policies and programs.

DISTRIBUTION OF GOVERNMENT DATA

Inevitably, formally published tabulations of governmental data cannot begin to exhaust the information contained in complex collections. At present, invaluable stores of information are never used. Computer technology now makes it possible to issue identity-free tapes of such data designed to meet the needs of particular research projects, thereby greatly multiplying the value of the stock of information, while guarding the rights of the individuals who provided it.

The Commission recommends that the various statistical agencies seek to maximize the public usefulness of the basic data by making identity-free tapes available to responsible research agencies.

237

MID-DECADE CENSUS

Our decennial censuses, together with our vital and migration statistics, provide the materials for developing quite accurate annual estimates of the nation's total population classified by age, sex, and race. They are wholly inadequate, however, to permit the construction of annual estimates for regions, states, and local areas, or to portray the intercensal social and economic status of the nation's constituent populations. The interval of 10 years between censuses—a leisurely pace established in the 18th century—is simply too long in view of the high mobility of our people. Under the best of circumstances, annual local estimates will be difficult to obtain, but the problems would be greatly reduced if the intervals between the total counts were five rather than 10 years. In addition, while sample surveys provide national data between censuses, decentralized decision making at the state and local level requires that these areas have reasonably current, detailed, quality data about their own areas. Only a national census (incorporating sampling principles as appropriate) can provide such data, because it alone can provide the standardization of content, definitions, and processing procedures which guarantee that a statistic for one place means the same as a statistic for another place.

The Commission recommends that the decennial census be supplemented by a mid-decade census of the population.

STATISTICAL USE OF ADMINISTRATIVE RECORDS

The addition of the county of residence to the information reported on the individual income tax return, and the inclusion of this entry in the taxpayer's identification file, would materially assist in the solution of problems now encountered by statistical agencies attempting to use taxpayer residence changes in the estimation of internal migration. Similarly, the Social Security Administration could greatly assist in estimating interstate and inter-area migration if its identity-deleted

238

one-percent sample of social security account holders were increased to a 10-percent sample.

> *The Commission recommends that the government give high priority to studying the ways in which federal administrative records, notably those of the Internal Revenue Service and Social Security Administration, could be made more useful for developing statistical estimates of local population and internal migration.*

INTERCENSAL POPULATION ESTIMATES

Close local and federal cooperation is essential for the construction of adequate annual estimates of population. Local people have special access to local data, but the problems of coordinating all the local estimates to state, regional, and national totals must be solved at the national level. The fund of professional experience for technical aid on methodological problems is also best located at the national level. The Census Bureau's program for local population estimates should be expanded to encompass annual estimates for all congressional districts, all metropolitan areas, and all cities and counties having 25,000 or more inhabitants. The Census Bureau's resources for developing, testing, and experimenting with improved sources and methods for population estimates should be expanded, and this support should also include resources for gaining access to, extracting, and processing relevant information from administrative records of federal, state, or local governments, such as tax records, school enrollment records, and the like.

> *The Commission recommends that the government provide increased funding, higher priority, and accelerated development for all phases of the Census Bureau's program for developing improved intercensal population estimates for states and local areas.*

SOCIAL AND BEHAVIORAL RESEARCH

The Center for Population Research of the Department of Health, Education and Welfare has responsibility for promoting and guiding research in both the biomedical aspects of reproduction and contraceptive development and in the social and behavioral concerns of population. The Center's role in the first area is acknowledged and reasonably well-developed. Social and behavioral research has not been given equal emphasis. This is perhaps because of a bias imposed by location of the Center within the National Institutes of Health. However, since the mandate of P.L. 91-572 includes investigation of the social and behavioral aspects of population, there is no reason that the Center or its successor, given adequate leadership and staff, cannot support a sufficient program in these areas as well.

Another reason that social and behavioral research has not been sufficient has been the general scarcity of funds for all types of population research. In fiscal year 1972, only $6.7 million of the $39.3 million spent on population research was devoted to behavioral aspects. Recent estimates are that federal support for social and behavioral research in population should be increased over the next several years to a total of about $50 million annually.[1] (See Chapter 11 for discussion of research into methods by which individuals may control their fertility.)

Research is needed on a broad range of topics in the behavioral sciences to develop the knowledge required for the formulation of population policy objectives and effective means to achieve them. A major component of this research must be directed toward increasing our knowledge of the effects of population changes on the many factors that determine the quality of life in the United States, such as economic growth, resources, environmental quality, and government services.

Since the effects of population change are diffuse and pervasive, the research questions are numerous and varied. The many gaps in our knowledge are abundantly clear in this Report. Many others are reflected by, and indicated in, the background papers commissioned for this Report, which will be published in several volumes.* The following paragraphs are intended only to illustrate the research needed.

Research on the consequences of population change must deal not only with population size and rates of change, but also with childbearing patterns (as reflected in ages at marriage and parenthood, lengths of intervals between births, and so forth), changing age composition, shifting geographic distributions, changing patterns of metropolitan and nonmetro-

* A list of these papers appears in the Appendix of this Report.

politan residence, increasing scales of social organization, density, and the like.

Studies should not be limited to "macro" phenomena, but should also explore the consequences of population dynamics at the family and individual level. For example, an important set of problems involves the immediate and long-term consequences, to mothers as well as children, of births to unmarried women. Other questions requiring investigation deal with the effects of family size and child-spacing patterns on the health and development of children.

The consequences of various migration patterns are of great importance to our society. For example, how do movements from rural to urban areas affect the quality of public services available in areas of origin and destination? How do great increases in the number of people in a jurisdiction affect the relationship of the citizen to his local government? How do various patterns of residential use affect the physical environment? What are the likely consequences of projected population decline in many metropolitan areas, associated with national population stabilization? Without answers to many of these questions, it is difficult to formulate reasonable policy objectives, either locally or nationally.

Also within the field of population distribution, research is needed which more clearly differentiates the factors perpetuating residential segregation. Racial discrimination is clearly an important factor, for even when economic differences between races are taken into account, residential segregation persists. Prejudice is not the only manifestation of racial discrimination. There are also institutional barriers which operate to keep racial minorities segregated residentially. These barriers need to be specified and their effects understood.

Another broad area of research requiring further development involves the determinants of population trends. Knowledge of the causes of population change is needed to permit the formulation of population policies that have a reasonable chance of helping us to achieve our objectives. For example, at the present time, it appears that if all couples had effective control of their fertility, we might achieve fertility rates consistent with the replacement, rather than the continued increase, of our population. However, we do not know whether current family-size preferences will change, and we know little about what causes these preferences to change. Following World War II, the United States, as well as a number of other developed countries, experienced a substantial rise in fertility after a century of decline. We understand very little about

241

why this happened, and we cannot be certain that a similar phenomenon will not occur again.

At the family and individual level, much more needs to be known about the factors affecting the control of fertility. We know, for example, that strongly motivated couples can limit their fertility with relatively ineffective contraceptive measures. On the other hand, even when highly effective measures are available, some couples have several unintended conceptions. There are many theories about the factors affecting success or failure in the control of fertility, but little solid knowledge.

An important area of research must involve the family as a dynamic institution. Not only do specific families change through the years, but the meaning and the functions of the institution itself change. Since population phenomena (births, deaths, and migration) inevitably involve the family, a major emphasis on the family is necessary in any research on the causes and consequences of population change. This will also necessarily lead to research on the changing roles of women in our society and the effects of these changes on the family and on reproduction.

Finally, increasingly important areas of research involve studies of the effectiveness of governmental programs and policies that affect population change. Of major importance now are family planning services. To what extent are they reaching the people who need them? To what extent are they helping couples to achieve their family-size and child-spacing goals? Do they affect the contraceptive practices of couples who no longer use the services offered? Beyond family planning, there are policy questions affecting fertility, migration, and mortality. For example, to what extent do various income-maintenance programs influence family-size and migration patterns? How do agricultural programs affect rural-urban population movements? How do family life education programs affect premarital sexual behavior and decisions to marry? The questions seem varied and unlimited, but research must begin to explore them if we are to learn how current and future programs and policies will affect the quantity and quality of our population.

The research needed in the social and behavioral sciences will require the expertise of many disciplines: demography, sociology, economics, anthropology, psychology, history, geography, and political science. To encourage and facilitate such research on population problems, a number of interdisciplinary population research centers should be supported in universities and other nongovernmental centers. In fiscal year 1972, federal support for such centers was only $1.5 million. Estimates are that about $11.5 million should be made available annually for this purpose within the next five years.[2] With the concerted efforts of scientists in such centers and elsewhere, we can build a solid foundation for intelligently dealing with population-related problems in our society.

The Commission recommends that substantial increases in federal funds be made available for social and behavioral research related to population growth and distribution, and for the support of nongovernmental population research centers.

RESEARCH PROGRAM IN POPULATION DISTRIBUTION

A center or sponsoring organizational unit and a funded research program should also be developed for those studies of population distribution needed for policy formation and program guidance in the fields of housing, urban and economic development, and transportation. The research program of this center should be carefully coordinated with the program of the Center for Population Research, which should continue to have responsibility for the general research on questions of population distribution and migration. The most abysmal ignorance exists concerning the nature and effects of changes in the population size of regions and communities in relation to economic, social, and governmental institutions and processes, and to the physical, human, and environmental factors of life. Yet hundreds of millions of dollars are spent on programs directly influencing them in the fields of transportation, housing, and community and regional development. There is an urgent need for the development of research capability for understanding how population redistribution affects government activities as well as how government programs affect population distribution.

The Commission recommends that a research program in population distribution be established, preferably within the proposed Department of Community Development, funded by a small percentage assessment on funds appropriated for relevant federal programs.

However, the establishment of this research program should

243

not be dependent upon the creation of the Department of Community Development. The Department of Housing and Urban Development has requested funds to begin such a program. We believe it should be initiated as quickly as possible.

FEDERAL GOVERNMENT POPULATION RESEARCH

In the economic field, the federal data-collection agencies have for years been conducting highly useful research and analytical work that has been widely used in the development of national policy. This is not so for federal demographic and social statistics. Here, most data-collection agencies have research programs dealing with their own techniques of collecting and processing data. This is necessary but not sufficient. To exploit adequately their special skills and knowledge, these agencies should also have staff and resources devoted to research that utilizes the data they produce and relevant data from other sources as well. A small but successful example is the Office of Health Statistics Analysis in the National Center for Health Statistics. Funding should provide core support for the agencies' own research work and for the grant and contract funding of projects that serve to stimulate the agencies' own work.

The Commission recommends that the federal government foster the "in-house" research capabilities of its own agencies to provide a coherent institutional structure for improving population research.

SUPPORT FOR PROFESSIONAL TRAINING

Finally, it should also be noted that the very large expansion of research and statistical work that has already taken place in the demographic field, not to mention that still to come, is creating heavy demands for able and highly trained personnel. The situation is extremely tight and inevitably will become worse unless strong measures are taken to increase the supply. Meanwhile, there are training facilities that suddenly have few students because of the curtailment of governmental support in spite of the continuing demand. Several years from now, if support for graduate training does not become available, there will be an even greater shortage of skilled personnel.

The Commission recommends that support for training in the social and behavioral aspects of population be exempted from the general freeze on training funds, permitting government agencies to support programs to train scientists specializing in this field.

CHAPTER 16. ORGANIZATIONAL CHANGES

A paradox exists within the federal government with regard to population. Although many departments and agencies administer programs which influence and are influenced by population growth and distribution, these subjects have not, until very recently, been of specific concern to either the executive or legislative branches. This Commission has made a number of recommendations directed toward: (1) increasing public knowledge of the causes and consequences of population change; (2) facilitating and guiding the processes of population movement; (3) maximizing information about human reproduction and its consequences for the family; and (4) enabling individuals to avoid unwanted fertility.

Many of these recommendations require governmental action, and some can be carried out by existing structures. But, in many cases, the recommendations illustrate the need for changes in governmental structure in order to acknowledge and deal with population issues, and to conduct research, develop policy, and administer programs more effectively. In addition, legislative review of population-related programs needs to be improved. We believe that both the executive and legislative branches of the federal government must give greater attention to population-related issues and programs.

The Commission recommends that organizational changes be undertaken to improve the federal government's capacity to develop and implement population-related programs; and to evaluate the interaction between public policies, programs, and population trends.

OFFICE OF POPULATION AFFAIRS, DEPARTMENT OF HEALTH, EDUCATION AND WELFARE

The Department of Health, Education and Welfare was the first federal agency to begin giving serious attention to population-related problems and is the major locus for both family planning services and population research. In 1967, the Secretary appointed a Deputy Assistant Secretary for Population and Family Planning. Subsequently, the title was changed to Deputy Assistant Secretary of Population Affairs. P.L. 91-572, passed in 1970, requires the Deputy Assistant Secretary to administer all family planning service and population research programs of the Department, provide and support training of personnel, serve as a clearinghouse for information, provide liaison with other agencies of the federal government that have responsibilities relating to family planning services and population research, and coordinate other Department of Health, Education and Welfare programs that relate to these fields.

During consideration of P.L. 91-572, the Department announced that, in addition to the proposed statutory powers, the Deputy Assistant Secretary would have line authority over the contraceptive evaluation program of the Food and Drug Administration, responsibility for preparation and presentation of budgets for family planning services and population research, and adequate staff to carry out his responsibilities. This authority would be exercised through two officials selected by the Deputy Assistant Secretary and who would have dual appointments within the Department. One would be named as an Assistant Director of the National Institutes of Health for Population Research, and the other as an Assistant Administrator of the Health Services and Mental Health Administration for Family Planning Services. Both would also serve as special assistants to the Deputy Assistant Secretary. Most of these arrangements have not yet been carried out.

Recently, the Secretary of the Department of Health, Education and Welfare gave the Deputy Assistant Secretary for Population Affairs overall departmental responsibility for coordinating population education. As yet, however, there is no staff and only a small budget has been requested to carry out this program.

We believe that creation of the position of Deputy Assistant

248

Secretary and the Office of Population Affairs was a step toward giving population-related programs in the Department the overall direction and coordination which they need. Although there has been some progress in this direction, it has been limited by failure to carry through on the specified arrangements.

We recommend that the capacity of the Department of Health, Education and Welfare in the population field be substantially increased by strengthening the Office of Population Affairs and expanding its staff in order to augment its role of leadership within the Department.

NATIONAL INSTITUTE OF POPULATION SCIENCES

As we noted earlier, the financial commitment to population research is not sufficient to deal with the problems presented. The Commission believes that the institutional framework for the population research program is also inadequate.

The primary focus of the federal population research program is the Center for Population Research—an operating unit of the National Institute of Child Health and Human Development. The Center supports research in the development of new contraceptives, the medical effects of existing methods of fertility control, and the social and behavioral aspects of population change. Although creation of the Center was a worthwhile development in 1968 when the government was first beginning to acknowledge the need for population research, the program has now outgrown this organizational arrangement.

In addition to population research, the National Institute of Child Health and Human Development houses research programs in aging and early childhood development. Both of these are important fields, requiring significant research efforts, but population research has been growing at a much faster rate than the other two programs. This results in two problems. First, advocates of research in aging and early childhood development believe that population research is being advanced at the expense of their programs. Second, administrators of the Institute have felt it necessary to maintain some balance among its programs. This appears to be at least part of the reason why population research has not been funded at its authorized levels. If all of the funds recommended by this Commission for population research in fiscal year 1973 were approved, it would be funded at a level greater than the other programs combined. It is apparent that the additional large increases recommended by the Commission for ensuing years will be difficult if not impossible to achieve under the present arrangement. All three areas of research—aging, early childhood development, and population research—could benefit from moving the population research program from the National Institute of Child Health and Human Development.

A greatly expanded and more focused population research effort is needed. In addition to strengthening programs in basic and applied reproductive research and evaluation of contraceptives, the behavioral research program must be significantly enlarged. In addition, the population research program must have the prestige to attract the very best investigators.

Creation of a separate institute should provide a stronger base from which this increased effort can be directed. It would facilitate acquisition of qualified personnel, laboratory and clinical space, and other resources necessary for a diversified research program. It would increase the visibility of the population research program, signal to the world that it ranks high among our research priorities, and should help in commanding the level of funding that we believe is necessary but which has not been forthcoming.

We therefore recommend the establishment, within the National Institutes of Health, of a National Institute of Population Sciences to provide an adequate institutional framework for implementing a greatly expanded program of population research.

DEPARTMENT OF COMMUNITY DEVELOPMENT

Programs affecting population distribution are scattered throughout the government. For example, the problems of growth and development of urban, suburban, and rural communities are closely related but, depending on their size, communities that seek help for planning and constructing public facilities must deal with one or more of three different departments that support these activities.

We believe it is necessary to make organizational changes

250

to coordinate and, in some cases, consolidate existing urban and rural development programs and provide a locus for the studies of population growth and distribution necessary for policy development and program implementation in the areas of housing, economic development, transportation, and other related fields.

Congress is currently considering legislation that would establish a new Department of Community Development.* Under this proposed reorganization, a single federal department would administer the major programs of assistance for the physical and institutional development of communities— for planning and building houses, for supporting public facilities and highways, and for strengthening state and local governmental processes. Among the programs which the reorganization would move to this Department would be all of the programs of the Department of Housing and Urban Development (except for the college housing program); the highway construction and mass transit programs of the Department of Transportation; the rural electrification, public facilities, and housing programs of the Department of Agriculture; the programs of financial and planning assistance for public works and development facilities (except business development) of the Economic Development Administration of the Department of Commerce, and that Department's Regional Action Planning Commissions; and the Community Action and "special impact" programs of the Office of Economic Opportunity.

This proposal is one of four submitted by President Nixon for reorganization of the federal departments. Each of them raises a great number of issues that are not our concern and on which we are not qualified to comment. However, from the perspective of better facilitating and guiding population distribution, coordination and consolidation of urban and rural development programs is essential. The proposal for the Department of Community Development does not include a specific provision for the increased research in population growth and distribution which we feel is necessary for adequate policy formulation and program development within its areas of concern. This should be provided for in the new Department.

We therefore recommend that Congress adopt legislation to establish a Department of Community Develop-

* A separate statement by Commissioner Alan Cranston appears on page 273.

ment and that this Department undertake a program of research on the interactions of population growth and distribution and the programs it administers.

There are other functions necessary to the formulation of a coherent national development policy which we believe cannot be handled adequately at the departmental level, but require a higher level of authority and perspective. These are discussed in the next section.

OFFICE OF POPULATION GROWTH AND DISTRIBUTION

Our government has no explicit population policy. Federal programs generally operate without regard to their effects upon population growth and distribution or how shifts in population patterns affect programs. The Commission believes that population-related factors must be given much more weight in the future development and implementation of a variety of federal policies and programs. Moreover, the content of a population policy would not be inflexible, but would need to be adjusted over time in the light of emerging developments, increased knowledge, and changing attitudes of both policy makers and the general public. To accomplish this requires much more than strengthening the Office of Population Affairs within the Department of Health, Education and Welfare or establishing a Department of Community Development. What is needed is an organizational unit with the ability to take the broadest possible view of population issues, to transcend individual departmental points of view, and to develop and formulate coherent population policies. This can be done most effectively from the Executive Office of the President which is able to coordinate the activities of all departments. This new office should:

Establish objectives and criteria for shaping national growth and distribution policies.

Monitor, anticipate, and appraise the effects on population of all governmental activities—including health, education, and welfare programs; urban and rural development programs; defense procurement policies; and tax laws—and the effect that population growth and distribution will have on the implementation of all governmental programs.

Provide for the review, integration, and coordination of population programs, giving consideration to the role played by nongovernmental resources and institutions.

Assume responsibility for preparation and submission of the biennial *Report on Urban Growth* required by the Housing Act of 1970.

Assist state and other units of government concerned about population matters in dealing with their problems.

In order to carry out effectively the monitoring of federal policies for their effect upon growth and distribution, the office should have the power to require, from federal agencies, statements indicating that an agency has given consideration to possible population-related effects of proposed programs and how programs in operation have affected population growth and distribution.

The Office should report to the President and the Congress annually. There should be an Advisory Committee composed of experts in various population-related fields, representatives of interested groups, and other citizens. It is essential that such an office be provided with the staff and funds necessary to carry out this range of activities. To create an office within the Executive Office of the President, and then require it to rely upon staff work from other federal agencies would hinder drastically the development of the broad and impartial perspective that is needed.

We therefore recommend the creation of an Office of Population Growth and Distribution within the Executive Office of the President.

There are a number of advisory bodies within the Executive Office of the President that have broad reponsibilities over other areas of concern. These agencies have not, in the past, given sufficient consideration to the effects of demographic variables on the nation's economic, social, environmental, and scientific life.

We therefore recommend the immediate addition of personnel with demographic expertise to the staffs of the Council of Economic Advisers, the Domestic Coun-

cil, the Council on Environmental Quality, and the Office of Science and Technology.

COUNCIL OF SOCIAL ADVISORS

Two years of study and deliberation have demonstrated to us that population is intimately tied to numerous social issues. Yet, innumerable social programs are undertaken by the government each year without having any of the overall direction that we have imposed upon our economic and environmental activities. The Council of Economic Advisers and the Council on Environmental Quality keep the President and the public informed of the effects of public needs and policies with regard to the economy and the environment and recommend programs to assist economic growth and stability and to preserve the environment. The Commission believes that population and related social matters require the same level of attention.

We therefore recommend that Congress approve pending legislation establishing a Council of Social Advisers and that this Council have as one of its main functions the monitoring of demographic variables.

If this legislation is passed, if the Council is adequately funded and staffed, and if it shows that it will give proper consideration to population problems, then it could and should take over the functions and role of the Office of Population Growth and Distribution.

JOINT COMMITTEE ON POPULATION

Congress has been the arm of government most interested in population problems. It was the hearings conducted by Senator Gruening, beginning in 1965, that first focused public attention on the need for federally subsidized family planning and population research programs. The urban growth policy provisions of the Housing Act of 1970 were a congressional initiative, and several bills urging the establishment of a Commission on Population were introduced in Congress as early as 1967.

However, jurisdiction over population-related programs is scattered among many committees of Congress. The P.L. 91-572 family planning services and population research programs are within the purview of the Interstate and Foreign Commerce Committee of the House of Representatives. But family planning services authorized by the Social Security Act and the Economic Opportunity Act fall under the jurisdiction of the Ways and Means and the Education and Labor Committees respectively. Housing legislation is handled by the banking committees of the House and Senate, while transportation is the concern of the commerce committees. It is impossible to combine jurisdiction over the many issues relating to population under one committee. However, if congressional review of population matters is to be most effective, some focal point within Congress is necessary. One committee should have responsibility for studying issues from the perspective of their effect upon population growth and distribution, for spotlighting problems, and for reviewing the implementation of federal programs in these areas.

In order to provide improved legislative oversight of population issues, the Commission recommends that Congress assign to a joint committee responsibility for specific review of this area.

STATE POPULATION AGENCIES AND COMMISSIONS

Many of the recommendations of this Commission require action by state and local governments. However, only a few states have agencies which give serious attention to the problems of population growth and distribution. One example of high-level attention to state population problems is the recent report and recommendations of the California State Assembly Science and Technology Advisory Council.

Only one state, Hawaii, has established a population agency, and it is temporary. A poll conducted by the State of Hawaii Commission on Population Stabilization showed that 22 states have no specific agency concerned with these problems. In most of the remaining states, population is the concern of planning, resource, or environmental agencies. However, in responding to the Hawaii poll, 27 states indicated that they considered population growth a problem; four states viewed population loss as a problem; and 12 states responded that distribution is a problem, including six which define the problem as one of both growth and distribution. Forty-one states reported that they would like to meet with representatives of other states to discuss population and what might be done at federal and state levels to influence growth. This interest and concern should be stimulated.

The Commission recommends that state governments, either through existing planning agencies or through new agencies devoted to this purpose, give greater attention to the problems of population growth and distribution.

PRIVATE EFFORTS AND POPULATION POLICY

We have taken the position that population growth, size, and distribution are too important to be left to chance in the formation of public policy, and that they require a continuing and conscious effort by government to assess the demographic impacts of alternative policy proposals. We believe that population problems are complex, that they are and will continue to be of critical importance to American society, that we are only in the beginning stages of learning how to deal with these problems as a matter of conscious policy and programming, and that these problems will require sustained attention over a period of years.

To maximize the government's ability to cope with population issues requires that the private sector use its independence and flexibility to facilitate policy formation. This may be done through policy-oriented research and analysis, monitoring and assessing change, education and training, and communication of the results of these processes to relevant publics. The private institutions which currently have some relationship to population policy include universities, voluntary and professional organizations, citizens groups, private corporations, and private foundations. The normal interests of these institutions, individually or collectively, do not presently ensure an adequate overall private effort.

For example, the normal interests of discipline-oriented academic institutions do not necessarily assign priority to studies essential to policy formation. Even when academic research produces findings directly relevant to policy formation, they

256

are often not made available in forms which are understandable to and usable by policy makers. Many critical policy-related studies in the last decade did not emerge as planned products of the academic research on which they were based, but rather as a result of reanalyses stimulated by groups closer to the policy-formation process.

Similarly, universities and other institutions which have as their primary focus the population problems of developing countries do not have the funds and personnel to be effective in policy formation at home. Domestic population questions are complex enough to require full-time concentration and commitment, free of pressure from other priorities.

This concept of private support for research and policy development has been utilized to deal with other issues. For example, several independent organizations are devoted to research, education, and publication in the field of economic policy. Among their purposes are aiding the development of sound public policies and promoting public understanding of issues of national importance. There is no reason to specify an exact organizational model for activity required in the population field, but we are at a stage of development in this area where major privately funded activities in development of population policy are required.

We therefore recommend that a substantially greater effort focusing on policy-oriented research and analysis of population in the United States be carried forward through appropriate private resources and agencies.

SEPARATE STATEMENTS

Separate Statement of Marilyn Brant Chandler

Beyond my own personal feelings, I oppose open abortion on demand and support limited therapeutic abortion laws for the following reasons:

1. The Commission report does stress that abortion should not be a substitute for birth control, but has not intimated that liberal abortion takes the responsibility away from sexual activity. Impulsive, irresponsible sexual involvement can be rationalized without fear of pregnancy if abortion is open, legal, and free.

2. My pragmatic feeling is that the United States is not ready for abortion on demand because:

Government agencies and politicians shy away from the issue.

Fifty states have 50 differing laws, though this is wrong, for laws should be uniform across the nation. These differing laws will take a long time to change. States will adopt a therapeutic law before adopting an open law.

Abortion is still a major moral issue.

Our Commission's public opinion poll indicates that, though 50 percent were pro-abortion on a patient-to-doctor relationship, the other half approves it not at all or half-heartedly.

Title X of the Public Health Service Act and the Economic Opportunity Family Planning Act will not fund or support abortion.

Conflicting state and federal court interpretations on the legal right of a fetus will not be resolved until a nationwide law or court decision is passed.

Until public opinion conclusively fights the strong groups opposing open abortion, the American Law Institute model presents a more acceptable alternative than open abortion.

261

This model, admittedly, has deficiencies in defining the mental health of a woman or in its egalitarian selection. However, I advocate therapeutic abortion on the basis that: (1) abortion is a decision between woman and physician; (2) it is approved by a hospital committee; (3) it is performed in a hospital or accredited clinic; and (4) the limit for the gestation period does not exceed 18 weeks.

Separate Statements of Paul B. Cornely, M.D.*

Legal Impediments for Minors

The recommendation that contraceptive information and services be made available to minors is indeed objectionable when it is applied to all minors. There is no question that this should be so in reference to those who are acknowledged to be emancipated minors, such as married teenagers or self-supported ones who may be living within or outside their parents' home. In this instance, the same guidelines and safeguards which have been noted for family planning services should apply. It should be voluntary, with due consideration given to the religious beliefs and culture of the individual; supporting services such as counseling and social service should be available; emphasis on privacy, consideration and the dignity of the individual should be always present; and there should be ease of accessibility for everyone.

On the other hand, when we as a society accept the responsibility of giving contraceptive advice and services to those who are minors living in a family unit, then we are striking at the foundation and roots of family life, which are already weakened by our misuse of affluence and technology. First of all, it should be stated that the age of menarche or beginning of menstruation is continually going downwards, so that today it is about 12.5 years. The implications of this are indeed obvious and need not be belabored. What is of greater importance is that our society has the responsibility to provide the kind of family life, education, neighborhood, recreational facilities, and creative outlets which would make it possible for all minors to live in an environment which would be conducive to the growth and development of the child which is due him. If this affluent society cannot do this, then it has failed miserably and does not deserve to continue to exist.

* See also concurrence with statement of Commissioner Otis Dudley Duncan on pages 274-275.

Contraceptive approach to minors is the cheapest and most irresponsible way for our society to solve this problem.

Abortion

The majority's recommendation that a nationwide abortion-on-demand law modeled after the New York State statute be adopted cannot be supported. Abortion in the opinion of this Commissioner is destruction of human life since it kills the fetus; and society through its laws has a responsibility to protect all human life. Support for this concern can best be expressed by discussing some of the issues raised in this section.

The Law: The argumentative posture of these paragraphs is exclusively that of the pro-abortionists, namely, that abortion legislation has been no more than a health measure postulated on the welfare of the *mother* only. This section of the report does not even make an attempt to provide a legal accounting for the unborn developing child.

The Moral Question: This section of the report proposes that only *one* moral principle be the controlling factor in the abortion situation: the woman's freedom to reproduce. Such moralistic monism, simplistic as it is, at bottom fails to consider the freedom of the unborn child to live. Overall, the arguments of this section would make some sense if the topic was a woman's right to use preventive contraceptive methods.

For all its language about moral sensitivities, the text seems completely oblivious of the fact, much less the implications, of defining a segment of humanity as "unwanted." The Commission does not face the question: What does it mean as public policy to legitimate the destruction of "unwanted children"?

Public Health: The report overrates the problems of illegal abortions as much as it overrates the feasibility of unrestricted abortion laws to solve what problems there really are. Most of the data cited in this section of the report come from New York City, and are based on a limited experience. This is concerned almost exclusively with the *short-range* effects of abortion on the mother's health (at that, there is no way of following up on the out-of-staters). The data from Russia, Eastern Europe, and Japan on the negative *long-range* effects of abortion on a woman's reproductive system are ignored.

It also should be noted that the overall maternal death rate, even with the presence of restrictive abortion laws, has been steadily declining for years. The role of positive maternal health care has been overlooked.

The *complete failure* to consider even the massive destruction of developing fetal life as some kind of balancing factor in public health is but an indictment of the myopic point of view of this section.

Family Planning: The report ignores the evidence in England, Japan, and the Eastern European countries that the easy availability of abortion destroys motivation to have consistent recourse to preventive contraception methods. As the text reads, the Commission would be saying that it believes that the transition from the abortion mentality to the preventive contraceptive mentality could be achieved by the simple presence of adequate contraceptive technology. If such would be the case, this would be the first time in human history that technology has ever solved a specifically human problem. This faith in technology is hardly justified, either historically as regards technology or specifically as regards family planning.

Demographic Context: It is highly ironic that a Commission concerned with population policy should settle for the kind of scattered information that is available regarding the demographic impact of abortion, yet would recommend unrestricted abortion as public policy. In this section, the Commission, practically writes off the demographic impact of abortion as a significant issue for the United States.

Population Stabilization

This Commissioner is one who identifies with the third position in Chapter 1 and firmly believes that population growth is indeed not the major problem in our society and that, of more import, is the need for a radical rearrangement of our values and priorities as well as the relationship of man to himself, of men to each other, and to the earth from which we sprang. As Rene Dubos stated in a speech which he made before the Smithsonian Institution on October 2, 1969, entitled "Theology of the Earth," the first chapter of Genesis tells man and woman to replenish the earth and subdue it; but of more importance is the second chapter wherein man is instructed to dress and keep the land. This means that man must be concerned with what happens to the land and its resources.

It is of particular importance to keep this in mind because, many times throughout the Report of the Commission, the need to speak in terms of statistics about people, rather than about people themselves, may leave the impression that human beings are looked upon as things or chattel which can be equated in terms of numbers or quantities; what it costs to produce them; what is the supply and demand; and how they can be moved or rearranged.

This then brings me to the recommendation of this chapter on population stabilization. I voted for it, but I would not want anyone to believe that the phrase, "the Commission recommends that the nation welcome and plan for a stabilized population," is intended to mean that I would support any national or state governmental policy or regulation which would in any way interfere with the desires, aspirations, and needs of any family concerning its size or number. For our government to interfere with this sacred trust given to each family would be to bring Orwell's 1984 prediction closer to reality. My intent is expressed by the following statement of goals by the Commission: . . . creating social conditions wherein the desired values of individuals, families, and communities can be realized; equalizing social and economic opportunities for women and members of disadvantaged minorities; and enhancing the potential for improving the quality of life.

Separate Statements of Alan Cranston

I agree with most of the views expressed in the final version of the Commission Report. Many of my early concerns over specific portions of prior drafts were eliminated in later revisions. But, as with the other Commissioners, my concurrence in this Report should not be interpreted as meaning that I necessarily agree with every statement or always with the wording chosen. I do want to make the following comments on the views expressed by the Commission on a few specific substantive points.

Resources and the Environment

I agree with the conclusion reached in this chapter that a lessening of population growth will buy us some time in the struggle to maintain a livable biosphere. The Commission's mandate was to study the effect of population growth on our environment and natural resources, and the models on which its studies were based emphasize the population factor. Those reading the Report should keep this in mind.

The Report argues that continued population growth inevitably speeds up the depletion of natural resources and requires rapid technological development—to meet the ever-increasing demand for goods and services—all of which increases environmental pollution.

Proceeding from this assumption, the Report attempts to show the impact of population on the environment by "using a quantitative model which shows the demand for resources and the pollution levels associated with different rates of economic and population growth." If the Commission's use of this quantitative model—appropriate for the Commission's function—were to be misunderstood, unintended and unjustified conclusions could be drawn from it about the Commission's view of the relationship between population growth and environmental degradation.

This bears clarification, for, in *The Closing Circle,* Barry

Commoner comments on the danger of this kind of approach to the environmental problem:

> This approach, it seems to me, is equivalent to attempting to save a leaking ship by lightening the load and forcing passengers overboard. One is constrained to ask if there isn't something radically wrong with the ship.

His point is well taken.

Population pressures did not lead soap manufacturers to switch to detergents.

Population pressures did not lead farmers to the use of pesticides and chemical fertilizers. -

Population pressures did not lead our cities to the abandonment of public transit systems nor to our public's dependence on the private automobile.

Population pressures did not develop the too-big and too-powerful American automobile.

Population pressures did not bring about the switch to flip-top beer cans and nonreturnable bottles.

Population pressures did not fill our homes with myriad electrical gadgets.

Most of our environmental disasters have been the technological successes of an economic system where the goal is to use technology to maximize profit.

The ecologically unsound technological developments of the past two decades would have created the environmental crisis even if the population had been stable during that period.

The final few pages of Chapter 4 tend to balance out the preceding emphasis on population as the cause of environmental deterioration. However, the Report states that: "Population growth is clearly not the sole culprit in ecological damage." I would like to point out the population growth is not the major culprit, either. The major culprit is the manner in which we use, control, and evaluate our technology.

Slowing population growth will give us time to reevaluate and change our technology, but it cannot substitute for the changes which must be made if we are to survive.

Population Education

The Commission recommends enactment of a Population Education Act and presents a persuasive case for a greatly enlarged federal effort. I was the Senate author of both provisions in the present law cited by the Commission dealing with federal assistance in the development and implementation of population education programs, materials, and curricula—in the Family Planning Services and Population Research Act (P.L. 91-572) and in the Environmental Education Act of 1970 (P.L. 91-516). As Chairman of the Special Subcommittee on Human Resources of the Senate Labor and Public Welfare Committee, I also conducted oversight hearings on the Administration's failure to implement these programs.

But I am not at present certain in my own mind whether it would be more appropriate to achieve our ends legislatively by amending existing laws or by enacting an entirely new statute.

Legal Impediments for Minors

The Commission recommends the elimination of legal barriers to, and the establishment of, programs for the distribution of contraceptive information and services to all, including unmarried teenagers. I support fully the Commission's purpose: to eliminate the suffering which an unwanted birth often produces both for mother and child. The means of implementing the Commission's recommendation that such information and services should be provided without parental consent to unmarried teenagers living in the home concern me, however.

I do not believe the Commission has placed sufficient stress on the role and responsibilities of parents regarding the provision of birth control information and services. Although I believe appropriate discussion of reproduction, birth control, and venereal disease should be included in the basic school curriculum for adolescents, I also believe it would be a mistake to place our principal emphasis on that method of education. Society and schools should make every effort to encourage child and parent to discuss these matters honestly and openly. Our educational programs should stress this.

I have similar concerns about medical authorities providing contraceptive services to unemancipated teenagers without parental consent or knowledge. I strongly believe that it should be the obligation of the health professional to counsel the unemancipated teenage patient to raise this issue with his or her parents. Nonetheless, despite my serious concerns on this question, I concur that it is poor public policy for pregnancy to be treated as a kind of moralistic punishment for what some may consider promiscuous sexual behavior.

269

Abortion

Although the Commission expresses strong concern—which I share fully—over the danger that abortion may be used as a means of birth control, the Commission also recommends the adoption of state laws permitting abortion upon a pregnant woman's request, provided it is performed by licensed physicians under conditions of medical safety.

I am unable to join in this recommendation because I hesitate to endorse governmental sanction of the destruction of what many people consider to be human life. I am particularly concerned by the social and ethical implications of such action now, given the general atmosphere of violence and callousness toward life in our society and in our world. Ours has become an incredibly violent time. Our people are involved in acts of violence both in our streets and in Southeast Asia. Meanwhile all mankind exists under the dark shadow of the strategy of nuclear terror with its threat of sudden death for all of us.

Has life ever been held more cheaply? Has there ever been greater indifference to the taking of life? Are we really aware of just how hardened we have become?

I wonder if, in this atmosphere, we are capable of making a wise decision on this issue involving our very attitude toward human life. Perhaps we should wait for a more compassionate and less callous time.

I want to make it plain that I recognize the inconsistencies and inequities involved in many existing state laws permitting abortions for "therapeutic" reasons. They have the effect of depriving low-income persons of equal access to medical procedures readily available to the more affluent. Such laws, along with the even more restrictive or prohibitive laws in some states, result in utter tragedy for women who, unable to afford travel to another state or abroad to obtain an abortion, turn in desperation to illegal abortions and suffer butchery that often destroys both the fetus and the mother.

I understand and respect the view that many people hold that abortion is fundamentally a question of a woman's inherent right to control her own body. But I also understand and respect the view of many others that a second body also is involved—a human fetus. And, as I have indicated, I am concerned about the effect of all this on still a third body—our society itself.

Illegal Aliens

The Commission recommends that Congress enact legislation to impose civil and criminal sanctions on employers of illegal border crossers or aliens who are in an immigration status which does not authorize employment. Such a statute would, in my judgment, impose on employers an onerous burden of having to ascertain in fact whether each individual is in a proscribed category. This could very well have a chilling effect on hiring in international border areas, thereby seriously jeopardizing employment opportunities for Mexican-Americans.

Only in the case of an employer who knows or has clear reason to know that an employee is within a proscribed category would I favor imposition of any criminal or civil penalty.

One burden I would place on the employer is that he inquire about the citizenship of each prospective employee. If the applicant states he is an alien, the employer should require submission of evidence of lawful admission for permanent residence or of authorized employment status. (I note that section 14 of S. 1373, currently pending before the Senate Committee on the Judiciary, contains such a provision. Also, a law recently enacted in California as section 2805 of the Labor Code penalizes employers who deprive lawful residents of jobs by knowingly hiring illegal aliens.)

I think we need to find better ways of halting the employment of illegal aliens, while at the same time not imposing onerous or counterproductive burdens or restraints on employers. Two that I am considering are:

1. Requiring that Social Security cards issued to aliens be of a different color, or in some way clearly distinguishable, from those issued to citizens. (We would need to make sure, however, that citizens are not unreasonably put to great trouble in producing evidence of citizenship in order to secure a Social Security card.)

2. Requiring each prospective employee to complete a non-notarized affidavit form regarding his or her United States citizenship. Material false statements would be punishable under the Federal False Statements Act.

It is important that in coping with the employment of illegal aliens, we consult with those population groups most directly affected. It is equally important that we do not choose a remedy that imposes special burdens on any geographical, ethnic, or racial group.

271

Depressed Rural Areas

In discussing the goals of our population policy as it relates to migration and economically depressed rural areas, concepts such as population maldistribution and the need for population dispersion take on real meaning only after careful analysis of the economic and social consequences of the changing structure of the agricultural industry. However, I wish to make certain observations about what *causes* people to leave rural America.

Of the 5.5 million individual farms that existed in 1950, only 2.9 million remain today. If present trends continue, there will be fewer than two million farms in 1980. In other words, 900,000 farms will disappear in the span of just eight years. Some 900,000 farm families will be forced to seek their livings outside of farming—often in already overcrowded urban centers where they are ill-equipped to compete in a job market that requires skills and training unacquired in rural life.

The structure of modern agriculture is changing dramatically. Twenty to 30 years ago, the rural landscape was dotted with family farms and small, thriving communities. Today, small farmers are being blown off their land by the winds of economic and technological change. Farms are increasingly large-scale and mechanized; the farming industry is increasingly dominated by giant corporations and conglomerates that buy up prime farmland and seek the total vertical integration of the industry from "seedling to supermarket." The production, processing, marketing, and distribution of agricultural commodities are increasingly controlled by huge corporate entities that have little, if any, stake in the rural community. With an economic base that is primarily urban, these agri-industries siphon off what few economic resources are left in rural America.

The Commission's statement that "many places have simply outlived their economic function" could be interpreted as an acceptance of the myth of the inevitability of bigness of agriculture. The unfortunate reality is that corporations and conglomerates are moving into farming not because smaller units are inefficient, but because present federal policies are encouraging these entities to diversify into agriculture by providing them with tax benefits and other economic incentives. Their presence in agriculture—and the nonfarm resources they control—make it virtually impossible for the independent farmer to compete successfully, even though he is likely to be the more efficient farmer.

If we are to discuss maximizing freedom of choice about where an individual wants to live and work—and I believe such freedom is essential—we must make it possible for the independent farmers and businessmen of rural America to survive economically. As the Commission notes, we must build up the economic and social base for the maintenance of rural communities so that people have a real choice about where to live and to work. We must also resist the temptation to assume that we can revitalize rural America only by bringing in new industry. Although rural communities desperately need infusion of new capital, industrialization alone will not provide jobs and economic stability there in a manner consistent with environmental and social quality.

It is vital that we examine these issues in more detail if we are to develop and implement viable national policies and priorities that can achieve a better rural/urban population balance.

Department of Community Development

The Commission recommends that Congress enact legislation to establish a Department of Community Development to undertake, among other things, research on the interactions between population growth and distribution, and the programs such a Department would administer. I agree that this research is necessary. An administration bill, S. 1618, to establish such a Department, is pending before the Senate Committee on Banking, Housing and Urban Affairs, of which I am a member. But until I am able to resolve all the difficult issues involved in creating this super-Department—including the implications of removing the community action program from the Office of Economic Opportunity—I believe it would be premature for me, as a member of the authorizing committee, to join in this Commission recommendation.

Separate Statement of Otis Dudley Duncan, concurred in by Paul B. Cornely, M.D.

We inquire what is the effect of a growing population on a "healthy economy." But the majority of the Commission, no doubt wisely, did not care to inquire into what may constitute "health" in regard to an economy. We accept projections to the effect that, three decades hence, "the average individual's consumption is expected to be more than twice what it is today" without inquiring whether a doubling of consumption every 30 years be a sign of "health," or, perchance, of some disease whose horrors will only be disclosed to us by degrees. The Commission cannot plead that the proper questions were not raised before it, for they are trenchantly stated in the paper, "Declining Population Growth: Economic Effects," prepared for the Commission by J. J. Spengler. I wish to conclude this statement with a quotation from Spengler's paper:

> Today it is assumed that the economic circle can be squared; for . . . it is supposed that a society may have guaranteed full employment, price-level stability, strong producer pressure groups (trade unions, business and agricultural groups, government employees), and freedom from direct economic controls. In reality, of course, it is impossible for these four objectives to be realized simultaneously; only two, possibly three, are compatible. The policies driving the American economy are much more directionless than those which animate the Strassburg goose and the Sumo wrestler to eat continuously, the one to become liver pâté and the other to "belly" one of his kind from the ring; for this economy, with its momentum based upon destruction of a finite earth's depleting resources, neglects the fundamental requirement for survival, namely, conducting its affairs in keeping with an infinite time or planning horizon.

Ultimately, attainability of a population goal compatible

274

with the finiteness of that part of the biosphere accessible to the American people turns on what happens in the moral realm—on determination of the content of this goal and construction of a penalty-reward system calculated to make the goal realizable. Market forces alone cannot assure its realization, for the reasons that make exchange, though the main organizing principle, inadequate without appropriate institutional and legal underpinnings. A population goal cannot be settled upon in isolation, but must be viewed as one of a set of interrelated goals, the attainability of any one of which turns on the weight attached to other goals within the framework of a finite physical as well as social environment.

Separate Statements of John N. Erlenborn

Child Care

In this section, the Report recommends a universally available child-care system. In the sense that the Commission holds voluntary participation to be essential, the Commission's position that participation in a child-care program not be a condition for other governmental assistance is not inconsistent. What is difficult to reconcile is the contention that a child-care system affords opportunities for learning, development, and companionship; but government should not require the people it supports to utilize these opportunities. These are the very people who, through little fault of their own, are otherwise isolated from these advantages and, as a consequence, from the mainstream of society. Thus, they are the very people who have the most to gain from exposure to child-care programs, but who may, understandably, be the most hesitant and apprehensive about volunteering.

In fairness to them, I believe they deserve priority in any child-care system financed by the federal government. In fairness to those who pay the bill for any government-sponsored program, I believe the government has the responsibility to set conditions which attempt to assure fulfillment of the program's goal. This should be no less true in the case of the welfare program, where one of the goals is to assist people in finding a meaningful and contributory niche in society, than it is in any other program.

All this is not to say I am prepared to support the Commission's recommendation for government to subsidize—beyond the tax relief recently enacted—a comprehensive child-care program of sufficient proportions to accommodate all those who want to participate. If the demand for child-care service continues to grow—and that seems to be the sign of the times —I believe those who want it should be willing to pay for it, if they can.

I am also convinced that pre-kindergarten education should

276

not be established as a separate federal school system, but should be integrated with other private and public education.

Children Born out of Wedlock

I agree with much of the analysis presented in this section on the need to reduce the social and moral stigma attached to children born out of wedlock. It is no fault of the child that the circumstances of his birth may have been deemed irregular by society. Thus, anything that this Commission's recommendations can do to reduce or eliminate the social and moral stigma is appropriate.

I am not, however, similarly convinced that the legal ramifications of the distinction between legitimacy and illegitimacy have been fully analyzed by the Commission in sufficient depth to enable it to recommend that the legal status of a child born out of wedlock be the same as a legitimate child. The purpose of the legal discrimination was not, as the Commission states, to protect the sanctity of family and discourage extramarital sex, so much as it was to clarify and make more certain the inheritance of property and the rights of individuals to legally obligate others. Even if the purpose had been to protect the family and discourage extramarital sex, the fact that the goal has not been realized causes me to argue against the relaxation of restrictions; it could easily be argued that the restrictions should be tightened, not weakened. By analogy, one could also argue that since laws against murder have not eliminated murder, they should be abolished.

The examples cited in the Report of reductions of discrimination only point out the complexities of the matter. For example, the amendments to the Social Security Act recognize, appropriately, certain conditions such as contributions to the support of the child by the father or a court decree identifying the father as a necessary precondition, a substitute, if you will, for marriage, "legitimizing" the status of the child. Unless there is some overt act of assumption of responsibility, the distinction is not removed.

Because of the complexities of the matter, I can agree that research and study by the American Bar Association, the American Law Institute, and other groups concerned with state laws are appropriate. I cannot, however, join in the Commission's recommendation that all legal distinctions between legitimate and illegitimate children be eliminated.

Women: Alternatives to Childbearing

Throughout this section, there runs the refrain that our primary object and goal is to provide greater freedom to the individual in society. In urging the adoption of the Equal Rights Amendment, the Commission may be inciting the substitution of greater regimentation and control rather than encouraging the expansion of individual freedom.

We are a pluralistic society. The vitality, the experimentation, the openness of our society is directly attributable, I believe, to the fact that we are free to march to the tune of different drummers. To force our citizens into a straitjacket of conformity and sameness would stultify individuality and undermine freedom. Yet I believe that in the name of equality such a course of action is being proposed here.

Women have been discriminated against in employment, in education, in legal arrangements, and in family relationships. I do not question this. To employ a blunderbuss, through enactment of the Equal Rights Amendment or the anti-sex-discrimination amendment to the education laws, however, can harm as many or more than it can help; and there is a better way to put an end to discrimination against women.

Wherever discrimination exists which deserves government action to overcome it, efforts should be made—and are being made—to provide remedies through measured steps, where facts are gathered, causal relationships established, and the margin for serious error reduced. In the enactment and now the strengthening of the Equal Employment Opportunity Act, this has been done. Similarly, it appears that both Houses of Congress have agreed upon the need to eliminate clearly illogical and harmful sex discrimination in the areas of vocational education and graduate higher education. Correctional action is also being taken to equalize the property rights of women and their status as heads of households.

The goal of the Equal Rights Amendment is to eliminate distinctions between men and women in the law, but there can be distinction without discrimination. Treating people differently, respecting their individual needs and desires, looking upon them as unique human beings—not as a part of a statistical herd—is not discrimination. Treating everyone alike, regardless of their preferences, however, is all too often discriminatory.

Many women find enjoyment and gratification in remaining home, being mothers, and rearing children. Eliminating laws

278

which protect that status is every bit as discriminatory as any efforts to impose such a status or role. Adoption of the Equal Rights Amendment, in particular, would not only have this effect, but would tie the hands of Congress and the people in efforts to recognize the uniqueness of individuals and their right to pursue their own objectives.

For over a century, organized labor has struggled to obtain protections for women who must or who choose to work. I would assume that, if polled, most women would elect to preserve these safeguards. Yet that which took many years to obtain would be undone overnight if the Equal Rights Amendment were adopted.

Serious erosion to individual freedom is also threatened in the area of education through either the enactment of the Equal Rights Amendment or legislation that permits the federal government to write admission policies where discrimination based upon sex has not been proven to exist. While no one can tolerate the denial of the opportunity for an education or fair consideration for employment in the field of education, the fact is that the great strength of America's educational system since the founding of the nation has been its freedom from government dictation and control. Diversity and autonomy have been its hallmarks. This has included the establishment of a variety of options which have been made available to students, ranging all the way from totally one-sex schools to equally balanced coeducation.

The organization of education has been based on that which is best educationally for the individual, not on what mathematical ratios dictate. To prohibit such diversity and autonomy through the imposition of uniform requirements would constitute a clear and present threat to our educational institutions.

In graduate, professional, and vocational education, and even in some of our public undergraduate schools, the evidence is clear that discrimination—not diversity—exists. This should be corrected, and corrective legislation is in the offing. However, we have seen no indication that those who seek an education at other levels and in other areas are prevented by reason of sex from attaining their goal.

While figures on elementary and secondary education are unavailable, the record discloses that, in undergraduate education, females continue to represent a larger percentage of total enrollment, increasing from 31.7 percent in 1946 to 41.1 percent in 1970. For first-time undergraduate enrollment, the percentage increased from 28.3 percent in 1945 to 44.7 percent in 1970. In these same years, females represented

56.8 percent and 50.5 percent of the number graduating from high school.

In sum, the fault I find with any remedy that attempts to cure a variety of ills with a single stroke of the pen is that it ignores the individual, removes the good with the bad, and erodes principles which only peripherally touch upon the ills at which the remedy is directed. Overall, the effect is to discriminate where discrimination does not exist, and to restrict rather than to free. I believe these pitfalls are inherent in the Equal Rights Amendment and the recommendation that the federal government direct the admissions of our elementary and secondary schools as they relate to sex. Specific legislation to correct proven problems will permit us to avoid these pitfalls.

Legal Impediments for Minors

I am compelled at the outset in commenting on this section to offer an observation: I do not believe the Report is proposing that contraceptive devices be sold through vending machines in school corridors, and I hope it will not be so construed.

As to contraception, the law, and minors, I wish the Commission had applied an age qualification to the term minor. Even so, I cannot join in the Commission's recommendation that all legal restrictions on access to contraceptive information and services should be eliminated to permit minors, youngsters under the age at which they are legally responsible for themselves, unlimited access to contraceptives and abortions.

As I have stated elsewhere, the goal of increasing the quality of life should not be paramount to the sanctity of life. The exercise of any right in excess can lead to license.

Throughout this report, the emphasis on the rights of the individual is used to justify increased individual freedom and responsibility. Yet, the facts cited in the report, particularly when dealing with questions of minors, show that minors are often inexperienced and ill-equipped to deal with the questions that the new freedom gives them.

I would have preferred that the Commission qualify its recommendation to give greater weight to circumstances and the need for parental guidance. I can fully support the recommendations that the consequences of illegitimacy and teenage pregnancy be reduced so that the mother will have a chance of enjoying a satisfying life. The tensions associated with what is, perhaps, an unwanted pregnancy should be reduced. At the same time, however, we should not detach ourselves, as the Commission does, from the related moral and social questions.

By eliminating any need or concern for parental guidance, the Commission essentially takes the view that the child knows better than the parent what his rights and responsibilities are. This, in my view, goes too far in placing emphasis on individual right, and tends to ignore responsibility for one's own actions.

A particular fear haunts me with regard to the lack of a recommendation that teenagers be exempted from laws permitting voluntary sterilization beyond the assumption that usual and accepted medical judgment will be exercised.

I do not know of any age a human being passes through that is more impressionable, more susceptible to suggestion, than the teen years. To couple this impressionability with access to sterilization without parental guidance can mean that many youngsters, in their zeal to be patriotic, to do something for mankind, will know more than a few moments of torment and regret.

It is no answer, to my mind, to these young people and others merely to suggest that sperm banks can alleviate concern about a change of mind. Technology in this area has not advanced to the stage that permits this guarantee. And, finally, the moral questions posed by artificial insemination remain unresolved.

Abortion

I cannot accept the recommendation that present state abortion laws be liberalized to allow abortions to be performed on request.

My basic premise is that we must include within our concern for the quality and enhancement of life a respect for life itself—indeed, it should be paramount. Otherwise, the concern for the enhancement or enrichment of life is entirely materialistic. Thus, I believe the Report should have resolved the moral and ethical issues it raised. The Report could have served a useful purpose at this point by a more wide-ranging discussion of these issues. Instead, it does nothing to clarify the fundamental bases on which people now quite rightly object to liberalized abortion.

A discussion of the moral and ethical issues, I realize, is not an easy task. How, for instance, do we distinguish between abortion and infanticide? The goal of relieving the mother of the burdens of child-rearing is the same; thus, some distinction between the means must lead to a recommendation of the one and not the other.

At what point in the development of the fetus do we consider it to be human life worthy of the protection of society? And what event signals the change of the fetus from the state of nonhuman to human? My own view is that the fetus is a new, separate human being from the moment of conception.

It would be helpful for those reading this report to be able to review the reasoning leading to the judgment that liberal abortion is morally defensible. In my own view, it is difficult, if not impossible, to reach that moral judgment, and yet stop short of justifying infanticide, euthanasia, or the killing of the severely mentally or physically handicapped.

I believe that the failure of the text to resolve these questions of moral judgment places the recommendation outside a moral context.

Viewed within a moral or ethical context, I do not believe that this society can accept the destruction of human life for the comfort or convenience of individuals within the society.

Furthermore, the recommendations do not reflect the complexity of potential situations in which abortion may be called for. It does not distinguish, for example, between the rights of married and unmarried women to request abortion. What may be appropriate for an unmarried woman to decide between herself and her doctor may be completely inappropriate for a married woman, who thus ignores the rights of her husband. Moreover, there are numerous distinctions of a medical nature which could be made to limit the scope of the recommendation.

In this section, the Commission notes the difficulty of assessing the demographic impact of liberalized abortion. Its impact would be small, no doubt less than that of immigration. And yet, abortion on request takes precedence as a recommendation over one concerning the limiting of immigration. Since this is a "Population" Commission and not a "Birth Control" Commission, what compelling consideration leads the Commission to make this very controversial recommendation when it has little or no population or demographic consequence?

In summary, for all of the reasons noted, I find it impossible to join with the Commission in these recommendations.

Methods of Fertility Control

A trait common to groups and organizations concerned about a particular problem is citing their issue as one of highest priority, but failing to view it in the context of other problems that confront us as a nation. Obviously, not all of the myriad dilemmas we are trying to solve can be classified as being of highest priority.

Specifically, the Commission recommends that this nation give *highest priority* to fertility control research and that the full $93 million authorized for this purpose for fiscal year 1973 be appropriated and allocated. Next, it recommends that federal expenditures for such research rise to a minimum of $150 million by 1975.

To put the full funding recommendation in perspective, it is necessary to examine the definition of the word "authorization" as it pertains to legislation. In simplest terms, it sets a limit on the amount that may be appropriated for a given purpose. It is a figure that, more often than not, is merely taken from thin air. Rarely does an authorization reflect a diligent inquiry into actual needs or a search for an amount that can be efficiently and effectively expended during a defined period.

If Congress were to heed the cry for full funding of each of the authorizations it makes, the federal budget would be more than three times the $246.3 billion requested for fiscal year 1973. The amount of the federal debt would be imponderable.

Viewed in this light, the necessity to evaluate each request for funds alongside all of the other requests in the budget as a whole is clearly evident. The Report notes that amount expended thus far by the federal government for fertility control research is modest in terms of total research expenditures, but no attempt is made to assess this demand for funds as they relate to the thousands of other funding demands.

In like manner, the Report makes specific recommendations for funding levels of family planning projects. We are not suggesting that the amounts recommended are either too high or too low, but rather that they are merely judgments; and we do not want to judge funding levels for these purposes in isolation from funding requests for all other programs.

Equally important, the discussions on funds do not take into account the fact that federal support for family planning services and fertility control research in fiscal year 1973 will rise to $240 million, a threefold increase since fiscal 1969.

Fertility-Related Services

The Commission recommends that both ". . . public and private health financing mechanisms should begin paying the full cost of all health services related to fertility, including prenatal, delivery, and postpartum services; pediatric care for the first year of life; voluntary sterilization; safe termination of unwanted pregnancy; and medical treatment of infertility." Moreover, the Commission suggests: "The same type of coverage could be built into existing private insurance programs."

Either way, it seems to me, the public pays. Indeed, perhaps the public is willing. I suggest, however, that in making that decision several considerations warrant examination.

First, of course, it is important to ascertain the present direction of private insurance. Those of us who do not earn our livelihood through the private insurance system know that health insurance (and my reference to health insurance includes the whole gamut—medical, surgical, hospital, major, and comprehensive) is costly. What is more, we know it does not provide all the benefits we seek and premiums go up when new benefits are added. We can probably all agree as well that the only way medical expenses are going to go is up. And we rightfully ask whether private insurance can provide a remedy.

In its 1971-72 report, the Health Insurance Institute tells us that some 170 million Americans under age 65 were protected by one or more forms of private health insurance in 1970. Despite Medicare, which serves those over age 65, over 11 million more persons, or 59 percent of the total population age 65 and over, carried private health insurance policies to supplement Medicare in 1970.

From its birth in 1950 until 1970, major medical expense insurance—wherein each individual pays the first $100 or so each year for health expenses and 10 to 15 percent of expenses over the deductible amount—had expanded to cover 78 million people.

Without a doubt, the system is responsive, flexible, and expandable, but nonetheless in need of improvement. The question is, what form marks improvement?

It is my conviction that additional expenditures, be they public or private, for health-related costs should be devoted to answering our needs for more medical personnel (a program already under way, I should point out), to allaying the

284

burden to individuals of prolonged or unusually heavy medical expenses, and to preventive medicine.

It seems to me we must recognize that this nation has basic needs that government can and must meet, but that our nation's capital is not a bottomless well from which we can pump endlessly without fear of the well running dry. There is a limit, and genuine priorities must be set. Surely public subsidy of sterilization and abortion should not come at the head of the list of priorities.

Separate Statement of D. Gale Johnson

After the Commission had approved "Racial and Ethnic Minorities," a study by Finis Welch of the Graduate Center, City University of New York and the National Bureau of Economic Research, came to my attention; this study throws new and important light on the returns to education for blacks and whites. The comparisons in the text on income by education are for males 25 years of age and older and seem to indicate that income gains from increased education, especially college education, are very small for blacks. Mr. Welch undertook a new analysis of the 1960 Census of Population data in which the data for both whites and blacks were analyzed by estimated years of work experience. In effect, the years of work experience was the number of years since each individual left school.

His conclusion with respect to the analysis of income and education data for 1969 was:

In the 1959 data, the evidence is that for persons with 1-4 years of experience, black earnings rise relative to white earnings as school completion levels increase. This point has not been previously noted. For persons with 5-12 years of experience, the black/white earning ratio is insensitive to schooling and for persons with 13-25 years of experience the relative earnings of blacks falls as schooling increases.

A similar analysis of data for 1966 reveals two results of great significance. First, for blacks who entered the labor force in 1959 or later, the percentage increase in income for each additional year was substantially greater than for whites. Second, blacks who entered the labor force between 1947 and 1958 retained the same percentage income gains from an additional year of schooling relative to the income gains for whites in 1966 as had been found for 1959.

These conclusions are consistent with the behavior of black young men and women. In the last two decades, there has been a substantial narrowing of the gap between the number of years of schooling completed by blacks and whites. In 1969, blacks who were 25 to 29 years old had a median years of school completed of 12.1 years compared to 12.6 years for whites. For persons who were 45 to 54 years old in 1969, the median years of schooling completed was 9.1 for blacks and 10.9 for whites.

Mr. Welch's study and, more importantly, the decisions made by young black men and women cast considerable doubt upon the quite strongly held view that the returns to education for recent entrants to the labor force is now substantially lower for blacks than for whites. That the returns to education for blacks who entered the labor force before the late 1940's is below the return realized by whites is not in doubt.

It is good that the data from the 1970 Census of Population will soon be available to permit further analysis of the returns to education.

Separate Statement of John R. Meyer

Forecasting economic events even for a few months into the future is a hazardous exercise. Making extrapolations for three decades or so, as one is required to do if one is to forecast the impact of demographic developments, is an even more uncertain undertaking. The Commission was therefore commendably cautious in asserting what it could identify as the probable economic impacts of slower population growth.

Nevertheless, there exists a growing body of highly interesting though speculative, literature on what the many different economic facts or aspects might be of slower population growth. Some of these contributions were done at the request of the Commission and will be issued as supplemental research reports. These comments, in fact, are largely drawn from those reports.

Perhaps the most important of these speculations concerns the possible impact of slower population growth on the extent and incidence of poverty in the United States. It seems highly probable that per capita incomes overall will be almost 100 percent higher than they are today by the end of this century if Americans adopt a two-child family as their norm and 75 percent higher if they opt for the three-child family. Certainly, such income increases should help reduce the absolute if not the relative incidence of poverty in our society.

However, reasons also exist for suspecting that slower population growth could help equalize the distribution of income as well. A slower growing population tends to be an older population, and it is a reasonably well-established economic fact that people save more in the later parts of their working lives, that is after the ages of 45 or 50 or so. Accordingly, some of the economists advising the Commission have suggested that these higher savings rates may depress the rate of return on capital and correspondingly increase the share of total national income going to labor. Since wage and salary income are more important to lower than higher income groups, and conversely for returns on investments, such a shift would suggest some equalization in the distribution of income.

Even without this effect, which is admittedly quite speculative, there are other reasons for suspecting that slower population growth could imply a more equal income distribution. Specifically, more unwanted births appear to have occurred historically among poorer families. Thus, the reduction of family size from slower population growth may be greater for these lower income families. In the late 1960's, in fact, the birthrate for women in families with incomes of less than $5,000 per annum declined by over 15 percent more than for the rest of our society. The poor still have a higher birthrate than the middle classes—but the recent trends suggest that this discrepancy may be disappearing. Thus, even if family or household incomes do not go up relatively more rapidly for poor families in the future—and as we have just noted there are some reasons for suspecting that they may—the per capita income available to members of lower income families could rise relatively because their family sizes will shrink relatively rapidly.

Another economic benefit that we might derive from slower population growth would be some simplification of the structural problems we now seem to face in absorbing labor force growth. This, in turn, could reduce the intensity and frequency of certain classes of unemployment problems that now bedevil our society. Many of our present unemployment difficulties, for example, are due to a sharp rise in unemployment of teenagers and those in their early twenties who are now a larger and increasing proportion of our society because of the post-war baby boom. To illustrate what this means, consider the years 1949 and 1971 which had virtually identical overall unemployment rates, 5.9 percent. In 1971, however, the 16- to 24-year-old unemployment rate was 12.7 percent, while in 1949 it was 10.8 percent. And again, do not forget that the higher percentage rate in 1971 was applied to a larger portion of the total population than in 1949. Or, to put the matter slightly differently, if we were to calculate the ratio of unemployment rates for those 16 to 19 years of age to the unemployment rate for those 25 years and over, we would find that the annual average of this ratio was approximately three times higher in the late 1960's than it was in 1949 or 1950; indeed, this ratio even in 1960 was 3.27, while at the end of the 1960's it was almost 6.0. Slower population growth implies (though it does not guarantee for reasons that are outlined elsewhere in this Report) a steadier and *relatively* smaller flow of young people into the labor market and this in turn should simplify planning their absorption into the labor force.

It should be stressed, though, that reduced entry pressures

on labor markets from slower population growth will not be realized quickly. Again, there is the momentum created by the post-war baby boom. Thus, the level of new entrants into the labor force during the 1970's should average approximately 3.5 million or almost 700,000 persons per year more than the annual average for the 1960's. By the 1980's, however, growth in the number of labor force entrants should be nominal. What happens in the 1990's, of course, depends on what our birthrates in the 1970's actually prove to be.

Adversities, of course, can flow from slower population growth as well as advantages. For example, some economists advised the Commission that slower population growth might complicate the problem of maintaining full employment in our economy. An equal number of economists advising us said just the opposite. As just noted, slower population growth might as well simplify as complicate certain aspects of achieving full employment. So, on balance, it would seem that the Commission was correct in concluding that unemployment would not be a serious consequence of slower population growth. In essence, an unemployment problem can be solved by wise fiscal and monetary policies. Slower population growth is a very cumbersome and imperfect substitute for such wisdom.

Another difficulty of slower population growth noted by the Commission is that an older labor force may lack the vigor or flexibility to keep productivity growing at historic rates. A question also arises of whether a work force more uniformly distributed by age brackets will provide as many incentives (opportunities for promotion) as the present pyramidal age structure. In essence, a more uniform distribution of workers by age, while it may simplify certain absorption problems at the lower end of the age spectrum, may create new structural problems elsewhere in the system.

Clearly, one approach to solving such new problems is, as the Commission suggested, development of new and better programs of continuing education. The required structural adaptation may necessitate certain other changes as well, such as reinforcement of the basic market or pricing mechanisms in our economy which we depend on for the realignment of resources and economic activities.

Separate Statement of Grace Olivarez

To brush aside a separate statement on the issue of abortion on the grounds that it is based on religious or denominational "hang-ups" is to equate abortion—a matter of life and death—with simpler matters of religion such as observance of the Sabbath, dietary restrictions, abstention from coffee and alcoholic beverages, or other similar religious observances. I prefer to believe that even nonreligious persons would be concerned with the issue of life and death, even as to the unborn.

My opposition to legalized abortion is based on several concerns that touch a variety of issues, not the least of which is the effect such a law would have on millions of innocent and ill-informed persons. These concerns center around the rights of women to control their own bodies, the rights of the unborn child, the poor in our society, the safety of abortion, our country's commitment to preventive as opposed to remedial measures and our future as a democratic society.

Rights of Women to Control Their Own Bodies

I fail to understand the argument that women have a right to control their own bodies. Control over one's body does not stem from a right, but depends on individual self-image and a sense of responsibility. I am not referring to the victim of rape or incest. *And* I am *not* referring to the poor for whom contraceptive services and techniques are not as accessible as we would want them to be.

With the recent advances in contraceptive technology, any woman who so desires is better able to control her fertility in a more effective way than has ever before been available. I accept the argument that, aside from total abstention, there is no perfect contraceptive; but no one can argue that effective contraceptives are more available now than ever before, but are effective only if used. Personal and contraceptive failures do not give women the "right" to correct or eliminate the so-called "accident" by destroying the fetus.

291

Advocacy by women for legalized abortion on a national scale is so anti-women's liberation and women's freedom that it flies in the face of what some of us are trying to accomplish through the women's movement, namely, equality—equality means an equal sharing of responsibilities *by* and *as* men and women.

With women already bearing the major burden for the reproductive process, men have never had it so good. Women alone must suffer the consequences of an imperfect contraceptive pill—the blood clots, severe headaches, nausea, edema, etc. Women alone endure the cramping and hemorrhaging from an intrauterine device. No man ever died from an abortion.

A more serious question is the kind of future we all have to look forward to if men are excused either morally or legally from their responsibility for participation in the creation of life. Women should be working to bring men into the camp of responsible parenthood, a responsibility that women have had to shoulder almost alone. Perhaps in our eagerness for equality, we have, in fact, contributed to the existing irresponsible attitude some men have toward their relationship to women and their offspring. Legalized abortion will free those men from worrying about whether they should bear some responsibility for the consequences of sexual experience. In the matter of divorce where children are involved, for instance, very few men fight or even ask for custody of their children. It is customary to measure their responsibility in terms of dollars and cents, rather than in terms of affection, attention, companionship, supervision, and warmth.

And laymen are not the only ones who reflect this attitude. Blame must also be placed on church*men*, who throughout the tumult and controversy surrounding legalized abortion, have expressed their concern only as abortion affects the moral and psychological problems of women, adroitly avoiding the issue of man's responsibility to decisions connected with his role in the reproductive process.

Abortion After Rape and Incest

Pregnancy as a result of forcible rape is not common. As a rule, forcible rape involves a struggle, the effects of which can be outwardly detected. An observing parent or adult can detect the effects of such a struggle in a young girl. There is a personal responsibility for reporting such assaults. To shirk this duty under the guise of privacy, pride, or dignity is to permit abuses to go unpunished and to condemn an innocent girl to live in anguish through no fault of her own. Forcible rape should be reported as the crime that it is. Under such circumstances, the victim is given medical attention and medication that can prevent her from getting pregnant.

The key words in the definition of rape are: "without her consent." There are varying degrees of consent and resistance. To permit abortion because a woman has had a change of mind or heart after intercourse, is to deny justice to the unborn child.

Generally speaking, incest is more prevalent. Proving incest is difficult. Pregnancies resulting from incest are seldom reported or recorded as such. As in rape, abortion in this instance is punishing the child and the young girl.

Rights of the Unborn Child

In relation to the rights of the unborn child, we seem to be confused as to the meaning of human life *before* and *after* birth. The fetus does not become "a life" at a specific magic moment in the process of development. Some biologists support the foregoing and I quote from one of them:

Everyone of the higher animals *starts life* as a single cell—the fertilized ovum. . . . The union of two such sex cells (male germ cell and female germ cell) to form a zygote constitutes the process of fertilization and *initiates the life* of a new individual." [Emphasis mine.] [Bradley M. Patten, *Foundations of Embryology,* New York: McGraw-Hill, 1964, page 2.]

Neither is it a "mass of cells," as anyone who has witnessed an abortion can testify to. Having witnessed some abortions, I would ask those in favor of abortion to visit any hospital where abortions are performed and request permission to see an aborted fetus. It will not be intact unless the abortion was performed by the saline method. Then it will be pickled, but intact.

"Wanted" and "Unwanted" Fertility

To talk about the "wanted" and the "unwanted" child smacks too much of bigotry and prejudice. Many of us have experienced the sting of being "unwanted" by certain segments of our society. Blacks were "wanted" when they could be kept in slavery. When that ceased, blacks became "unwanted"—in white suburbia, in white schools, in employment. Mexican-American (Chicano) farm laborers were "wanted" when they could be exploited by agri-business. Chicanos who fight for their constitutional rights are "unwanted" people. One usually wants objects and if they turn out to be unsatisfactory, they are returnable. How often have ethnic minorities heard the statement: "if you don't like it here, why don't you go back to where you came from?" Human beings are not returnable items. Every individual has his/her rights, not the least of which is the right to life, whether born or unborn. Those with power in our society cannot be allowed to "want" and "unwant" people at will.

The Poor in Our Society

I am not impressed nor persuaded by those who express concern for the low-income woman who may find herself carrying an unplanned pregnancy and for the future of the unplanned child who may be deprived of the benefits of a full life as a result of the parents' poverty, because the fact remains that in this affluent nation of ours, pregnant cattle and horses receive better health care than pregnant poor women.

The poor cry out for justice and equality and we respond with legalized abortion.

The Commission heard enough expert testimony to the effect that increased education and increased earnings result in lower fertility rates. In the developed countries of the world, declining fertility rates are correlated with growing prosperity, improved educational facilities and, in general, overall improvement in the standard of living.

But it is not necessary to go beyond our own borders to verify this contention. Current data indicate that the same holds true for minority groups in this country. The higher the education attained by minorities and the broader the opportunities, the lower the fertility rate.

Thus, the sincerity of our concern for population growth (because of its effect on the quality of life for all people) will be tested, if, in the face of incontrovertible facts, we move rapidly to utilize alternatives to abortion in order to reduce fertility.

The Safety of Abortion

The general public has not been given all the facts on the dangers, risks, and side effects resulting from abortion. On the contrary, we have been told that abortion is a "safe and simple" procedure, as easy as "extracting a tooth."

These are the facts. In Japan, Hungary, Yugoslavia, Sweden, England, and the United States, studies and surveys indicate that abortions are not that safe.

In Japan, for example, a survey conducted in 1969 by the Office of the Prime Minister revealed an increasing percentage of five different complaints reported by women after abortion. These include increases in tubal pregnancies, menstrual irregularities, abdominal pain, dizziness, headaches, subsequent spontaneous miscarriage, and sterility.

Although one could argue that abdominal pain, dizziness, and headaches can be experienced by anyone, sterility, tubal pregnancy, and subsequent miscarriages are after-effects that have been reported in other countries.

From the Hungarian *Women's Journal*, April 17, 1971, No. 16, come the following statistics:

At every 87th abortion, surgery (uterus) perforation occurs.

At every 40th abortion, hemorrhaging complications set in, to such degree that the woman has to be hospitalized and again requires medical help.

Every 55th abortion is followed by inflammation.

Totaled up, this means that complications can be expected at every 25th abortion; or, out of every 100,000 abortions, 4000 patients must be hospitalized and require close medical attention. There were 12 maternal deaths out of 278,122 abortions recorded in New York after abortion became available on request.

Dr. Donald L. Hutchinson, Chief of the Department of Obstetrics and Gynecology at the University of Pittsburgh School of Medicine, was quoted in the *Los Angeles Times*, February 16, 1971, as follows:

A survey of complications following 1,400 therapeutic abortions showed that about 10%, or 140, of the women had significant medical complications following the procedure. The most serious complication was one death which occurred during surgery made necessary by the failure of the method—injection of salt—used to induce the abortion. . . . Among 1000 women aborted by the "D and C" method (dilation and curettage) there were six that required major surgery as a result of laceration of the wall of the womb. In several cases the womb had to be removed. Among the 400 women on whom the salt solution injections were used, the most serious complications resulted from the injection of the solution into blood vessels. In three other cases there was evidence that the salt had gotten into the circulatory system and had been carried around the body . . . in another case there were transient signs of brain damage while other cases included infections and the loss of blood through hemorrhaging, with the result that 5% of the 1,400 required blood transfusions.

Numerous other statistics on the after-effects of abortion exist, but are not included for lack of space. However, the New York experience, which is being touted as "highly successful" cannot go unchallenged.

Mr. Gordon Chase, New York City Health Services Administrator, in testimony before the Commission's hearings in New York City on September 27, 1971, reported that New York had experienced a birth decline since the advent of the abortion law. The fact is that the entire nation experienced a birth decline during the same period without legalized abortion.

The reduction in maternal deaths in New York, as reported by Mr. Chase, was credited to abortions. This is an assumption and not a proven fact. The decline in birthrates obviously, in itself, accounts for the decline in maternal mortality. Besides, maternal mortality declined throughout the country.

Recent statistics indicate that over 60 percent of abortions performed in New York were performed on out-of-state residents. Complications and deaths occurring as a result of abortions performed in New York on out-of-state women would not be recorded in New York; therefore, any New York statistics on the safety of abortion are challengeable at every level. Statistics can be categorized in different ways to support different conclusions.

Infant mortality rates are *not* reduced by killing an *unborn* child. How sad and incriminating that quality health facilities and services, denied to the poor for lack of money, are being *used* for performing abortions instead of being *utilized* for healing of the sick poor. But then, one represents a profit and the other an expense. It is all a matter of values.

Our Commitment to Preventive Measures

Although we pride ourselves on being a nation that believes in "a stitch in time saves nine," we really do not practice it. The Commission's Report includes a section on "Methods of Fertility Control" which I consider an excellent exposé of this nation's lack of commitment to the development of safer and more effective preventive measures for fertility control. If it is true that this society does not want to see abortion used as a means for population control, then I, for one, will expect an *immediate* and dramatic allocation and distribution of resources into the field of research on reproductive physiology; the development of safer, more effective, and more acceptable methods of fertility control for everyone—men and women—plus wide-scale distribution of same throughout the country. The degree of swiftness this nation employs in moving in that direction will measure the extent of its commitment to check population growth through preventive measures and not with abortion.

Our Future as a Democratic Society

The ease with which destruction of life is advocated for those considered either socially useless or socially disturbing instead of educational or ameliorative measures may be the first danger sign of loss of creative liberty in thinking, which is the hallmark of a democratic society. [Leo Alexander, M.D., *The New England Journal of Medicine,* Vol. 241, July 14, 1949.]

In order to persuade the citizen that he controls his destiny, that morality informs decisions and that technology is the servant rather than the driving force, it is necessary today to distort information. The ideal of informing the public has given way to trying to convince the public that forced actions are actually desirable action . . . we are consenting to our own deepening self-destruction. [Ivan Illich, *Celebration of Awareness,* New York: Anchor Books, Doubleday & Co., Inc., page 4.]

297

When one considers that medical science has developed four different ways for killing a fetus, but has not yet developed a safe-for-all-to-use contraceptive, the preceding quotes cannot be dismissed as the ramblings of extremists.

I believe that, in a society that permits the life of even one individual (born or unborn) to be dependent on whether that life is "wanted" or not, all its citizens stand in danger.

As long as we continue to view abortion as a solution, we will continue to avoid facing the real issue—that abortion treats the symptom and neglects the disease. When you consider that more than half of all abortions performed in New York were performed on women under 24 years of age (and not on "those unfortunate women who could not face the prospect of still another child"), you begin to get a glimpse of one aspect of the "disease." When you consider the current rush to reform the welfare system because the cost has gotten out of hand supposedly as a result of "all those children being born to those lazy women," but subsidies to profit-making entities suffer not one iota, one begins to get a glimpse of the disease.

When all of our people have access to the same benefits, advantages, and opportunities, abortion will not be necessary.

Separate Statements of James S. Rummonds

Perspective on Population

I do not agree that "the policies recommended here all lead in the right directions for this Nation, and generally at low costs." It seems to me that too many of the policies we have recommended, both explicitly and implicitly, are in the wrong direction and have heavy social-psychological environmental costs associated with them. While I agree that it is critically important that population growth be stabilized, I would go beyond that and say that the present size and distribution of the population in the United States is inconsistent with the traditional values of individual freedom, individual justice, and the true spirit of democracy. As stated in the introduction, the population issue raises profound questions of what people want, what they need, and what people are for. It is against this broader perspective that we have to measure the cost and direction of our population policies.

A common thread which underlies many aspects of the "population problem" is the rapid growth of urban areas of unprecedented size. The rapid rate and extent of population concentration is clearly illustrated in the growth of urban areas of one million or more people:

Year	Number of such areas	Percent of total pop.
1940	12	28%
1960	23	38%
1980	39	54%
2000	44+	63%

If we had wished to avoid this massive concentration of people we could have done so by avoiding, not only population growth, but economic growth. Our huge urban areas are essentially creatures of economic forces evolved for economic ends. The motivating forces have been economies of scale, specialization and division of labor, profit to the developer,

299

and efficiency in production. Thus, there is a direct linkage between our economy and population problems.

The result of these unbridled economic forces has been the creation of an almost totally manmade living environment—built initially by economic necessity and now reflective of only a narrow portion of the full range of human needs and concerns. As we rapidly become a nation that is almost totally urban-industrial, our manmade environments will increasingly shape our individual and collective behavior. Since we are presently products of environments of our own uncertain and narrow making, it seems obvious we had best be sure we are "making man" deliberately and consonant with his highest human potentials in the future.

In earlier times our deference to economic forces for ordering our existence was necessitated by the struggle for subsistence. The pressure for sheer physical survival in an agriculturally based economy made a virtue of pursuing one's own competitive self-interest. However, our rapidly increasing affluence makes survival concerns more and more inappropriate as goals around which to order our lives. The decreasing importance of survival concerns is reflected in the growth of our real family incomes which were roughly $2,400 in 1939, $9,400 in 1969, and are expected to be in excess of $21,000 by the year 2000. Another indication of our new-found affluence is shown by the fact that the proportion of the population in poverty has dropped from roughly 60 percent in 1929 to 12 percent today.

It seems clear, then, that a few select nations are rapidly entering a new age of human history where an increasing majority will live far beyond subsistence. However, our present values and institutions have been evolved for the express purpose of coping with the problem of marginal survival. Now, man has suddenly been deprived of his traditional economic purpose. We have been caught off guard by our success. We have only begun to realize how far we have come, let alone to think what might lie beyond. Thus, the fundamental question of our time arises: Are our contemporary values and institutions, inherited from a subsistence era, adequate or even desirable in coping with the problems and potentials of relative affluence, sophisticated technologies, and huge population agglomerations? There is mounting evidence which suggests that our continued reliance upon traditional economic forces will lead us into a population distribution future, as well as a larger American future, that is neither wanted nor desirable.

Economic—Research data shows that our larger urban areas are growing because of the momentum of natural increase and in-migration rather than because of any significant economies of scale associated with their size. It appears that an urban place of 200,000 people is as efficient as one of several million. Therefore, the economic rationale for allowing the size of our urban areas to increase is marginal at best.

Political—We value our democratic processes yet, other things being equal, it appears to be more difficult to exercise our democratic prerogatives as the size of the political unit increases. First, as the number of citizens increases, the time that can be spent with any one of them by a government official decreases. Second, as urban size increases there is a more than proportionate increase in public service demanded; thereby putting an even greater burden upon the democratic processes. Third, with size comes a complexity which makes it increasingly difficult for the average citizen to maintain the "relative political maturity" necessary to effectively participate in the decision-making processes. Fourth, the trend toward metropolitan government will aggravate the first three impediments to a "grass-roots" democracy.

Social—We tend to judge the "goodness" of our urban concentrations by whether or not they seem to induce such behavioral extremes as criminality, mental illness, high divorce rates, etc. The few crude studies that have been conducted have been largely inconclusive but the implicit conclusion has been: Since our big cities don't produce much bad behavior, they therefore must be good places to live. However, since man is so highly adaptable, he can tolerate very undesirable environments without exhibiting pathological behavior. Clearly, reliance upon crude "tolerance" indicators to measure our social well-being will insure our living in an environment without the beauty and serenity of the countryside, without the stability and sense of community of a small town, and within the culturally desolate confines of a homogeneous suburban social layer.

Environmental—It has been conclusively documented in the Commission's research that large population agglomerations aggravate environmental problems. This includes increasing air pollution, increasing noise pollution, decreasing access to open spaces, increasing travel time to work, increasing respiratory ailments, and adverse climatic changes. To make things worse, our research has also shown that it is oftentimes more expensive to cope with these difficulties in a larger urban environment.

Diversity—We value diversity as a precondition to freedom since freedom of choice is meaningless without something to choose from. And yet, a continuation of present distribution trends will largely narrow living choices to large urban agglomerations and will thereby eliminate a major element of diversity from our lives.

Opinion Polls—We are becoming an increasingly urban nation against the will of an absolute majority of the population. Our opinion poll survey showed that 53 percent of the population preferred a small town or country environment. Over 50 percent wanted the federal government to slow the growth of the large urban areas and over 50 percent wanted the federal government to encourage growth of smaller places. Implementation of policies consistent with these preferences would give people a greater diversity of living environments to choose from.

It seems clear, then, that we are blundering into a population distribution pattern which is unwanted by the majority of Americans. Historically, the pattern of urbanization has been a by-product of the economic imperatives of industrialization. Thus, we have trusted the control of our population distribution patterns largely to the workings of the marketplace. Only now are we learning the central weakness of the market system: the market has no inherent direction, no internal goal other than to satisfy the forces of supply and demand. With increasing abundance the market system continues to direct human activities into accustomed economic channels—yielding an increasing production and consumption of an ever larger volume of ever less valued goods. Robert Heilbroner notes that ". . . the danger exists that the market system, in an environment of genuine abundance, may become an instrument which liberates man from *real* want only to enslave him to purposes for which it is increasingly difficult to find social and moral justification." What is required, then, is a realization that to solve the "population problem" requires us to create a new relationship between the economic aspects of existence and human life in its totality. Our affluence not only makes it possible but makes it imperative that we go beyond strictly economic concerns and become creative architects rather than passive pawns of our own environment. What we need as a starting point are national goals or guiding principles which go beyond a concern for mere quantity—in short, a quality of life manifesto. I present the following as a suggestive listing of those individual and collective goals we might want to pursue as we become a post-industrial society:

1. *Efficiency*: Efficient production is desirable but not so desirable that in an affluent society it should take precedence over higher human values. In other words, we should be willing to accept some economic inefficiency as an inevitable but necessary price in realizing noneconomic values.

2. *Growth*: Just as population growth can reach disastrous proportions, so can economic growth. For example, if the rest of the world were consuming at our level we would quickly exhaust available resources. Our continued high rates of growth are predicated upon continuing disparities among nations of the rest of the world. Therefore, we need to moderate our growth ethic and begin to create the society envisioned by John Stuart Mill: ". . . in which while no one is poor, no one desires to be richer, nor has any reason to fear being thrust back by the efforts of others to push themselves forward. . . . There would be as much scope as ever for all kinds of mental culture, and moral and social progress; as much room for improving the Art of Living and much more likelihood of its being improved, when minds ceased to be engrossed by the art of getting on."

3. *Equity*: Elimination of poverty in an affluent society through overall increases in real income is too slow and unjust. Further, large disparities in income will only serve to encourage further demands for economic growth as those less advantaged note their relative rather than absolute income position. A reduction in inequity is a necessary precondition to justice as well as to the gradual attainment of a dynamic, steady state economy.

4. *Democracy*: Big business requires big government to control, big unions to bargain effectively, and big cities as productive economic mechanisms. In each case the individual comes to feel that he just "can't make a difference" as his political power is swamped by huge, complex organizations. Therefore, if we prize our democratic processes we had best be willing to design our institutions so that they are compatible with democracy.

5. *Environment*: We can no longer assume the arrogant

303

role of mastery over nature; rather, we must learn to live in balance and harmony with our environment. This means we must be sensitive to the possibility of world-wide depletion of resources and to the domestic aspects of environmental degradation—particularly in our large urban areas.

6. *Life Style*: Finally, and perhaps most important, we need to insure a physical environment that is conducive to a variety of life styles. Underlying this is a recognition of the supremacy of the individual. This was well stated by the Eisenhower Commission on National Goals: "The first national goal to be pursued . . . should be the development of each individual to his fullest potential. . . . Self-fulfillment is placed at the summit. . . ." All other goods are relegated to lower orders of priority. . . ." But what conditions are most conducive to self-fulfillment? Do the expressed and implied policies in this report enhance the creation of a physical and social environment compatible with human actualization? Too often they do not. The following points will briefly illustrate why.

Work—We have become a very productive society but at great expense to the fulfillment to be gained through our work. Most people are now alienated from their work, viewing it only as a means of acquiring the money to satisfy other needs. The excessive specialization and division of labor deprives the worker of a sense of completion and purpose in his productive process.

Nature—Our manmade environments have isolated man from his historical habitat and thus deprived him of an important life perspective. Whereas the agrarian environment forced a realization of man's finitude in relation to the ecologic totality of the earth, the urban environment allows an arrogance of power since man is living in a world of his own making. Seldom is there a sense that man has not created all. The hubris engendered by this anthropocentric environmental perspective may help to explain our current despoilation and disregard for that seemingly outside of man's created domain.

Community—In our search for personal identity through goods acquired and occupational status achieved we have been willing to move to wherever there were the greatest economic opportunities. These high rates of geographic mobility in search of social status have destroyed our sense of community.

Family—with the transition to an urban-industrial economy we have had to forsake the extended family since it was no longer an economically productive mechanism. With its economic reason to exist undermined, the social rationale was not sufficient to insure its continuity. With further industrialization came specialized demands for education and the traditional educational role of the family was subsequently lost as well. Now, with further economic "progress" we have a developing interest in childcare centers for working mothers. Although I can grant the pragmatic desirability of such institutions within an urban-industrial context, it saddens me to think that we may soon see the day when the last significant role of the family—the love and warmth of the mother—will soon disappear just as did the economic and educational roles.

In conclusion, as a rural-agrarian society, we had many of the life style elements that we now look for in vain: Our sense of belonging to, and finding identity in, the family and community; knowing that there was understanding, concern, and compassion deep felt by our peers and neighbors; being able to exert influence on the political and economic institutions of our community and society. These parts of our lives and more are being lost in our passion for affluence and in the overwhelming surge of sheer numbers of people. Surely it is time for those in control of our political and economic institutions, our leaders, to begin to create conditions wherein the highest qualities of human existence can more fully come to fruition.

I believe it was to this end that Dr. Lee A. DuBridge, then President Nixon's science advisor, wrote: "The prime task of every human institution should be to halt population growth . . . the first great challenge of our time is insuring that there are no more births than deaths. Every human institution, school, university, church, family, government, and international agency, should get this as its prime task."

The Economy

The Commission asks, what effect will slowing population growth have on the health of the economy? It concludes, with minor exceptions, that slowing population growth will not be detrimental to the economic interests of the American people. The Commission does not ask what effect the American economy has on the noneconomic interests and values of the people of this country and the world; a world increasingly characterized by overcrowding, resource depletion, ecological imbalances, and individual alienation. Put another way, is an economic system predicated on the principles of productivity and efficiency and characterized by ever-increasing concentration of the ownership of the means of production, capable of responding to the individual's need for security, purpose, and dignity? Is an economic system motivated by profit and oriented to mass consumption as an end in itself capable of guarding the values of individuality, family, and community?

While the Commission is correct in concluding that slowing population growth will not necessarily prejudice economic interests, there is considerable evidence to suggest that the system itself is destructive of a broad range of values closely held by the American people, including the job security of significant numbers of people.

Unemployment will continue to be a difficult problem for the next several years. The reason is that the rate of increase in the supply of human resources will be high, and continuing competitive pressure for efficiency will reduce demand for labor per unit of work output.

The best predictor of the increase in the labor supply each year is the number of people born about 20 years earlier. In 1950, about 3.65 million people were born in the United States, and these people entered labor force pool about 20 years later, in 1970. By 1955, births had increased to 4.13 million, so the labor force will have to accommodate more new laborers in 1975 than in 1970 if the unemployment rate is to stay constant at its present level. By 1957, births had reached 4.33, so by 1977, the labor force will have to accommodate an increase of almost 20 percent over the number of new workers as in 1970.

The problem of absorbing this increasing number of new workers into the labor force each year will be rendered particularly difficult by the strong pressure for efficiency. Each year, the work output per worker is expected to increase. This means that the number of workers required for a given amount of work is constantly dropping. Thus, at the very period in the nation's history when a great many new jobs are required, the pressure for efficiency is reducing the demand for new workers.

The magnitude of the drop in demand for workers over the last several years is quite surprising.

For example, in 1950, scheduled air carriers employed 8.1 personnel for every million revenue passenger miles of transportation provided. By 1968, only 2.6 personnel were employed to provide the same amount of transportation.

From 1950 to 1968, the number of men employed in the oil and gas industries to deliver one quadrillion British Thermal Units of energy dropped from 28.4 to 11.5.

From 1950 to 1969, the number of people employed on farms to deliver 100 units of farm output decreased from 11.6 to 3.8.

The tremendous reduction in number of workers required per unit of work delivered in all existing industries and businesses means that there must be a tremendous increase in the number of new enterprises in the next 10 years if unemployment is to be kept at a level of six percent of the labor force.

The problem is compounded, because not only will there be continuing reduction in the number of workers per unit work output, but, in addition, there are a number of major industries in which there will be a reduction in the amount of work output, because of market saturation.

A particularly striking example is the aerospace industry. In 1970, the total number of jet aircraft used by all scheduled airlines in the world was only about 5,000 Boeing 707 equivalents. In 1972, at least seven major new models of large jet aircraft are being manufactured in several countries. The number of copies of these models that would have to be produced in order for the manufacturers to yield to a reasonable return on invested capital is very large. In fact, the world jet fleet would have to be at least doubled from its present size. Since load factors (percent of seats filled) in commercial scheduled airlines had dropped to less than 50 percent in the early 1970's, and domestic demand for seats only increased two percent in 1971, it is difficult to see how demand for new models of aircraft can hold up. Consequently, there will probably be still more layoffs in the aerospace industry in the next few years. This could have an important effect on the entire economy, for two reasons. First, the industry uses about 60,000 workers for each new model of aircraft manufactured; this is about one-tenth of one percent of the entire labor force. Second, jet aircraft is the most important single export item of the nation. Slackening of sales would intensify an already deteriorating balance of trade situation.

These problems are compounded by the prospect of increased costs resulting from environmental deterioration and escalating demands on our social and political institutions. What this suggests is that demographic trends, like environmental pollution, impose costs that the market economy traditionally has externalized or failed to take into consideration. That the present economic system is no longer representative of the beneficial interests of the American people and in fact, in conflict with the material conditions of the modern world, should not be discounted.

307

Government

The Commission has asked: "Can government adapt to the new realities and fragility of our existence as the pace of our lives accelerates, the world grows more crowded, technology multiplies life's complexities, and the environment is increasingly threatened?" It concludes, ". . . slowing down the rate of population growth would ease the problems facing government in the years ahead. . . ." This is not a particularly responsive answer to the question posed. Perhaps the Commission did not intend otherwise.

Government has been defined as, "that form of fundamental rules and principles by which a nation or state is governed, or by which individual members of a body politic are to regulate their social action." Accordingly, the question posed by the Commission cannot be answered by statistical projections or cost benefit analysis. Rather, we must ask if the rules and principles of government and social behavior are adequate to meet both the just demands of the people and the dictates of demographic and ecological imperatives. This question can profitably be viewed as three distinct inquiries.

First, what are the rules and principles of government in the United States; or, in other words, what is government for. One response to this question has been given by Arthur S. Miller of the George Washington University Law faculty and a contributor to the Commission's research project: "The raw material of modern government is business, taxation, utility regulation, agricultural control, labor relations, housing, banking and finance, control of the security market—all our major domestic issues—are phases of a single central problem: namely, the interplay of economic enterprise in government. . . ." While it cannot be denied that modern government undertakes programs to accomplish noneconomic objectives, it can readily be seen that there is considerable truth in the observation that, "the business of government is business." Indeed, the dominant analytical perspective taken throughout this report supports a predominantly economic interpretation of the role of government.

The second question is to what ends are the rules and principles of government applied. This can be answered in a number of ways. For example, the ends can be equated with "values." It is generally agreed that one of the primary *stated* goals or values of government in the United States is the promotion and enhancement of individual freedom for all the people. Thus, the "government" pursues the goal of "freedom" through the vehicle of the "free market" and the maintenance of competitive economic conditions. Fundamental to this particular notion of "freedom" is a reliance on the "invisible hand" or classical laissez-faire economics.

Another end or goal of the rules and principles of government can be ascertained by analyzing the distribution of wealth in society. By this standard, the end of "government" can reasonably be understood as seeking to maximize the satisfactions of the dominant forces in society, that is, the owners of the means of production. However, it has been forcibly argued by the sociologist Max Weber that freedom and wealth are, in fact, one and the same:

> The exact extent to which the total amount of 'freedom' within a given legal community is actually increased depends entirely upon the concrete economic order and specifically on property distribution. In no case can it be simply deduced from the content of the law.

The final question is, can the present political economy (government) of the United States cope with the demands presently being placed upon it. A. E. Keir Nash, formerly a director of research and now a consultant for the Commission, responded to this question as follows:

> There is good reason to doubt the capacity of the American governmental system to accommodate a third 100 million citizens in the final decades of the 20th century. There are strong grounds for doubting the ability of the government both to maintain political order and to attain social justice among a citizenry of 300 million.

Dr. Nash goes on to note two fundamental failures of American government. First, is an historical failure to fulfill its basic promises of freedom and equality. Second, is the failure of government, "to shift government actions—so as to make them appropriate to the increasingly crowded world in which we live."

> Legislative and executive policymaking continues largely to be based upon log-rolling and incremental solutions to problems in the society and the economy which are not genuine solutions at all. Such a pseudo-problem-solving may work respectably when the basic structures of the economy, the society and the environment are not in flux.

309

They may be admirable in a largely empty and unsettled country, half slave and half free. Yet they are wholly unsuited to the problems which confront Americans today. The politics of yesterday is simply not suited to the needs of tomorrow.

The Commission chose to reject the evidence militating toward this conclusion. I cannot.

Separate Statement of Howard D. Samuel

Although I fully share the goals ending discrimination and providing equal opportunity for women, I disagree that passage of the Equal Rights Amendment would be a useful step in that direction. On the one hand, the Equal Rights Amendment would accomplish very little for women; what is needed is a specific body of legislation, federal and state, to end discriminatory practices and open up opportunity. On the other hand, the Equal Rights Amendment would have a destructive effect in that it would render invalid present state laws protecting women—particularly women workers—against certain kinds of injustice and hardship. For this reason, I do not support the recommendation endorsing the Equal Rights Amendment.

Separate Statement of George D. Woods

I believe the Commission should leave decisions on the amounts of funds necessary to the proper authorities. Such amounts may be either lesser or greater than those recommended in these sections.

REFERENCES

Chapter 2. Population Growth

1. Ansley J. Coale, "Alternative Paths to a Stationary Population" (prepared for the Commission, 1972).
2. U.S. National Center for Health Statistics, *Vital Statistics of the United States,* Volume I, *Natality,* 1968.
3. U.S. National Center for Health Statistics, *Vital Statistics of the United States,* Volume II, Section 5, *Life Tables,* 1968.
4. James Mooney, "The Aboriginal Population of America North of Mexico," *Smithsonian Miscellaneous Collection,* 1928, Vol. 80, No. 7.
5. Irene B. Taeuber, "Growth of the Population of the United States in the Twentieth Century" (prepared for the Commission, 1972).
6. U.S. Bureau of the Census, *Current Population Reports,* Series P-23, No. 36, "Fertility Indicators: 1970," 1971.
7. U. S. Bureau of the Census, *Current Population Reports,* Series P-20, No. 232, "Birth Expectations Data: June 1971," 1972.
8. See note 1.
9. National Education Association, *NEA Research Bulletin,* 1971, Vol. 49, No. 3.
10. Estimates developed from Census Bureau data on the population by age, 1960 and 1970, and data on the volume of arrests for crime index offenses as reported for 1960 and 1970 in U.S. Federal Bureau of Investigation,

Uniform Crime Reports—1970, by direct standardization methods.

11. Denis F. Johnston, "Illustrative Projections of the Labor Force of the United States to 2040" (prepared for the Commission, 1972).

Chapter 3. Population Distribution

1. Philip M. Hauser, in hearings before the Commission, Chicago, Illinois, June 21-22, 1971.
2. Irene B. Taeuber, "The Changing Distribution of the Population of the United States in the Twentieth Century" (prepared for the Commission, 1972).
3. Jerome P. Pickard, "U.S. Metropolitan Growth and Expansion, 1970-2000, With Population Projections" (prepared for the Commission, 1972).
4. See note 2. Also, U.S. Bureau of the Census, *Census of Population and Housing: 1970, General Demographic Trends for Metropolitan Areas,* 1960 to 1970, Final Report PHC(2), 1971.
5. See note 2.
6. U.S. Bureau of the Census, "Regional Metropolitan Projections" (special tabulations prepared for the Commission).
7. U. S. Bureau of the Census, *Current Population Reports,* Series P-20, No. 210, "Mobility of the Population of the United States: March 1969 to March 1970," 1971.
8. See note 4.
9. See note 2.
10. See note 4.
11. William Alonso, "The System of Intermetropolitan Population Flows" (prepared for the Commission, 1972).
12. U.S. Bureau of the Census, *Census of Population: 1970, Number of Inhabitants,* Final Report PC(1), 1971.
13. U.S. Department of Agriculture, *The Economic and Social Condition of Rural America in the 1970's* (prepared for the Senate Committee on Government Operations, 1971).
14. Mariah Gilmore, in hearings before the Commission, Little Rock, Arkansas, June 7-8, 1971.
15. The impact of rural repopulation was determined by subtracting the resident population of the United States in 1970 from a hypothetical population wherein all counties in the country had been repopulated to their historical maximum. This figure was adjusted to remove

some of the bias attributable to the exodus from some of our central cities, since our intent was to focus on the effects of rural repopulation only. It was found that rural repopulation under the conditions described above would absorb no more than 11 million people, or about five years worth of national growth as projected under the 2-child family assumption.

16. Glenn V. Fuguitt, "Population Trends of Nonmetropolitan Cities and Villages in the United States" (prepared for the Commission, 1972).
17. Ira S. Lowry, "Housing Assistance for Low-Income Urban Families: A Fresh Approach" (prepared for the House Committee on Banking and Currency, 1971).
18. See note 4.
19. See note 6.
20. George Romney, Secretary of the Department of Housing and Urban Development (address to Metropolitan Washington Council of Governments, 1971).
21. National Public Opinion Survey conducted for the Commission by the Opinion Research Corporation, 1971.
22. James J. Zuiches and Glen V. Fuguitt, "Residential Preferences: Implications for Population Redistribution in Nonmetropolitan Areas" (prepared for the 138th Meeting of the American Association for the Advancement of Science, Philadelphia, 1971).
23. See note 21.
24. See note 3.
25. See note 6.
26. Edward E. Murray and Ned Hege, "Growth Center Population Redistribution 1980-2000" (prepared for the Commission, 1972).
27. See note 3.
28. See note 21.

Chapter 4. The Economy

1. U.S. Bureau of the Census, "Projections of Family Income to the Year 2000" (unpublished tabulations prepared at the request of the Commission). These Census tabulations, which also provide estimates of per capita income, were developed in part from projections of the Gross National Product prepared at the request of the Commission by the Office of Business Economics, Department of Commerce. Both the family income and GNP projections utilized labor force projections from a paper

prepared for the Commission by Denis F. Johnston of the Bureau of Labor Statistics.

2. These data were derived from projections of the Gross National Product prepared for the Commission by the Office of Business Economics (see note 1).

3. U.S. Bureau of the Census, *Current Population Reports,* Series P-60, No. 81, "Characteristics of the Low-Income Population, 1970," 1971.

4. Denis F. Johnston, "Illustrative Projections of the Labor Force of the United States to 2040" (prepared for the Commission, 1972).

5. John A. Howard and Donald R. Lehman, "The Effect of Different Populations on Selected Industries in the Year 2000" (prepared for the Commission, 1972).

6. Robert O. Anderson, "Population, Productivity, and the Environment," in hearings before the Commission, New York, September 28, 1971.

7. Irene B. Taeuber, "Growth of the Population of the United States in the Twentieth Century" (prepared for the Commission, 1972).

8. Edgar M. Hoover, "Reduced Population Growth and the Problems of Urban Area" (prepared for the Commission, 1972).

Chapter 5. Resources and the Environment

Nearly all of the source material for this chapter came from the resource and environmental research done for the Commission by Resources for the Future, Inc. Their work includes a summary chapter on the resource and environmental consequences of population growth in the United States by Ronald G. Ridker, as well as more detailed supporting work which includes an analysis of pollution, recycling, adequacy of non-fuel minerals, energy, outdoor recreation, agriculture, water supplies, and urban scale.

1. James G. Edinger, in hearings before the Commission, Los Angeles, May 4, 1971.

2. Paul R. Ehrlich and John P. Holdren, "One-Dimensional Ecology," *Science and Public Affairs,* Spring, 1972, forthcoming.

Chapter 6. Government

1. Jack Appleman, William P. Butz, David H. Greenberg, Paul L. Jordan, and Anthony H. Pascal, "Population Change and Public Resource Requirements: The Impact of Future United States Demographic Trends on Education, Welfare and Health Care" (prepared for the Commission, 1972).
2. John G. Grumm, "Population Change and State Government Policy" (prepared for the Commission, 1972).
3. Michael N. Danielson, "Differentiation, Segregation, and Political Fragmentation in the American Metropolis" (prepared for the Commission, 1972).
4. Robert F. Drury, "Local Governments and Population Change" (prepared for the Commission, 1972).
5. National Public Opinion Survey conducted for the Commission by the Opinion Research Corporation, 1971.
6. Roy W. Bahl, Jr., "Metropolitan Fiscal Structures and the Distribution of Population Within Metropolitan Areas" (prepared for the Commission, 1972).
7. Richard Lehne, "Population Change and Congressional Representation" (prepared for the Commission, 1972). Also, Roger H. Davidson, "Population Change and Representational Government" (prepared for the Commission, 1972).
8. Kenneth N. Vines, "Population Increase and the Administration of Justice" (prepared for the Commission, 1972).
9. *The Report of the President's Commission on an All-Volunteer Armed Force*, 1970.
10. A.F.K. Organski, Alan Lamborn, and Bruno Bueno de Mesquita, "The Effective Population in International Politics" (prepared for the Commission, 1972).
11. William Alonso, "Problems, Purposes, and Implicit Policies for a National Strategy of Urbanization" (prepared for the Commission, 1972).
12. Allen D. Manvel, "Metropolitan Growth and Governmental Fragmentation (prepared for the Commission, 1972).
13. Dorn C. McGrath, Jr., "Population Growth and Change: Implications for Planning" (prepared for the Commission, 1972).
14. Lawrence B. Christmas, in hearings before the Commission, Chicago, Illinois, June 21-22, 1971.

15. Tom Bradley, in hearings before the Commission, Los Angeles, California, May 3, 1971.

Chapter 7. Social Aspects

1. Lincoln H. Day, "The Social Consequences of a Zero Population Growth Rate in the United States" (prepared for the Commission, 1972).
2. U. S. National Center for Health Statistics, *Vital Statistics of the United States,* Volume II, Section 5, *Life Tables,* 1968. Excludes immigration.
3. The 1970 data and population projections used throughout this chapter are drawn from U. S. Bureau of the Census, *Current Population Reports,* Series P-25, No. 470, "Projections of the Population of the United States by Age and Sex: 1970 to 2000."
4. U.S. Bureau of the Census, *Historical Abstract of the United States, Colonial Times to 1957,* 1960.
5. U.S. Bureau of the Census, *Current Population Reports,* Series P-60, No. 81, "Characteristics of the Low-Income Population, 1970," 1971.
6. U.S. Bureau of the Census, *Census of Population and Housing: 1970, General Population Characteristics: U.S. Summary,* Final Report PC(1)-B1.
7. See note 2.
8. U.S. Bureau of the Census, *Current Population Reports,* Series P-20, No. 212, "Marital Status and Family Status: March 1970," 1971.
9. U.S. Bureau of the Census, *Current Population Reports,* Series P-20, No. 223, "Social and Economic Variations in Marriage, Divorce, and Remarriage: 1967," 1971.
10. Luman H. Long, ed., *The 1972 World Almanac and Book of Facts* (New York: Newspaper Enterprise Association, Inc., for *The Washington Daily News,* 1971).
11. See note 9.
12. Kingsley Davis, "The American Family in Relation to Demographic Change" (prepared for the Commission, 1972).
13. U.S. Bureau of the Census, *Census of Population and Housing,* for 1970 and 1960, *Number of Inhabitants: U.S. Summary,* Final Report PC(1)-A1.
14. U.S. Bureau of the Census, *Census of Population and Housing: 1970, Number of Inhabitants: New York,* Final Report PC(1)-A34.
15. U.S. National Institute of Mental Health, "Psycho-

Ecological Aspects of Population," by John B. Calhoun, 1966.

16. Jonathan L. Freedman, "A Positive View of Population Density," *Psychology Today,* September 1971.

17. Jonathan L. Freedman, "Population Density, Juvenile Delinquency, and Mental Illness in New York City" (prepared for the Commission, 1972).

18. These estimates are based on the number of children ever born to 35- to 44-year-old women according to their ethnic origin (U. S. Bureau of the Census, *Current Population Reports,* Series P-20, No. 226, "Fertility Variations by Ethnic Origin: November 1969," 1971). The number of children theoretically required for replacement was calculated by multiplying the number of women in each ethnic group by 2.07 (the average number of children per woman 35 to 44 consistent with completed fertility at the replacement level). This "hypothetical" number of children was then subtracted from the actual number of children born to women in each ethnic group, to estimate fertility in excess of replacement needs.

19. The data for poor and nonpoor women were developed in the same manner (see note 18), utilizing U. S. Bureau of the Census, *Current Population Reports,* Series P-20, No. 211, "Previous and Prospective Fertility: 1967," 1971. Partly estimated.

20. Births throughout the sixties (1960-1968), were obtained from the U.S. National Center for Health Statistics, *Vital Statistics of the United States,* Volume I, *Natality,* and subtracted from the total January 1, 1969 population to determine their relative impact. Spanish-origin births were estimated.

21. U.S. Bureau of the Census, *Current Population Reports,* Series P-23, No. 36, "Fertility Indicators: 1970," 1971. On this point and others in this section, see Reynolds Farley, "Fertility and Mortality Trends Among Blacks in the United States" (prepared for the Commission, 1972).

22. Benjamin Bradshaw, "Some Aspects of the Fertility of Mexican-Americans" (prepared for the Commission, 1972).

23. Dr. Eugene S. Callender, in hearings before the Commission, New York, September 27-28, 1971.

24. Naomi Gray, in hearings before the Commission, Washington, D.C., April 14-15, 1971.

25. Manuel Aragon, in hearings before the Commission, Los Angeles, California, May 3-4, 1971.

26. Rev. Jesse Jackson, in hearings before the Commission, Chicago, Illinois, June 21-22, 1971.

27. National Public Opinion Survey conducted for the Commission by the Opinion Research Corporation, 1971.

28. U.S. Bureau of the Census, *Current Population Reports*, Series P-60, No. 80, "Income in 1970 of Families and Persons in the U. S.," 1971.

29. U.S. Bureau of the Census, *Current Population Reports*, Series P-20, No. 224, "Selected Characteristics of Persons and Families of Mexican, Puerto Rican, and Other Spanish Origin: March 1971," 1971.

30. Irene B. Taeuber, "Growth of the Population of the United States in the Twentieth Century" (prepared for the Commission, 1972).

31. See notes 2 and 4.

32. Robert E. Roberts and Cornelius Askew, "A Consideration of Mortality in Three Subcultures" (paper presented at the annual meeting of the Population Association of America, Washington, D. C., 1971).

33. U.S. Department of Health, Education and Welfare, "Natality and Mortality of American Indians Compared with U. S. Whites and Nonwhites," by Charles Hill and Mozart Spector, in *HSMHA Health Reports*, March 1971.

34. Evelyn M. Kitagawa, "Socioeconomic Differences in Mortality in the United States and Some Implications for Population Policy" (prepared for the Commission, 1972).

35. Sonny Walker, in hearings before the Commission, Little Rock, Arkansas, June 7-8, 1971.

36. Irene B. Taeuber, "The Changing Distribution of the Population of the U.S. in the Twentieth Century" (prepared for the Commission, 1972).

Chapter 8. Population and Public Policy

1. U.S. Bureau of the Census, *Current Population Reports*, Series P-23, No. 36, "Fertility Indicators: 1970," 1971.

2. Estimated from data on population 65 to 74 years old, and survival rates, in U.S. Bureau of the Census, *Current Population Reports*, Series P-25, No. 470, "Projections of the Population of the United States, by Age and Sex: 1970 to 2020," 1971.

3. U.S. Bureau of the Census, *Current Population Reports*, Series P-60, No. 81, "Characteristics of the Low-Income Population, 1970," 1971.

322

Chapter 9. Education

1. National Public Opinion Survey conducted for the Commission by the Opinion Research Corporation, 1971.
2. Stephen Viederman, "Population Education in the Elementary and Secondary Schools of the United States" (prepared for the Commission, 1972).
3. Sue T. Reid and Alan P. Bates, "Undergraduate Sociology Programs in Accredited Colleges and Universities," *American Sociologist*, May 1971, Vol. 6.
4. Ritchie H. Reed and Susan McIntosh, "Costs of Children" (prepared for the Commission, 1972).
5. Jane A. Menken, "Teenage Childbearing: Its Medical Aspects and Implications for the United States Population" (prepared for the Commission, 1972).
6. U.S. Bureau of the Census, *Current Population Reports* Series P-20, No. 223, "Social and Economic Variations in Marriage, Divorce and Remarriage: 1967," 1971.
7. White House Conference on Children, *Report to the President*, 1970.
8. See note 7.
9. Barry M. Popkin, "Economic Benefits from the Elimination of Hunger in America," Discussion Paper No. 102-71 (University of Wisconsin, Institute for Research on Poverty, 1971).
10. F. Glen Loyd, "Finally, Facts on Malnutrition in the United States," *Today's Health*, September 1969.
11. Heinz F. Eichenwald and Peggy Crooke Fry, "Nutrition and Learning," *Science*, September 1970, Vol. 163.
12. Curt Stern, "The Place of Genetics in Medicine," *Annals of Internal Medicine*, October 1971, Vol. 75, No. 4.
13. This information was contained in a background memorandum from Joseph D. Beasley, M.D.
14. Sol Gordon, "Family Planning Education for Adolescents" (prepared for the Commission, 1972).
15. Elizabeth Hendryson, "The Case for Sex Education," *The PTA Magazine*, May 1969.
16. Interfaith Commission on Marriage and Family Life, *Interfaith Statement on Sex Education*, 1968.
17. *The Report of the Commission on Obscenity and Pornography*, September 1970.
18. See note 17.
19. Hariette Surovell in hearings before the Commission, New York, September 27-28, 1971.

20. John F. Kantner and Melvin Zelnik, "Sexuality, Contraception, and Pregnancy Among Pre-Adult Females in the United States" (prepared for the Commission, 1972).

21. U. S. Bureau of the Census, *Current Population Reports,* Series P-23, No. 36, "Fertility Indicators: 1970," 1971.

22. Joe Blount, National Communicable Disease Center, Atlanta, Georgia, unpublished data.

23. See note 17.

Chapter 10. The Status of Children and Women

1. U.S. Department of Health, Education and Welfare, Maternal and Child Health Service, *Promoting the Health of Mothers and Children, FY 1971.*

2. Charlotte F. Muller and Frederick S. Jaffe, "Financing Fertility-Related Health Services in the United States, 1972-1978, A Preliminary Projection," *Family Planning Perspectives,* January 1972.

3. U.S. Bureau of Labor Statistics, *Children of Women in the Labor Force, March 1970,* Special Labor Force Report 134, 1971.

4. White House Conference on Children, *Report to the President,* 1970.

5. Based on per child estimates contained in U. S. Congress, Senate, Committee on Labor and Public Welfare, *Economic Opportunity Amendments of 1971,* S. Rept. 92-331, to accompany S. 2007, 92nd Cong., 1st sess., 1971.

6. *Revenue Act of 1971,* P.L. 92-178.

7. Jane Menken, "Teenage Childbearing: Its Medical Aspects and Implications for the U. S. Population" (prepared for the Commission, 1972). Also, U. S. National Center for Health Statistics, *Vital Statistics of the United States,* Volume I, *Natality,* 1968.

8. Philip J. Keeve, M.D., "Fertility Experience of Juvenile Girls: A Community-Wide 10 Year Study" (paper presented to the American Public Health Association, Detroit, Michigan, November 12, 1968).

9. Commissioner Sidney P. Marland, Office of Education, speaking before Conference on Improving Services to School-Age Parents, Florida, December 1971.

10. U. S. Bureau of the Census, *Current Population Reports,* Series P-23, No. 36, "Fertility Indicators: 1970," 1971.

11. "Bastards," *American Jurisprudence* 2nd, Volume 10, sec. 62.

12. United Nations, *Study of Discrimination Against Persons*

Born Out-of-Wedlock, by V. Saario, 1967.

13. *Social Security Act,* 64 Stat. 492, 42 U.S.C. sec. 416(H) (3) (1965).

14. The analysis of adoption is developed from information available from the U. S. Dept. of Health, Education and Welfare, National Center for Social Statistics and National Center for Health Statistics.

15. See note 10.

16. National Public Opinion Survey conducted for the Commission by the Opinion Research Corporation, 1971.

17. Judith Blake, "Coercive Pronatalism and American Population Policy" (prepared for the Commission, 1972).

18. U. S. Department of Labor, Bureau of Labor Statistics, *Marital and Family Characteristics of Workers, March 1970,* Special Labor Force Report 130, 1971.

19. U. S. Bureau of the Census, *Census of Population: 1960, Women by Number of Children Ever Born,* Final Report PC(2)-3A.

20. U.S. Department of Labor, *1969 Handbook of Women Workers,* Women's Bureau Bulletin No. 294; *Negro Women in the Population and in the Labor Force,* December 1967.

21. U.S. Bureau of Labor Statistics, *Marital and Family Characteristics of Workers, March 1971,* Special Labor Force Report, September 1971.

22. U.S. Bureau of Labor Statistics, *Why Women Start and Stop Working, A Study in Mobility,* Special Labor Force Report 59, September 1965.

23. See note 21.

24. Jeanne Clare Ridley, "Family Planning and the Status of Women in the United States" (unpublished) and U. S. Department of Health, Education and Welfare, Office of Education, *Earned Degrees Conferred: 1969-1970, Summary Data,* by Mary Evans Hooper.

25. U.S. Department of Health, Education and Welfare, *Report of the Women's Action Program,* January 1972.

26. The President's Task Force on Women's Rights and Responsibilities, *A Matter of Simple Justice,* April 1970.

27. Elliott Morss, "The Influence of Federal Government Activities on the Family Decision to Have a Child" (prepared for the Commission, 1972).

28. John T. Noonan, Jr., and Mary Cynthia Dunlap, "Unintended Consequences: Laws Indirectly Affecting Population Growth in the United States" (prepared for the Commission, 1972).

29. U.S. Department of Health, Education and Welfare, National Center for Social Statistics, *Findings of the 1969 AFDC Study: Data by Census Division and Selected States, Part I: Demographic Program Characteristics*, NCSS Report AFDC-3(67) July 1970, and NCSS Report AFDC-3(69) December 1970.
30. Telephone conversation with Jule M. Sugarman, Human Resources Administrator and Commissioner of Social Services, New York.
31. These proposals are discussed in Daniel Callahan, "Ethics, Population, and the American Tradition" (prepared for the Commission, 1972).

Chapter 11. Human Reproduction

1. 1970 National Fertility Study conducted by Office of Population Research, Princeton University. See Norman B. Ryder and Charles F. Westoff, *Reproduction in the United States: 1965* (Princeton: Princeton University Press, 1971).
2. Hans Forssman and Inga Thuwe, "One hundred and twenty children born after application for therapeutic abortion refused," *Acta Psychiat. Scand.*, 1966.
3. President's Message on Population, July 18, 1969.
4. U.S. National Center for Health Statistics, *Vital Statistics Rates in the United States, 1940-1960,* 1968. Current figures were obtained from the Statistical Research Section, Division of Vital Statistics, National Center for Health Statistics.
5. Jane A. Menken, "Teenage Childbearing: Its Medical Aspects and Implications for the U.S. Population" (prepared for the Commission, 1972).
6. Harriet Pilpel and Peter Ames, "Legal Obstacles to Freedom of Choice in the Areas of Contraception, Abortion, and Voluntary Sterilization in the United States" (prepared for the Commission, 1972).
7. Harriet Pilpel and N. F. Wechsler, "Birth Control, Teen-Agers and the Law: A New Look, 1971," *Family Planning Perspectives,* 1971, Vol. 3, No. 3.
8. See note 1. Also Harriet Presser and Larry Bumpass, "Demographic and Social Aspects of Contraceptive Sterilization in the United States: 1965-1970" (prepared for the Commission, 1972.)
9. See note 6, and Cyril C. Means, Jr., "The Law of New York Concerning Abortion and the Status of the Foetus,

1664-1968: A Case of Cessation of Constitutionality," 14 *New York Law Forum* 411 (1968). As a New York court has recently observed: "It is generally believed that abortion of a quick child was a high crime at Common Law . . . although one commentator has argued persuasively that, in fact, it was not, that abortion was a purely ecclesiastical offence punishable only by spiritual penalties and that the secular crime of abortion was created by the imagination of Sir Edward Coke who felt strongly that abortion after quickening should be punishable and that the purely spiritual penalties of the ecclesiastical courts would not deter the people from it. (See, generally, Means, 'The Phoenix of Abortional Freedom: Is a penumbral or Ninth-Amendment Right About to Arise from the Nineteenth-Century Legislative Ashes of a Fourteenth-Century Common-Law Liberty?' 17 [*New York Law Forum* 335 (1971)])." Byrn v. N.Y. City Health and Hosp. Corp. 167 *New York Law Journal* No. 39, p. 5, col. 1 (N.Y. App. Div., 2d Dep't. February 24, 1972).

10. Daniel Callahan, "Abortion: A Summary of the Arguments" (prepared for the Commission, 1972).
11. City of New York Health Services Administration, *Bulletin on Abortion Program,* December 1971.
12. Gordon Chase, in hearings before the Commission, New York, September 27-28, 1971.
13. Personal communication from Karl Tyler, National Communicable Disease Center, Atlanta, Georgia.
14. James W. Brackett, "The Demographic Consequences of Legal Abortion," in *Abortion, Obtained and Denied Research Approaches,* Sidney H. Newman, Mildred B. Beck, and Sarah Lewit, eds. (New York: The Population Council, 1971).
15. Christopher Tietze, "The Potential Impact of Legal Abortion on Population Growth in the United States" (prepared for the Commission, 1972).
16. Elise F. Jones and Charles F. Westoff, "Attitudes Toward Abortion in the United States in 1970 and the Trend Since 1965" (prepared for the Commission, 1972).
17. National Public Opinion Survey conducted for the Commission by the Opinion Research Corporation, 1971.
18. Some of the material in this section is based on Sheldon Segal, "Possible Means of Fertility Control: Distant or Near" (prepared for the Commission, 1972).
19. U.S. Congress, Senate, "Report of the Secretary of HEW, Submitting Five-Year Plan for Family Planning Services

and Population Research Programs," prepared for the Special Subcommittee on Human Resources of the Senate Committee on Labor and Public Welfare, October, 1971.

20. Carl Djerassi, "Birth Control After 1984," *Science,* September 4, 1970.

21. Estimated from "Population Research: A Prospectus," Committee Report to the Assistant Secretary for Health and Scientific Affairs, U.S. Department of Health, Education and Welfare. Reprimand in U.S. Congress, House, Committee on Interstate and Foreign Commerce, *Family Planning Services, Hearings* before the Subcommittee on Public Health and Welfare, 91st Cong., 2nd sess., August 3, 4, and 7, 1970, p. 162. Also from Oscar Harkavy and John Maier, "Research Conducted in Contraception and Reproduction," *Family Planning Perspectives,* July, 1971.

22. Title IV and X, *Public Health Service Act* as amended, 242 U.S.C. 281-289c and 42 U.S.C. 201.

23. U. S. Department of Health, Education and Welfare, *Population and Family Planning,* Report of the President's Committee on Population and Family Planning, November, 1968. And also, "Population Research: A Prospectus" (note 21).

24. See note 19.

25. See note 21.

26. Estimate as of January 1, 1972, based on projections in Five-Year Plan (see note 19). Much of the material in this section is based on Frederick S. Jaffe, "Family Planning Services in the United States" (prepared for the Commission, 1972).

27. See note 19.

28. Sec. 59.5, *Fed. Reg.* Doc. 71-13560, filed 9-14-71.

29. Material in this section is taken from Charlotte F. Muller and Frederick S. Jaffe, "Financing Fertility-Related Services in the United States, 1972-1978: A Preliminary Projection," *Family Planning Perspectives,* January, 1972.

30. See note 19.

31. John F. Kantner and Melvin Zelnik, "Sexuality, Contraception, and Pregnancy Among Pre-Adult Females in the United States" (prepared for the Commission, 1972).

32. See note 11.

33. Sol Gordon, "Family Planning Education for Adolescents" (prepared for the Commission, 1972).

34. See note 17.

Chapter 12. Population Stabilization

1. Norman B. Ryder, "A Demographic Optimum Projection for the United States" (prepared for the Commission, 1972). Also Ansley J. Coale, "Alternative Paths to a Stationary Population" (prepared for the Commission, 1972).

2. Tomas Frejka, "Demographic Paths to a Stationary Population; The U.S. in International Comparison" (prepared for the Commission, 1972); and, "Reflections on the Demographic Conditions Needed to Establish a U.S. Stationary Population Growth," *Population Studies,* November 1968.

3. U.S. Bureau of the Census, *Current Population Reports,* Series P-23, No. 36, "Fertility Indicators: 1970," 1971.

4. See Ryder, note 1.

5. Jane A. Menken, "Teenage Childbearing: Its Medical Aspects and Implications for the United States Population" (prepared for the Commission, 1972).

6. National Public Opinion Survey conducted for the Commission by the Opinion Research Corporation, 1971.

7. U.S. Bureau of the Census, *Current Population Reports,* Series P-20, No. 212, "Marital Status and Family Status: March 1970," 1971.

8. Christopher Tietze, "The Potential Impact of Legal Abortion on Population Growth in the United States" (prepared for the Commission, 1972).

9. Michael Teitelbaum, "International Experience with Fertility at or Near Replacement Level" (prepared for the Commission, 1972).

10. U.S. Bureau of the Census, *Current Population Reports,* Series P-25, No. 470, "Projections of the Population of the United States, by Age and Sex: 1970 to 2020," 1971.

11. Judith Blake, "Coercive Pronatalism and Population Policy" (prepared for the Commission, 1972), and other papers cited above in discussion of institutional pressures.

12. Ellen Peck, in hearings before the Commission, Chicago, Illinois, June 21-22, 1971.

13. The Population Council, "Japan: Interim Report of the Population Problems Inquiry Council," *Studies in Family Planning,* No. 56, August 1970. See also note 10.

Chapter 13. Immigration

1. Irene B. Taeuber, "Growth of the Population of the United States in the Twentieth Century" (prepared for the Commission, 1972). For this chapter, see also Charles B. Keely, "Immigration: Considerations on Trends, Prospects, and Policy" (prepared for the Commission, 1972).
2. See note 1.
3. Richard Irwin and Robert Warren, "Demographic Aspects of American Immigration" (prepared for the Commission, 1972).
4. U.S. Immigration and Naturalization Service, *1971 Annual Report of the Immigration and Naturalization Service.*
5. See note 3.
6. U.S. Bureau of the Census, *Current Population Reports,* Series P-25, No. 470, "Projections of the Population of the United States, by Age and Sex: 1970 to 2020," 1971.
7. Ansley J. Coale, "Alternative Paths to a Stationary Population" (paper prepared for the Commission, 1972).
8. U.S. Bureau of the Census, "Regional Metropolitan Projections" (special tabulations prepared for the Commission).
9. See note 4.
10. See note 4.
11. J. N. Haug and B. C. Martin, *Foreign Medical Graduates,* American Medical Association, 1971. On professional immigration, see also Judith Fortney, "Immigration Into the United States With Special Reference to Professional and Technical Workers" (prepared for the Commission, 1972).
12. Estimate based on figures appearing in: U. S. Bureau of the Census, *Statistical Abstract of the United States: 1970.*

Chapter 14. National Distribution and Migration Policies

This chapter draws primarily on the following papers prepared for the Commission:

William Alonso, "Problems, Purposes, and Implicit Policies for a National Strategy of Urbanization."

Gordon Cameron, "The Relevance to the United States of British and French Regional Population Strategies."

Michael Danielson, "Differentiation, Segregation, and Political Fragmentation in the American Metropolis."

Niles M. Hansen, "The Case for Government-Assisted Migration."

Edgar M. Hoover, "Policy Objectives for Population Distribution."

Allen Manvel, "Metropolitan Growth and Governmental Fragmentation."

Dorn C. McGrath, Jr., "Population Growth and Change: Implications for Planning."

Peter A. Morrison, "Dimensions of the Population Problem in the United States"; "Population Movements: Where the Public and Private Interests Conflict"; and "Population Movements and the Shape of Urban Growth: Implications for Public Policy."

Chapter 15. Population Statistics and Research

1. "Population Research: A Prospectus," Committee Report to the Assistant Secretary for Health and Scientific Affairs, U.S. Department of Health, Education and Welfare. Reprinted in U.S. Congress, House, Committee on Interstate and Foreign Commerce, *Family Planning Services, Hearings* before the Subcommittee on Public Health and Welfare, 91st Cong., 2nd sess., August 3, 4, and 7, 1970, p. 162.
2. See note 1.

Chapter 16. Organizational Changes

This chapter draws primarily on the following:

U.S. Congress, Senate, Committee on Labor and Public Welfare, *Expanding, Improving, and Better Coordinating the Family Planning Services and Population Research Activities of the Federal Government*, S. Rept. 91-1004, To Accompany S.2108, 91st Cong., 2nd sess., 1970.

U.S. Congress, Senate, Committee on Labor and Public Welfare, *Full Opportunity Act, Hearings* before the Special Subcommittee on Evaluation and Planning of Social Problems, on S.5, 91st Cong., 1st and 2nd sess., July 7, 8, 10, 18; December 18, 1969; and March 13, 1970.

U.S. Congress, Senate, Committee on Labor and Public Welfare, *Full Opportunity and National Goals and Priorities Act, Hearings* before the Special Subcommittee on Evaluation and Planning of Social Programs, on S.5, 92nd Cong., 1st sess., July 13, 1971.

U.S. Executive Office of the President, *Papers Relating to the President's Departmental Reorganization Program, A Reference Compilation*, March 1971.

U.S. Dept. of Health, Education and Welfare, *Toward a Social Report*, January 1969.

APPENDIX

RESEARCH PAPERS

Alonso, William
Institute of Urban and Regional Development and Department of City and Regional Planning, University of California, Berkeley
Problems, Purposes, and Implicit Policies for a National Strategy of Urbanization
The System of Intermetropolitan Population Flows

Appleman, Jack, William P. Butz, David H. Greenberg, Paul L. Jordan, and Anthony H. Pascal
Rand Corporation
Population Change and Public Resource Requirements: The Impact of Future United States Demographic Trends on Education, Welfare, and Health Care

Ayres, Robert U., and Ivars Gutmanis
International Research and Technology Corporation
Technological Change, Pollution and Treatment Cost Coefficients in Input-Output Analysis

Bachrach, Peter
Department of Political Science, Temple University
and
Elihu Bergman
Center for Population Studies, Harvard University
Participation and Conflict in Making American Population Policy: A Critical Analysis

335

Bahl, Roy W., Jr.
Department of Economics, Syracuse University
Metropolitan Fiscal Structures and the Distribution of Population Within Metropolitan Areas

Beale, Calvin L.
Economic Research Service, U.S. Department of Agriculture
Rural and Nonmetropolitan Population Trends of Significance to National Population Policy

Berry, Brian J. L.
Center for Urban Studies, University of Chicago
Population Growth in the Daily Urban Systems of the United States, 1980-2000

Blake, Judith
Department of Demography, University of California, Berkeley
Coercive Pronatalism and American Population Policy

Bollinger, W. LaMar
Department of Economics, College of Idaho
The Economic and Social Impact of the Depopulation Process Upon Four Selected Counties in Idaho

Bradshaw, Benjamin S.
Population Research Center, University of Texas
Some Aspects of the Fertility of Mexican-Americans

Cain, Glen G.
Department of Economics, University of Wisconsin
The Effect of Income Maintenance Laws on Fertility in the United States

Callahan, Daniel, ed.
Institute of Society, Ethics and the Life Sciences
Ethics, Population, and the American Tradition

Cameron, Gordon
Department of Applied Economics, University of Glasgow
The Relevance to the United States of British and French Regional Population Strategies

Carr, A. Barry, and David W. Culver
Economic Research Service, U.S. Department of Agriculture
Agriculture, Population, and the Environment

Christmas, Lawrence Barroll
Northeastern Illinois Planning Commission
Continued Metropolitanization: The Chicago Experience

Cicchetti, Charles J.
Resources for the Future, Inc.
Outdoor Recreation and Congestion in the United States

Coale, Ansley J.
Office of Population Research, Princeton University
Alternative Paths to a Stationary Population

Commoner, Barry
Center for the Biology of Natural Systems, Washington University
The Environmental Cost of Economic Growth

Cutright, Phillips
Department of Sociology, Indiana University
Illegitimacy in the United States: 1920-1968

Danielson, Michael N.
Woodrow Wilson School of Public and International Affairs, Princeton University
Differentiation, Segregation, and Political Fragmentation in the American Metropolis

Darmstadter, Joel
Resources for the Future, Inc.
Energy

David, Henry P.
Transnational Family Research Institute, American Institutes for Research; and Preterm Institute
Unwanted Pregnancies: Costs and Alternatives

Davidson, Roger H.
Department of Political Science, University of California, Santa Barbara
Population Change and Representative Government

Davis, Kingsley
International Population and Urban Research and Department of Sociology, University of California, Berkeley
The American Family in Relation to Demographic Change

Day, Lincoln H.
Demographic and Social Statistics Branch, Statistical Office, United Nations
The Social Consequences of a Zero Population Growth Rate in the United States

Demeny, Paul
East-West Population Institute, University of Hawaii
Welfare Considerations in United States Population Policy

Drury, Robert F.
Consultant
Washington, D.C.
Local Governments and Population Change

Ehrlich, Paul R.
Department of Biological Sciences, Stanford University
    and
John P. Holdren
Lawrence Radiation Laboratory, University of California, Berkeley
Impact of Population Growth

Elazar, Daniel J.
Department of Political Science, Temple University
Population Growth and the Federal System

Farley, Reynolds
Population Studies Center, University of Michigan
Fertility and Mortality Trends Among Blacks in the United States

Fischman, Leonard L.
Economic Associates, Inc.
    and
Hans H. Landsberg
Resources for the Future, Inc.
Adequacy of Nonfuel Minerals and Forest Resources

Fortney, Judith A.
Department of Sociology and Center for the Study of Aging and Human Development, Duke University
Immigration Into the United States With Special Reference to Professional and Technical Workers

Freedman, Jonathan L.
Department of Psychology, Columbia University
A Conceptualization of Crowding
Population Density, Juvenile Delinquency, and Mental Illness in New York City

Frejka, Tomas
The Population Council
Demographic Paths to a Stationary Population: The U. S. in International Comparison

Fuguitt, Glen V.
College of Agricultural and Life Sciences, University of Wisconsin
Population Trends of Nonmetropolitan Cities and Villages in the United States

338

Gold, Neil M.
Suburban Action Institute
The Mismatch of Jobs and Low-Income People in Metropolitan Areas and Its Implication for the Central-City Poor

Gordon, Sol
College for Human Development and Center for Family Planning and Population Information, Syracuse University
Family Planning Education for Adolescents

Grumm, John G.
Department of Government, Wesleyan University
Population Change and State Government Policy

Hansen, Niles M.
Center for Economic Development, University of Texas
The Case for Government-Assisted Migration

Hetrick, Carl C., A. E. Keir Nash, and Alan J. Wyner
Department of Political Science, University of California, Santa Barbara
Population and Politics: Information, Concern, and Policy Support Among the American Public

Hoch, Irving
Resources for the Future, Inc.
Urban Scale and Environmental Quality

Hoover, Edgar M.
Department of Economics, University of Pittsburgh
Policy Objectives for Population Distribution
Reduced Population Growth and the Problems of Urban Areas

Howard, John A., and Donald R. Lehman
Graduate School of Business, Columbia University
The Effect of Different Populations on Selected Industries in the Year 2000

Irwin, Richard, and Robert Warren
U. S. Bureau of the Census
Demographic Aspects of American Immigration

Jaffe, Frederick S.
Center for Family Planning Program Development, Planned Parenthood-World Population
Family Planning Services in the United States

Johnston, Denis F.
U. S. Bureau of Labor Statistics and Department of Sociology, Georgetown University
Illustrative Projections of the Labor Force of the United States to 2040

Jones, David
Department of Economics, Indiana University
Projections of Housing Demand to the Year 2000, Using Two Population Projections

Jones, Elise F., and Charles F. Westoff
Office of Population Research, Princeton University
Attitudes Toward Abortion in the United States in 1970 and the Trend Since 1965

Kantner, John F., and Melvin Zelnik
Department of Population Dynamics, School of Hygiene and Public Health, Johns Hopkins University
Sexuality, Contraception, and Pregnancy Among Pre-Adult Females in the United States

Keely, Charles B.
Department of Sociology, Western Michigan University
Immigration: Considerations on Trends, Prospects, and Policy

Keller, Suzanne
Department of Sociology, Princeton University
The Future Status of Women in America

Kelley, Allen C.
Department of Economics, University of Wisconsin
Demographic Changes and American Economic Development: Past, Present, and Future with *Comment* by Richard Easterlin, Department of Economics, University of Pennsylvania

Kitagawa, Evelyn M.
Department of Sociology and Population Research Center, University of Chicago
Socioeconomic Differences in Mortality in the United States and Some Implications for Population Policy

Lehne, Richard
Department of Political Science, Rutgers University
Population Change and Congressional Representation

Leibenstein, Harvey
Department of Economics, Harvard University
The Impact of Population Growth on the American Economy with *Comment* by Edgar M. Hoover, Department of Economics, University of Pittsburgh

Leven, Charles L.
Institute for Urban and Regional Studies, Washington University
Changing Sizes, Forms, and Functions of Urban Areas

340

Lowi, Theodore
Department of Political Science, University of Chicago
Population Policies and the American Political System

Manvel, Allen D.
Consultant
Washington, D.C.
Metropolitan Growth and Governmental Fragmentation

McGrath, Dorn C., Jr.
Department of Urban and Regional Planning, School of Government and Business Administration, George Washington University
Population Growth and Change: Implications for Planning

Menken, Jane A.
Office of Population Research, Princeton University
Teenage Childbearing: Its Medical Aspects and Implications for the United States Population

Miller, Arthur S.
National Law Center, George Washington University
Population Policy-Making and the Constitution

Mills, Edwin S.
Department of Economics, Princeton University
Economic Aspects of City Size

Morrison, Peter A.
Rand Corporation
Dimensions of the Population Problem in the United States
The Impact of Population Stabilization on Migration and Redistribution
Population Movements: Where the Public and Private Interests Conflict
Population Movements and the Shape of Urban Growth: Implications for Public Policy

Morss, Elliott R.
Commission on Population Growth and the American Future
The Influence of Federal Government Activities on the Family Decision to Have a Child

Murray, Edward E., and Ned Hege
Urban Land Institute
Growth Center Population Redistribution 1980-2000

Noonan, John T., Jr., and Mary Cynthia Dunlap
School of Law, University of California, Berkeley
Unintended Consequences: Laws Indirectly Affecting Population Growth in the United States

ternational Institute for Study of Human Reproduction, Columbia University
and

Larry L. Bumpass
Department of Sociology and Center for Demography and Ecology, University of Wisconsin
Demographic and Social Aspects of Contraceptive Sterilization in the United States: 1965-1970

Preston, Samuel H.
Department of Demography, University of California, Berkeley
Female Employment Policy and Fertility

Reed, Ritchie H., and Susan McIntosh
Commission on Population Growth and the American Future
Costs of Children

Ridker, Ronald G.
Resources for the Future, Inc.
Resource and Environmental Consequences of Population Growth in the United States: A Summary
The Economy, Resource Requirements, and Pollution Levels
Future Water Needs and Supplies, with a Note on Land Use
The Model (with H. W. Herzog, Jr.)

Ridley, Jeanne Clare
School of Public Health and Administrative Medicine and International Institute for Study of Human Reproduction, Columbia University
On the Consequences of Demographic Change for the Roles and Status of Women

Rindfuss, Ronald R.
Office of Population Research, Princeton University
Recent Trends in Population Attitudes

Rundquist, Barry S., P. G. Bock, Anthony M. Champagne, and Karl F. Johnson
Department of Political Science, University of Illinois, Urbana-Champaign
The Impact of Defense Cutbacks on Employment and Migration

Ryder, Norman B.
Office of Population Research, Princeton University
A Demographic Optimum Projection for the United States

Ryder, Norman B., and Charles F. Westoff
Office of Population Research, Princeton University
Unwanted Childbearing in the United States: 1970

Segal, Sheldon
The Population Council
Possible Means of Fertility Control: Distant or Near

Smith, Frank Austin
Center for the Environment and Man, Inc.
Waste Material Recovery and Reuse

Smith, Frederick J.
Graduate School of Design, Harvard University
Ecological Perspectives

Spengler, Joseph J.
Department of Economics, Duke University
Declining Population Growth: Economic Effects with *Comment* by Warren Robinson, Department of Economics, Pennsylvania State University

Taeuber, Irene B.
Office of Population Research, Princeton University
Growth of the Population of the United States in the Twentieth Century
The Changing Distribution of the Population of the United States in the Twentieth Century

Teitelbaum, Michael S.
Office of Population Research, Princeton University
International Experience with Fertility at or Near Replacement Level
Some Genetic Implications of Population Policies

Tietze, Christopher, M.D.
The Population Council
The Potential Impact of Legal Abortion on Population Growth in the United States

Viederman, Stephen
The Population Council
Population Education in the Elementary and Secondary Schools of the United States

Vines, Kenneth N.
Department of Political Science, State University of New York, Buffalo
Population and the Administration of Justice

CONSULTANTS

James E. Allen, Carolina Population Center, University of North Carolina

William Alonso, Institute of Urban and Regional Development and Department of City and Regional Planning, University of California, Berkeley

Peter Ames, Member, Connecticut Bar

Peter Bachrach, Department of Political Science, Temple University

Edward Banfield, Department of Government, Harvard University

Calvin L. Beale, Economic Research Service, U.S. Department of Agriculture

Benjamin S. Bradshaw, Population Research Center, University of Texas

Benjamin Branch, M.D., Medical Director, Preterm, Washington, D.C.

Richard Burton, The Urban Institute, Washington, D.C.

Daniel Callahan, Institute of Society, Ethics and the Life Sciences

William D. Carey, Arthur D. Little, Inc., Washington, D.C.

Lenora T. Cartright, Center for Urban Studies, University of Illinois

Robert Lee Chartrand, Legislative Reference Service, Library of Congress

Preston Cloud, Department of Geological Sciences, University of California, Santa Barbara

Ansley J. Coale, Office of Population Research, Princeton University

Barry Commoner, Center for the Biology of Natural Systems, Washington University

Phillips Cutright, Department of Sociology, Indiana University

Michael N. Danielson, Woodrow Wilson School of Public and International Affairs, Princeton University

Kingsley Davis, International Population and Urban Research and Department of Sociology, University of California, Berkeley

Robert G. Dixon, Jr., National Law Center, George Washington University

Robert Dorfman, Department of Economics, Harvard University

Anthony Downs, Real Estate Research Corporation, Chicago, Illinois

Edwin D. Driver, Department of Sociology, University of Massachusetts

Robert F. Drury, Consultant, Washington, D.C.

Richard A. Easterlin, Department of Economics, University of Pennsylvania

Paul R. Ehrlich, Department of Biological Sciences, Stanford University

Stephen Enke, General Electric TEMPO, Center for Advanced Studies, Washington, D.C.

Edward J. Ennis, Attorney at Law, New York, New York

Cynthia Fuchs Epstein, Queens College of The City University of New York and Bureau of Applied Social Research, Columbia University

Judith A. Fortney, Department of Sociology and Center for the Study of Aging and Human Development, Duke University

Maurice Fulton, President, The Fantus Company, Chicago

Sol Gordon, College for Human Development and Center for Family Planning and Population Information, Syracuse University

Naomi T. Gray, Naomi Gray Associates, Inc., New York, New York

John Grumm, Department of Government, Wesleyan University

Robert E. Hall, M.D., Department of Obstetrics and Gynecology, College of Physicians and Surgeons, Columbia University

Niles M. Hansen, Center for Economic Development, University of Texas

Edgar M. Hoover, Department of Economics, University of Pittsburgh

John A. Howard, Graduate School of Business, Columbia University

Richard Irwin, U.S. Bureau of Census

Frederick S. Jaffe, Center for Family Planning Program Development, Planned Parenthood-World Population

John F. Kain, Department of Economics, Harvard University

Allen C. Kelley, Department of Economics, University of Wisconsin

Donald R. Lehman, Graduate School of Business, Columbia University

Harvey Leibenstein, Department of Economics, Harvard University

Seymour Martin Lipset, Department of Government, Harvard University

Allen D. Manvel, Consultant, Washington, D.C.

Alan Margolis, Department of Obstetrics/Gynecology, University of California Medical Center, San Francisco

Donald R. Matthews, The Brookings Institution

Donald N. Michael, Institute for Social Research, University of Michigan

Arthur S. Miller, National Law Center, George Washington University

Edwin S. Mills, Department of Economics, Princeton University

Peter A. Morrison, RAND Corporation

Frank W. Notestein, Office of Population Research, Princeton University

A.F.K. Organski, Department of Political Science, University of Michigan

Anthony Pascal, RAND Corporation

Edmund S. Phelps, Department of Economics, Columbia University

Jerome P. Pickard, Appalachian Regional Commission

Harriet F. Pilpel, Member, New York Bar

Ronald J. Pion, M.D., School of Public Health, University of Hawaii

James W. Prothro, Carolina Population Center, University of North Carolina

Ronald G. Ridker, Resources for the Future, Inc.

Randall B. Ripley, Department of Political Science, Ohio State University

Warren C. Robinson, Department of Economics, Pennsylvania State University

Norman B. Ryder, Office of Population Research, Princeton University

Richard Scammon, Election Research Center, Washington, D.C.

Allan Schick, The Brookings Institution

Sheldon J. Segal, The Population Council

M. Brewster Smith, University of California, Santa Cruz

Robert G. Smith, Management Consultant, Washington, D.C.

Frank J. Sorauf, Department of Political Science, University of Minnesota

Joseph J. Spengler, Department of Economics, Duke University

J. Mayone Stycos, Department of Sociology, Cornell University

James L. Sundquist, The Brookings Institution

Conrad Taeuber, U.S. Bureau of the Census

Irene B. Taeuber, Office of Population Research, Princeton University

Michael S. Teitelbaum, Office of Population Research, Princeton University

Vaida D. Thompson, Carolina Population Center, University of North Carolina

Christopher Tietze, M.D., The Population Council

Stephen Viederman, The Population Council

Ben J. Wattenberg, Author and Consultant, Washington, D.C.

Charles V. Willie, Vice President for Student Activities and Organization, Syracuse University

Robert C. Wood, President, University of Massachusetts

CONSULTING ORGANIZATIONS

Institute of Society, Ethics and the Life Sciences, Hastings-on-Hudson, N.Y.

Opinion Research Corporation, Princeton, N.J.

RAND Corporation, Santa Monica, Calif.

Resources for the Future, Inc., Washington, D.C.

ULI—The Urban Land Institute, Washington, D.C.

U.S. Department of Commerce, Bureau of the Census, Washington, D.C.

U.S. Department of Commerce, Office of Business Economics, Washington, D.C.

PARTICIPANTS IN PUBLIC HEARINGS

(in order of appearance)

Washington, D.C., April 14-15, 1971

The Hon. Donald Rumsfeld, Counsellor to President Richard M. Nixon

The Hon. John G. Veneman, Under Secretary, U.S. Department of Health, Education and Welfare
> Gooloo Wunderlich, Demographer, Office of Population Affairs
> Carl Schultz, M.D., Director, Office of Population Affairs

Wilma Scott Heide, National Chairwoman, National Organization for Women

General Andrew O'Meara (USA Ret.), National Chairman, Population Crisis Committee, Washington, D.C.

Phyllis T. Piotrow, Consultant, Population Crisis Committee, Washington, D.C.

Donald Paarlberg, Director, Agricultural Economics, U.S. Department of Agriculture
> Lynn M. Daft, Assistant Deputy Administrator, Economic Research Service

The Hon. Stewart Udall, Lawyer, Environmental Columnist; former Secretary of the Interior

Rev. Monsignor James T. McHugh, Director, Family Life Division, United States Catholic Conference, Washington, D.C.

Alan C. Guttmacher, M.D., President, Planned Parenthood-World Population

Milo Macura, Director, Population Division, United Nations

Roger Revelle, Chairman, Department of Demography, School of Public Health, Harvard University

George Hay Brown, Director, Bureau of the Census
        Conrad Taeuber, Associate Director
        Herman P. Miller, Chief, Population Division

Carl Pope, Washington Representative, Zero Population Growth

Naomi T. Gray, President, Naomi Gray Associates, Inc., Family Planning Consultants, New York, N.Y.

Rufus E. Miles, President, Population Reference Bureau, Washington, D.C.

John Tanton, National Chairman, Sierra Club Population Committee

Carl H. Madden, Chief Economist, Chamber of Commerce of the U.S., Washington, D.C.

Bradley Byers and Gerald Barney, Arlington Committee on Optimum Growth, Arlington, Va.

Rev. David O. Poindexter, Director, Population Communications Center, United Methodist Church, New York, N.Y.

Robert Lamson, Staff Associate, Plans and Analysis Office, National Science Foundation, Washington, D.C.

Los Angeles, California, May 3-4, 1971

S. I. Hayakawa, President, San Francisco State College,
        John Westfall, Chairman, Geography Department

The Hon. Jerome Waldie, U.S. House of Representatives, 14th C. District, California

Mrs. Tee Bertha Spring, Member, Board of Directors, Los Angeles Regional Planning Council

Henry Gibson, Television Entertainer, Malibu

Kingsley Davis, Professor of Sociology, International Population and Urban Research and Dept. of Sociology, University of California, Berkeley

Frederic G. Styles, Executive Director, Science and Technology Advisory Council, California State Assembly

Eduardo Arriaga, University of California, Berkeley

Manuel Aragon, Jr., General Manager, City of Commerce Investment Company; former Executive Director, Economic and Youth Opportunity Agency, Los Angeles County

Kenneth M. Mitzner, President, Mobilization for the Unnamed, Los Angeles

Joe C. Ortega, Associate Counsel, Mexican-American Legal Defense and Education Fund, Inc.

Walter R. Trinkaus, President, Right to Life League of Southern California; Professor of Law, Loyola University of Los Angeles

Judith Ayala, Registered Nurse, Los Angeles

Johnson C. Montgomery, Attorney, representing Zero Population Growth, Palo Alto

Stuart W. Knight, Attorney, Anaheim

The Hon. Tom Bradley, Los Angeles City Council

Addie Klotz, M.D., Director of Student Council Services, San Fernando Valley State College, and three students

David S. Hall, Senior Public Health Educator, Los Angeles County Public Health Department

Laura Anderson, Coordinator, Comprehensive Family Planning Program, Berkeley

Calvin S. Hamilton, Director of Planning, City of Los Angeles

Clarence R. Allen, Professor of Geology and Geophysics, Seismological Laboratory, California Institute of Technology, Los Angeles

Walt Thompson, Chairman, Journalism Department, Laney College, Oakland

Alfred Heller, Director, California Tomorrow, San Francisco

Ernest Loebbeke, Past President, California State Chamber of Commerce, Los Angeles

Robert Sassone, President, League for Infants, Fetuses and the Elderly, Santa Ana

353

James Edinger, Associate Professor of Meteorology, University of California, Los Angeles

Rits Tadema, Westminster

Little Rock, Arkansas, June 7-8, 1971

The Hon. John L. McClellan, U.S. Senate, Arkansas

The Hon. David Pryor, U.S. House of Representatives, 4th C. District, Arkansas
> Eddie White, Seasonal Farm Worker, Altheimer

Colin Clark, International Economist; Fellow of Monasch University, Melbourne, Australia

William (Sonny) Walker, Director, Equal Opportunity Division, U.S. Department of Housing and Urban Development, Little Rock

Gordon D. Morgan, Professor of Sociology, University of Arkansas, Fayetteville

The Hon. Winthrop Rockefeller, Former Governor of Arkansas, Little Rock

Calvin L. Beale, Economic Research Service, U.S. Department of Agriculture, Washington, D.C.

Mariah Gilmore, Trainee in Operation Mainstream, a project funded by Opportunities Industrialization Center, Little Rock
> Mrs. Mitchell, Counselor, Opportunities Industrialization Center, Little Rock

Barton A. Westerlund, Director, Industrial Research and Extension Center, College of Business Administration, University of Arkansas, Fayetteville

Jason Rouby, Executive Director, Metroplan, Little Rock

John H. Opitz, Executive Director, The Ozarks Regional Commission, Washington, D.C.

William W. Blunt, Jr. Chief Counsel, Economic Development Administration, U.S. Department of Commerce, Washington, D.C.

William C. Nolan, Jr., Vice President, El Dorado Chamber of Commerce

Paul Stabler, Field Representative for the Oklahoma Indian Affairs Commission, Tulsa, Oklahoma

Russell Thomas, Director of Industrial Relations, Wolverine Toy Company, Cooneville

David L. Barclay, M.D., Professor and Chairman of the Department of Obstetrics and Gynecology, University of Arkansas Medical Center
   Rex Ramsey, M.D., Director of Maternal and Child Health Division, Arkansas State Health Department

Trusten H. Holder, Private Consultant in the areas of ecological studies, outdoor recreation, environmental planning, Little Rock

Pratt Remmel, Jr., Director, Arkansas Ecology Center, Little Rock

The Hon. Dale Bumpers, Governor of Arkansas

E. L. Bud Stewart, Jr., Federal Co-Chairman, the Ozarks Regional Commission, Washington, D.C.

Chicago, Illinois, June 21-22, 1971

Philip M. Hauser, Professor of Sociology, University of Chicago

The Hon. Alderman Marilou Hedlund, Member Chicago City Council

Jeffrey R. Short, Jr., President, J. R. Short Milling Company, Chicago

Richard Babcock, Attorney, Past President, American Society of Planning Officials, Chicago

Lawrence B. Christmas, Technical Director, Northeastern Illinois Planning Commission, Chicago

Norman Lazarus, President, N. Lazarus Company, Chicago

John Yolton, Administrative Assistant to Olga Madar, Vice President of the United Auto Workers, Detroit, Michigan

Conrad E. Terrien, Chemical Engineer, Villa Park

Rev. Don C. Shaw, Executive Director, Midwest Population Center, Chicago

Ellen Peck, Author, Baltimore, Maryland.

Rev. Jesse Jackson, National Director, Operation Breadbasket, Chicago

Anthony Downs, Senior Vice President, Real Estate Research Corporation, Chicago

Jean Phillips, Senior at Northeastern Illinois State College, Chicago

John E. Lester, student, Northeastern Illinois State College, Chicago

Frances Frech, Housewife, Kansas City, Missouri

The Hon. William Cousins, Member, Chicago City Council

Ione Du Val, Director of Immigrant Services, The Travelers Aid Society of Metropolitan Chicago

Fred Domville, Oak Park

New York, New York, September 27-28, 1971

The Hon. Percy Sutton, President, Borough of Manhattan

Gordon Chase, Health Services Administrator, City of New York, and Chairman, Health and Hospital Corporation

Timothy Costello, Deputy Mayor, City of New York

George Trombetta, M.D., Chief of Obstetrics and Gynecology, Highland Hospital, Rochester
      Alyce Friend, Family Planning Counselor, Rochester

Sylvester Charleston, Student, Bernard Baruch College, New York, N.Y.

Harriet Surovell, High School Women's Coalition, New York, N.Y.

Frank Febus, Student, New York Institute of Photography

Bill Baird, Lecturer on Abortion and Birth Control; Director of the Parents' Aid Society, Hempstead, Long Island

Robert M. Byrn, Professor of Law, Fordham University School of Law

Bernard Pisani, M.D., Director, Department of Obstetrics and Gynecology, St. Vincent's Hospital, New York, N.Y.

Alvin F. Moran, Executive Vice President, Planned Parenthood of New York, N.Y.

Donald Hohl, Assistant Director of Migration and Refugee Services, U.S. Catholic Conference, Washington, D.C.

Edward J. Logue, President, New York State Urban Development Corporation

Mr. Magee, New York, N.Y.

Paul Ylvisaker, Professor of Public Affairs and Urban Planning, Princeton University

Betty Rollin, Author, New York, N.Y.

Patricia Cooper, Director, Pennsport Civic Association, Philadelphia
Mrs. Fizur, Community Worker, Philadelphia

Joseph Monserrat, New York City Board of Education, former Director of Migration Services, Department of Labor, Puerto Rico

Robert O. Anderson, Chairman of the Board, Chief Executive Officer, Atlantic-Richfield Company, New York, N.Y.

Irving Stern, Director of Local 342, Amalgamated Meat Cutters and Retail Food Store Employees Union; International Vice President, Amalgamated Meat Cutters and Butchers Union; Vice President, New York City Central Labor Council

Eugene S. Callender, President, New York Urban Coalition

MANDATES

Public Law 91-213
91st Congress, S. 2701
March 16, 1970

AN ACT

To establish a Commission on Population Growth and the American Future.

Be it enacted by the Senate and House of Representatives of the United States of America in Congress assembled, That the Commission on Population Growth and the American Future is hereby established to conduct and sponsor such studies and research and make such recommendations as may be necessary to provide information and education to all levels of government in the United States, and to our people, regarding a broad range of problems associated with population growth and their implications for America's future.

Commission
on Population
Growth and
the American
Future.
Establish-
ment.

MEMBERSHIP OF COMMISSION

Sec. 2. (a) The Commission on Population Growth and the American Future (hereinafter referred to as the "Commission") shall be composed of—

(1) two Members of the Senate who shall be members of different political parties and

358

who shall be appointed by the President of the Senate;

(2) two Members of the House of Representatives who shall be members of different political parties and who shall be appointed by the Speaker of the House of Representatives; and

84 STAT. 67

(3) not to exceed twenty members appointed by the President.

84 STAT. 68

(b) The President shall designate one of the members to serve as Chairman and one to serve as Vice Chairman of the Commission.

(c) The majority of the members of the Commission shall constitute a quorum, but a lesser number may conduct hearings.

COMPENSATION OF MEMBERS OF THE COMMISSION

Sec. 3. (a) Members of the Commission who are officers or full-time employees of the United States shall serve without compensation in addition to that received for their services as officers or employees of the United States.

(b) Members of the Commission who are not officers or full-time employees of the United States shall each receive $100 per diem when engaged in the actual performance of duties vested in the Commission.

(c) All members of the Commission shall be allowed travel expenses, including per diem in lieu of subsistence, as authorized by section 5703 of title 5 of the United States Code for persons in the Government service employed intermittently.

80 STAT. 499;

83 STAT. 190.

DUTIES OF THE COMMISSION

Sec. 4. The Commission shall conduct an inquiry into the following aspects of population

growth in the United States and its foreseeable
social consequences:

(1) the probable course of population
growth, internal migration, and related demographic developments between now and the
year 2000;

(2) the resources in the public sector of
the economy that will be required to deal with
the anticipated growth in population;

(3) the ways in which population growth
may affect the activities of Federal, State, and
local government;

(4) the impact of population growth on
environmental pollution and on the depletion
of natural resources; and

(5) the various means appropriate to the
ethical values and principles of this society by
which our Nation can achieve a population level
properly suited for its environmental, natural
resources, and other needs.

STAFF OF THE COMMISSION

Sec. 5. (a) The Commission shall appoint an
Executive Director and such other personnel as
the Commission deems necessary without regard 80 STAT. 378.
to the provisions of title 5 of the United States 5 USC 101 et
Code governing appointments in the competitive
service and shall fix the compensation of such per- 80 STAT. 443,
sonnel without regard to the provisions of chapter 459.
51 and subtitle II of chapter 53 of such title relating to classification and General Schedule pay
rates: *Provided,* That no personnel so appointed
shall receive compensation in excess of the rate
authorized for GS-18 by section 5332 of such title.

(b) The Executive Director, with the approval 34 F. R. 9605.
of the Commission, is authorized to obtain ser- 5 USC 5332
vices in accordance with the provisions of section note.
3109 of title 5 of the United States Code, but at 80 STAT. 416.
rates for individuals not to exceed the per diem
equivalent of the rate authorized for GS-18 by
section 5332 of such title.

(C) The Commission is authorized to enter into contracts with public agencies, private firms, institutions, and individuals for the conduct of research and surveys, the preparation of reports, and other activities necessary to the discharge of its duties.

Contract authority

84 STAT. 68

84 STAT. 69

GOVERNMENT AGENCY COOPERATION

Sec. 6. The Commission is authorized to request from any Federal department or agency any information and assistance it deems necessary to carry out its functions; and each such department or agency is authorized to cooperate with the Commission and, to the extent permitted by law, to furnish such information and assistance to the Commission upon request made by the Chairman or any other member when acting as Chairman.

ADMINISTRATIVE SERVICES

Sec. 7. The General Services Administration shall provide administrative services for the Commission on a reimbursable basis.

REPORTS OF COMMISSION:
TERMINATION

Sec. 8. In order that the President and the Congress may be kept advised of the progress of its work, the Commission shall, from time to time, report to the President and the Congress such significant findings and recommendations as it deems advisable. The Commission shall submit an interim report to the President and the Congress one year after it is established and shall submit its final report two years after the enactment of this Act. The Commission shall cease to exist sixty days after the date of the submission of its final report.

Sec. 9. There are hereby authorized to be appropriated, out of any money in the Treasury not otherwise appropriated, such amounts as may be necessary to carry out the provisions of this Act.

Approved March 16, 1970